Re-engineering the Uptake of ICT in Schools

Frans Van Assche • Luis Anido-Rifón
David Griffiths • Cathy Lewin • Sarah McNicol
Editors

Re-engineering the Uptake of ICT in Schools

Forewords by Giovanni Biondi and Patricia Manson

Editors
Frans Van Assche
Department of Computer Science
University of Leuven
Leuven, Belgium

David Griffiths
Institute of Educational Cybernatics
University of Bolton
Bolton, UK

Sarah McNicol
Education and Social Research Institute
Manchester Metropolitan University
Manchester, UK

Luis Anido-Rifón
Telematics Engineering Department
ETSI Telecommunication
University of Vigo
Vigo, Spain

Cathy Lewin
Education and Social Research Institute
Manchester Metropolitan University
Manchester, UK

ISBN 978-3-319-36603-6 ISBN 978-3-319-19366-3 (eBook)
DOI 10.1007/978-3-319-19366-3

Springer Cham Heidelberg New York Dordrecht London

Softcover reprint of the hardcover 1st edition 2015

Printed on acid-free paper

Springer International Publishing AG Switzerland is part of Springer Science+Business Media (www.springer.com)

Foreword

"The future classroom is not about the environment or about the furniture or the technology either. It's about how the students learn". This is how one iTEC teacher in the UK sums up iTEC (Innovative Technology for an Engaging Classroom), a 4-year European project on designing the future classroom.

The evidence gathered from more than 2500 classrooms involved in the project between 2010 and 2014 suggests that iTEC has succeeded in improving learning by allowing teachers to innovate in their classroom practice. Key to the success of the iTEC project, and what makes it different from other, technology-focused education initiatives, is that it allows teachers to take a step back from their everyday practice to visualise and create scenarios of how learning could be.

The iTEC project, which was a cooperation between Ministries of Education, educational technology providers and pedagogical experts, as well as primary and secondary teachers in classrooms across Europe, has developed a "scenario-driven learning design" process. This process facilitates teachers innovating in their teaching practice, supported with ICT and ensures that use of technology in schools is informed, not by "blue-sky" thinking, but by meaningful pedagogical visions of how it can best engage and support students.

The Future Classroom methodology developed by iTEC has already had an impact in classrooms across 20 countries; it is not only allowing schools to rethink how they are currently using ICT but is also helping to close the "mainstreaming gap"—when technology is not fully integrated in teaching and learning, both inside and outside of school.

This book provides an overview of the results of the iTEC project: its scenarios, innovative Learning Activities and tools, its mix of vision and practice, its engagement with partners and communities, its outcomes and results, and its remarkable journey towards widespread sharing and adoption.

European Schoolnet
Brussels, Belgium

Giovanni Biondi

Digital technologies are transforming all sectors of our societies, including education. Technology has the potential to make the learning process more transparent, more personal, and motivating. It connects teachers and learners to each other and beyond the classroom walls to the world around us in a way that has not been possible before. Technology can make learning accessible 24/7—and help transform the way we acquire knowledge and skills in the twenty-first century.

However, digital technologies are not a magic wand that makes learning happen without effort from teachers and students. We need to understand how and when to put it to best use in the classroom—and in so doing we can make sure the classroom is a place of discovery, passion, and joy. Just as technology helps to connect people, it helps each individual learner to find individual learning paths and to be master of her and his own learning.

The iTEC project was a flagship project of the European Commission which brought these new methods and experiments in teaching and learning to over 2500 classrooms across Europe. It was supported by a large number of Ministries of Education and has pushed forward the change agenda towards twenty-first century classrooms in Europe. We are confident that the effects of this change will multiply and cascade widely, and that today's future classroom will become a reality for all our classrooms in the not-too-distant future.

European Commission
Luxembourg

Patricia Manson

Preface

This book reports on the results of the iTEC project,[1] a comprehensive effort to re-engineer the uptake of ICT in schools, which was undertaken in response to the European Commission's call for proposals for large-scale pilots as part of the "Learning in the 21st-Century Research Challenge". Over the course of the project, educational tools and resources were piloted in over 2500 classrooms across 20 European countries, with the goal of providing a sustainable model for fundamentally redesigning teaching and learning.

Teachers, head teachers, and policymakers may benefit from reading how novel scenarios can be elaborated, adapted to a local context, and implemented in the classroom; how new technologies can support this process for teachers and their national/regional communities; how teachers and other stakeholders can be educated in such a re-engineering process; how the approach can be scaled up through MOOCs, ambassador schemes, and train-the-trainer programmes; how future classroom labs can inspire teachers, head teachers, and policymakers; how teachers and, above all, learners can become more engaged in learning through the adoption of the iTEC approach.

Readers with a more technical focus may also be interested in the discussion of recommender systems, the flexible provision of resources and services, the deployment of the cloud in schools, and systems for composing technological support for lesson plans. In particular, Chap. 4 is intended for readers with a technical background.

The book is organised as follows. First, the whole concept of re-engineering the uptake of ICT in schools, its motivation, and an overview of the main results of the project's work are given. Second, the basic concepts of Scenarios and Learning Activities are introduced along with an explanation of the experiences and lessons learned. Third, the technologies supporting the uptake of ICT are introduced. These

[1] The iTEC project was co-funded by the European Commission's FP7 Programme. The content of this book is the sole responsibility of the authors and it does not represent the opinion of the European Commission and the Commission is not responsible for any use that might be made of information contained herein.

technologies range from tools to compose the learning design, tools to provide access to content resources as well as events and experts, tools for making recommendations about learning designs and resources, and an architecture that allows for cross-platform integration of these tools and resources. Finally, the book ends with the presentation of 15 key evaluation findings addressing: how the iTEC approach impacted on learners and learning, how the iTEC approach impacted on teachers and teaching, and the potential of the iTEC approach for system-wide adoption in schools.

This book could not have been written without the contributions of all partners, associated partners, and so many volunteering teachers in the iTEC project. This 12.5 million Euro project, coordinated by the European Schoolnet, involved 26 project partners, including Ministries of Education or national agencies representing ministries (MoE), technology providers, and research organisations. The partnership of iTEC consisted of:

European Schoolnet (BE)
Bundesministerium für Bildung und Frauen (MoE AT)
Centre of Information Technologies in Education (MoE LT)
Centre National de Documentation Pédagogique (MoE FR)
Direção-Geral da Educação (MoE PT)
EduBIT.eu (MoE BE)
Educatio (MoE HU)
Istituto Nazionale di Documentazione, Innovazione e Ricerca Educativa (MoE IT)
MAKASH (MoE IL)
National Ministry of Education (MoE TR)
Norwegian Centre for ICT in Education (MoE NO)
Swiss Agency for ICT in Education (MoE CH)
The Information Technology Foundation for Education (HITSA) (MoE EE)
UNI•C (MoE DK)
Elfa (SK)
Knowledge Markets Consulting (AT)
Promethean (UK)
SMART Technologies (DE)
Aalto University (FI)
Institute of Education of University of Lisbon (PT)
Katholieke Universiteit Leuven (BE)
Manchester Metropolitan University (UK)
National Foundation for Educational Research (UK)
University of Bolton (UK)
University of Namur (BE)
University of Vigo (ES)

Our special thanks goes to the European Schoolnet and all the Ministries of Education that inspired thousands of teachers to participate, making iTEC the largest pan-European validation of ICT in schools yet made. We are in debt to Claire

Bélisle, Roberto Carneiro, Nick Kearney, Demetrios Sampson, Mikolt Csap, and Liina-Maria Munari for their expert advice and recommendations.

Our final thanks go to Will Ellis, for managing this huge endeavour and leading it towards successful completion.

Leuven, Belgium — Frans Van Assche
Vigo, Spain — Luis Anido-Rifón
Bolton, UK — David Griffiths
Manchester, UK — Cathy Lewin
Manchester, UK — Sarah McNicol

Contents

Contributors

Victor Alonso-Roris University of Vigo (ES), Pontevedra, Spain

Victor Alvarez Department of Computer Science, University of Leuven, Leuven, Belgium

Luis Anido-Rifón Telematics Engineering Department, ETSI Telecommunication, University of Vigo, Vigo, Spain

Michael Aram Knowledge Markets Consulting G.m.b.H., Wien, Austria

Douglas Armendone Swiss Agency for ICT in Education, Bern, Switzerland

Roger Blamire European Schoolnet, Brussels, Belgium

Manuel Caeiro-Rodríguez University of Vigo (ES), Pontevedra, Spain

Agustin Cañas-Rodríguez University of Vigo (ES), Pontevedra, Spain

Jean-Noël Colin University of Namur, Namur, Belgium

Sue Cranmer Department of Educational Research, Lancaster University, Lancaster, UK

Erik Duval Department of Computer Science, University of Leuven, Leuven, Belgium

Will J.R. Ellis European Schoolnet, Brussels, Belgium

Manuel Fernández-Iglesias University of Vigo (ES), Pontevedra, Spain

Javier García-Alonso University of Vigo (ES), Pontevedra, Spain

Miguel Gómez-Carballa University of Vigo (ES), Pontevedra, Spain

David Griffiths Institute of Educational Cybernatics, University of Bolton, Bolton, UK

Anna Keune Aalto University, Espoo, Finland

Joris Klerkx Department of Computer Science, University of Leuven, Leuven, Belgium

Teemu Leinonen Aalto University, Espoo, Finland

Cathy Lewin Education and Social Research Institute, Manchester Metropolitan University, Manchester, UK

Martín Llamas-Nistal University of Vigo (ES), Pontevedra, Spain

Mario Manso-Vázquez University of Vigo (ES), Pontevedra, Spain

Sarah McNicol Education and Social Research Institute, Manchester Metropolitan University, Manchester, UK

Rubén Míguez-Pérez University of Vigo (ES), Pontevedra, Spain

Marcos Mouriño-García University of Vigo (ES), Pontevedra, Spain

Roberto Pérez-Rodríguez University of Vigo (ES), Pontevedra, Spain

Kris Popat University of Bolton, Bolton, UK

Manuel Caeiro Rodríguez University of Vigo (ES), Pontevedra, Spain

Juan Santos-Gago University of Vigo (ES), Pontevedra, Spain

Bernd Simon Knowledge Markets Consulting G.m.b.H., Wien, Austria

Tarmo Toikkanen Aalto University, Espoo, Finland

Mary Ulicsak JISC, Bristol, UK

Frans Van Assche Department of Computer Science, University of Leuven, Leuven, Belgium

Abbreviations

API	Application programming interface
CPD	Continued professional development
DSRM	Design science research methodology
FCL	Future classroom lab
FCT	Future classroom toolkit
FOAF	Friend of a friend
HLG	High level group; a group of senior advisors to the iTEC project
ICT	Information and communication technology
IEC	iTEC educational cloud
ITE	Initial teacher education
iTEC	Innovative technologies for an engaging classroom, the name of the project co-funded by the European Commission
iTEC-PDH	iTEC protocol for data harvesting
JISC	Joint Information Systems Committee (UK)
LTI	Learning technology interoperability; a specification of IMS Global
MCDA	Multiple criteria decision analysis
MOOC	Massive open online courses
NPC	National Pedagogical Coordinator; a role in the iTEC project
NTC	National Technical Coordinator; a role in the iTEC project
OECD	Organisation for Economic Co-operation and Development
REST	Representational state transfer
RTE	Run-time environment
SAAS	Software as a service
SDE	Scenario development engine
SDK	Software development kit
SUS	System usability scale
TEL	Technology enhanced learning
TPC	Technical pedagogical coordinator
UMAC	User management and access control system developed in iTEC

Chapter 1
Innovative Technologies for an Engaging Classroom (iTEC)

Will J.R. Ellis, Roger Blamire, and Frans Van Assche

Abstract The iTEC project developed a process that allows schools to rethink how they are currently using ICT, and which provides concrete guidance and tools to help them close what is being called the "mainstreaming gap", where technology is not yet fully harnessed as a systemic part of everyday classroom practice that integrates learning both in and out of school. A key element in the approach is to bring together policy makers, researchers, technology suppliers and teachers to develop future classroom scenarios. These scenarios both engage and challenge schools to rethink their current practice and allow them to develop pedagogically advanced Learning Activities that enable a school to upscale its use of ICT and adapt to changing socio-economic conditions. A "Future Classroom Toolkit" has been produced to support wide-scale adoption of the iTEC approach to help schools to design innovative Learning Activities and carry out classroom pilots. This piloting has been carried out on a scale never before attempted in a pan-European project; over 2500 classrooms piloted Learning Activities based on the iTEC Future Classroom scenarios. It is increasingly clear from work in iTEC that the mainstreaming gap needs bottom-up as well as top-down actions, and particularly requires each school to be able to innovate with ICT and develop a sustainable change management process on its own terms and at its own pace.

Keywords Uptake of ICT • Re-engineering • Innovative technologies • School education • Policy making

W.J.R. Ellis (✉) • R. Blamire
European Schoolnet, Brussels, Belgium
e-mail: willellis.work@gmail.com; roger.blamire@eun.org

F. Van Assche
Department of Computer Science, University of Leuven, Leuven, Belgium
e-mail: frans.van.assche@gmail.com

F. Van Assche et al. (eds.), *Re-engineering the Uptake of ICT in Schools*,
DOI 10.1007/978-3-319-19366-3_1

Rationale for Re-engineering the Uptake of ICT in Schools

Reaping the benefits of ICT in education is, however, not an easy endeavour. Research confirms broad benefits; however demonstrators are not scaling up as expected—and cost is only part of the problem. The project was set up with a back drop that too many previous future classroom designs had been technology-driven, based on blue-sky thinking or a "rigorous imagining" approach that had little visible impact on schools and teachers. A number of the scenarios that have been influential at European level in terms of technology-enhanced learning research have even declared the school to be redundant or "over". However, at the time this project was conceived, Ministries of Education were not calling for more blue-sky visions. On the contrary, the view from some ministries was that while radical future classroom scenarios involving emerging technologies may provide useful food for thought, they can also intimidate or even alienate many teachers and could be counterproductive as far as mainstreaming is concerned.

Therefore, the focus of our work was to address the transition from new ideas to a full uptake of developed products, services and processes, based on solid principles.

Among the approaches taken into consideration for addressing this issue were the adoption life cycle for Learning Technologies by CETIS,[1] the design science approach of Hevner and Chatterjee (2010), the design science research methodology for IS research (Peffers et al. 2007), and the benefits realisation management (BRM) approach (Bradley 2010). A simple model is depicted in Fig. 1.1.

iTEC's strategic vision is grounded in the belief that the greatest impact can be achieved by **improving the mainstreaming process of current and emerging technologies into evolving educational contexts**. From this perspective, one of the most substantial contributions the project has made to the educational community is an approach (supported by appropriate tools, techniques and frameworks) that can

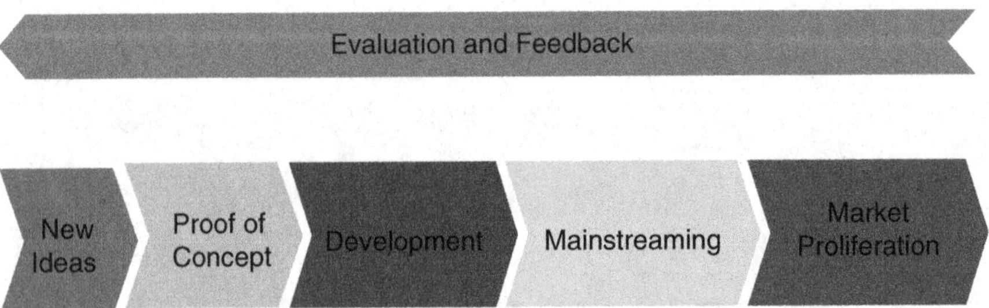

Fig. 1.1 The innovation cycle

[1] http://www.cetis.ac.uk/

stand the test of time and be used for future emerging technologies and that can be used across Europe. There is an old saying: "Give a man a fish and you feed him for a day; teach a man to fish and you feed him for a lifetime". Similarly, iTEC sought to improve, exemplify and support a mainstreaming *approach* rather than to provide a few isolated and unsustainable examples of successful Research and Development showcases of hyped technology, out of date in 5 years.

Education systems adapt slowly for reasons which in some cases are understandable (social cohesion, transmission of enduring values, political pressure) yet technology (and its promise for learning) is evolving at an increasing speed. In such a context, the effectiveness of mainstreaming processes is often the most significant determining factor in changing practice and capitalizing on what ICT can offer. Mainstreaming processes should not only foster the uptake of innovative practices and of technologies but also improve the detection of risks and barriers, in order to avoid mainstreaming efforts that are likely to fail.

Barriers to the mainstreaming of technologies have been studied since the beginning of Technology Enhanced Learning (TEL). For example, the first large scale European project about TEL in schools, e.g., he Web for Schools project of 1996 (see Van Assche 1998), as well as more recent studies (European Commission 2013) reported the limited time of teachers, the lack of good ICT practice in teacher education, the constraints of the curriculum, the lack of teacher confidence (teachers being scared and intimidated by their student's increasing knowledge about Internet and communication devices), lack of pedagogical teacher education; lack of suitable educational software, limited access to ICT; rigid structure of traditional education systems, etc.

Typically, such barriers are part of the debate about innovation versus traditional approaches. A NESTA report on this subject (Luckin et al. 2012, p. 63) confirms many of these barriers but also identifies opportunities and confirms the iTEC findings while concluding:

> *We found proof by putting learning first. We have shown how different technologies can improve learning by augmenting and connecting proven learning activities... there is also a great deal that can be done with existing technology. It is clear that there is no single technology that is 'best' for learning.*

Most significantly, with the increasing confidence of practitioners, the prevailing culture of education practice is changing towards an understanding that innovation and experimentation should be embraced as a solution to challenges in the classroom.

iTEC has been working towards a vision in the future where the pace of change in the classroom has become significantly more aligned with the pace of change and use of technology in society; where technologies supporting creativity, collaboration and communication have become common in the workplace and everyday lives, and the ubiquitous nature of this technology, and the affordances it brings, is mirrored by its use in schools across Europe; where schools are no longer an oasis of "low tech" and traditional didactic interaction.

Supporting the Uptake of ICT in Schools

The uptake of ICT in schools was in iTEC supported by eight strands of activity (Ellis 2014), based on the iTEC evaluation findings, ongoing consultation with partners and the recommendations of the external experts. These strands are (see Fig. 1.2):

1. The Future Classroom Toolkit (the main output)
2. An Initial Teacher Education network and emerging network of Future Classroom Labs
3. The Future Classroom Ambassador scheme
4. Continuing Professional Development (CPD)
5. A family of related projects (see below for examples)
6. Influencing national policy and strategy
7. Exploitation of iTEC technical research and industry collaboration
8. Further engagement with school leaders and teacher communities

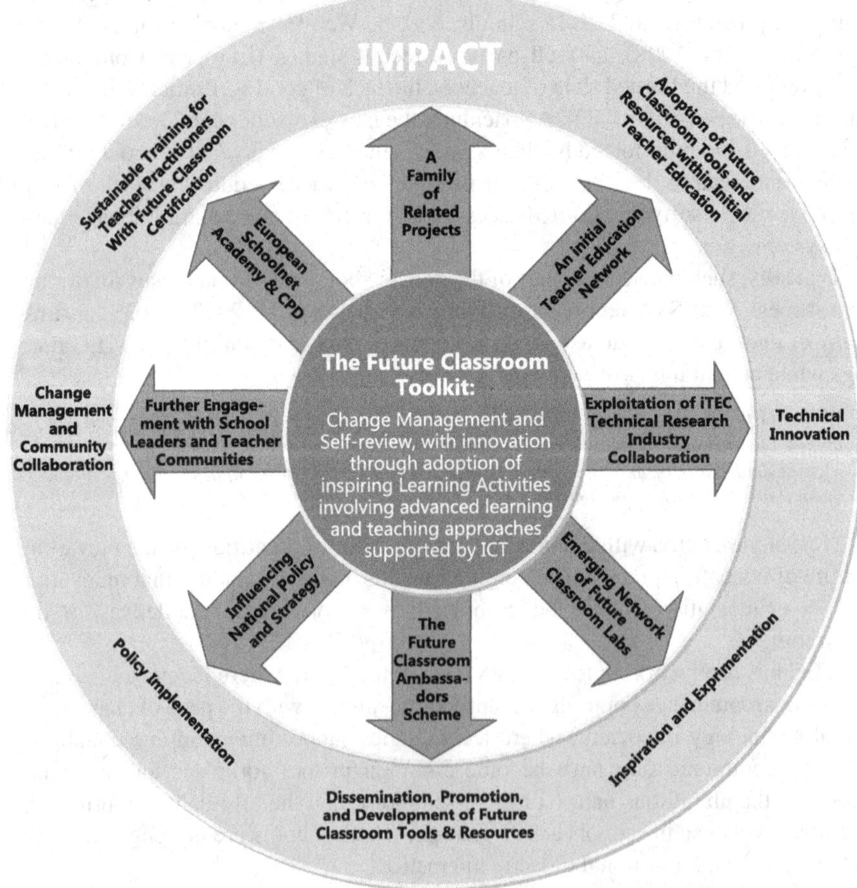

Fig. 1.2 Eight strands of ICT uptake that reinforce each other

The Future Classroom Toolkit

The iTEC project partnership was very successful in developing and adapting the processes for scenario development and learning activity design. The consortium delivered a well thought through set of tools and techniques for achieving this through the Future Classroom Toolkit, including a solid bank of Future Classroom Scenarios and Learning Activities.

This Future Classroom Toolkit provides a "clear narrative" for a "change management" oriented workflow that starts with creating a vision of innovation, captured in scenarios. In iTEC, a **scenario** is defined as a narrative description of teaching and learning that provides a vision for innovation and advanced pedagogical practice, making effective use of ICT. Next, the workflow proceeds through to the practical implementation of Learning Activities and classroom validation. These **Learning Activities** are detailed descriptions of novel (at least in the iTEC context) teaching and learning in classrooms. These detailed descriptions include the resources to be used, the context (e.g., the location), the roles of participants, etc.

This workflow is supported by tools for learning design, maturity modelling, finding resources, etc. In guiding users through the tools and processes, the toolkit itself acts as a method of training and professional development, rather than simply a resource repository. The toolkit takes the following into consideration:

- Target Audience—Initially school leaders and advanced teachers, but also targeting other groups particularly Initial Teacher Education organisations, Continuous Professional development (CPD) providers and ICT suppliers.
- Inclusion of video materials, learner stories and teacher stories (repository of experiences).
- Perspectives of school leaders and learners.

There are different strategies for developing scenarios and Learning Activities. While initially it may be advisable to centrally manage, in a top-down manner, the creation of scenarios and Learning Activities, eventually it should be possible for other stakeholders to replicate the processes in order to create their own resources. The strategy to devolve the design processes across the iTEC partnership was an essential first step in enabling the ongoing development of relevant scenarios and Learning Activities, and ensuring that these outputs meet the local needs of users, e.g., by responding to local trends, opportunities and constraints.

A Teacher Education Network and Emerging Network of Future Classroom Labs

Teacher competencies are at the heart of effective education systems, yet consultation with partners and Initial Teacher Education (ITE) organisations has revealed that teacher education does not adequately cover innovation and change, and technology-supported pedagogical practices.

Workshops with ITE organisations have confirmed that the design of Learning Activities is well suited to preparing trainee teachers for their classroom practice. This has led to the set-up of an ITE network that will work collaboratively to research and summarise current developments and trends in teacher education. The ITE providers within the network will assess the effectiveness of the iTEC/Future Classroom model and its potential for use in other European countries.

The expected outcomes of this network are:

- A Future Classroom Toolkit, tailored for adoption and adaptation by ITE providers.
- A published set of case studies showing how a diversity of ITE providers can adopt the tools and resources within their own training provision.
- A sustainability plan showing how the Future Classroom training programme and resources can be maintained and adopted at scale by ITE organisations.

A second approach to establishing this network is to link interested parties with the development of a network of Future Classroom Labs. The project decided that an important part of the iTEC 'value proposition' would be to provide physical environments in which iTEC Future Classroom Scenarios, Learning Activities and best practices could be showcased and demonstrated to policy makers, industry partners, school leaders and teachers. The Future Classroom Lab[2] (FCL) concept was developed by European Schoolnet in parallel to the iTEC project and is now an independently funded initiative supported by European Schoolnet and 35 industry partners. The FCL consists of a room designed as an interactive classroom, to illustrate how a traditional classroom setting can use technology to enhance interactivity and student participation, plus a large reconfigurable open space equipped with the latest technology. As iTEC results and training courses were heavily promoted via the Future Classroom Lab over the last 18 months of the project, one totally unforeseen consequence of this iTEC activity has been an increasing interest from both Ministries of Education and schools in replicating elements of the Future Classroom Lab at the European Schoolnet[3] in Brussels, in a variety of countries. Teaching rooms inspired by this lab, have now been established in schools in Ancona in Italy, Ghent in Belgium, Setubal in Portugal, Crema in Italy, Zagreb in Croatia, and Tallinn in Estonia, and many others are in the process of implementation. See examples in Figs. 1.3 and 1.4.

[2] Future Classroom Lab, http://flc.eun.org

[3] European Schoolnet is a network of 30 European Ministries of Education. See http://www.eun.org/

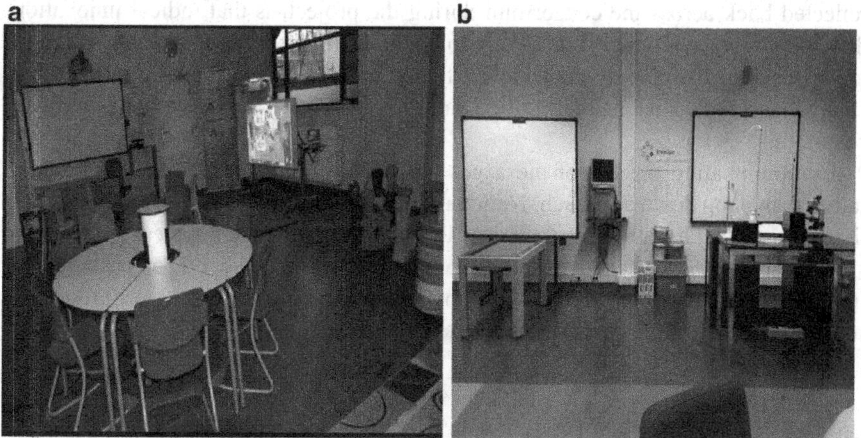

Fig. 1.3 The Future Classroom Labs in Ghent (Belgium) and Setubal (Portugal)

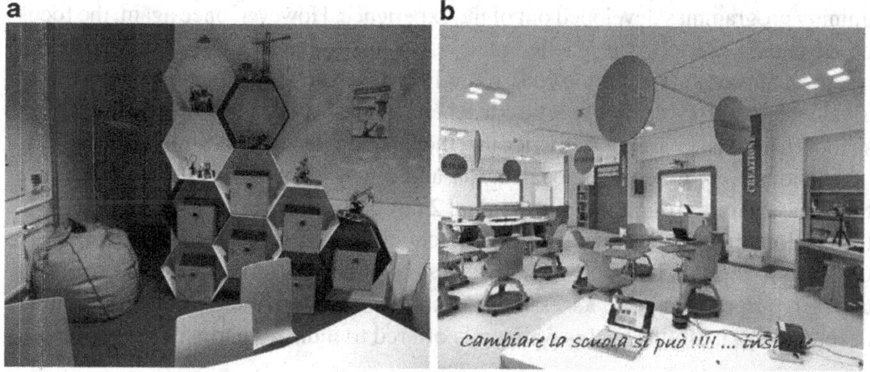

Fig. 1.4 The Future Classroom Labs in Tallinn (Estonia) and Ancona (Italy)

A Future Classroom Ambassadors Scheme

Communicating iTEC to a wider audience has been a challenge, and the "Future Classroom" discussion regularly opens up a debate about innovation verses traditional approaches. However, the iTEC project has presented some clear and well-targeted messages, which have helped engage stakeholders. Perhaps the most important message has been to emphasise that iTEC is about advances and innovation in learning and teaching, not about "pushing" ICT into schools. Whilst evidence shows that teachers largely appreciate the value of technology, they can still be understandably threatened by initiatives which put the technology before the needs of learners, or the reality of the classroom. Another message, that was reflected back across the consortium during the project, is that radical innovation driven by new technology is not likely to be mainstreamed. Pilots were designed to move teachers sufficiently outside of their comfort zone to ensure sustainable change, and tools such as the Future Classroom Maturity Model were designed to ensure this.

Communicating this set of messages has been through an advocacy approach, rather than a top down approach. National Coordinators, in touch with teacher realities were critical to the early success of the project and, in later cycles, the work to spread iTEC resources and ideas was taken on by the teachers who had participated in pilots. The value of teacher ambassadors either formally appointed, or informally self-appointed in some cases, has been demonstrated.

Continuing Professional Development

Already for decades, teacher professional development initiatives are mostly seen as a key component of using ICT in the classroom, with a variety of online and offline training programmes developed out of the experience. However, once again, the focus on advancing pedagogical practice rather than just technical skills is the subtle but powerful approach. The Future Classroom Lab (FCL) has continued to prove itself as a valuable asset in this, supporting teachers as they carry out pilots in their own schools using the Learning Activities that they have collectively developed in the Lab.

Obviously, CPD requires localization and a way of achieving this is through a train-the-trainers programme. In an initial 2 day course, partners get training on how to develop their own course for local schools based on the use of the Future Classroom Toolkit. This will include access to course materials and resources that can be repurposed and full access to the Future Classroom Toolkit (including future developments). Similarly, this training is offered to industry partners.

Continued and Related Research and Development

An important part of the overall vision for the uptake of ICT in schools has been to ensure that the iTEC's R&D is not a stand-alone activity but is part of a 'family' of related R&D efforts. Examples of such continued and related R&D are:

The CPD*Lab* project[4] which was consciously designed to leverage, consolidate and help sustain the work being carried out in iTEC related to the professional

[4] Continuing Professional Development Lab (CPDLab), http://cpdlab.eun.org

development of teachers. The 5-day Future Classroom Scenarios course developed in CPD*Lab* was first delivered in the FCL in Brussels in summer 2013 to teachers who had received Comenius funding and a second version of this course (*Future Classroom—adapting pedagogical practice*) was offered in spring 2014. Shorter versions of the course have also been run in two-day workshops for eTwinning[5] teachers in the FCL.

The second project, Living Schools Lab[6] (LSL), has explored new models for mainstreaming innovative practice by establishing a network where Advanced Practitioners work with Advanced Schools based around regional clusters. As well as impacting on the extensive professional development programme that has been provided for LSL teachers, iTEC and LSL started to put in place a new mechanism to allow exchanges with head teachers to take place on a regular basis under the FCL umbrella.

The third project, Creative Classrooms Lab[7] (CCL) is carrying out a series of policy experimentations on the use of tablets in schools involving nine Ministries of Education. In the first year of the project, policy makers and teachers in CCL followed the iTEC process to create tablet scenarios (related to collaboration, content creation, flipped classroom, and personalisation) and Learning Activities that were piloted in 45 classrooms in eight countries. As in iTEC, the CCL scenarios are included within a new bank of Future Classroom Scenarios and Learning Activities.[8]

Influencing National Policy and Strategy

For the outcomes of iTEC to feature in any emerging policy or strategy initiative, the timing of policy-making, competing political pressures, and economic considerations all have to be factored in. While in some countries the political context does support a top down intervention, this approach is not viable in every case. There are indeed cases where the political system does not support any intervention e.g., Portugal and the Slovak Republic where there is no specific policy initiative likely to focus on education and ICT, and in Flemish Belgium where it is accepted that the role of government is not to intervene in learning and teaching. Therefore, iTEC sought to achieve impact in a more direct way, through engagement with the different agencies and mechanisms that exist in each country, with the role of putting national policy into practice.

[5] http://www.etwinning.net/

[6] Living Schools Lab (LSL), http://lsl.eun.org

[7] Creative Classrooms Lab (CCL), http://creative.eun.org

[8] http://creative.eun.org/scenarios

Assessment by a Group of Senior Advisors

The iTEC project established a High Level Group (HLG) of senior advisors and policy makers (that included two former ministers of education) which assessed the iTEC outcomes, identifying a number of challenges and enabling factors for the uptake of ICT in schools.

Implementation Challenges

Despite widespread support from participants and stakeholders in iTEC, a key challenge in the exploitation of the results was engaging the attention and support of a wider group of key education influencers and persuading them to mainstream the project's innovative practices. To achieve this, project outputs must continue to be communicated effectively to those key influencers to encourage them and move them to action.

Clear messaging must continue to be developed and communicated, for those specific stakeholders. Messaging should highlight compelling evidence, and address where appropriate, factors that might be used to diminish or undermine progress. HLG members, representing the perspective of senior policy makers provided valuable insight into perceptions of such stakeholders and identified challenges that might present barriers to policy maker engagement.

Different Results in Different Countries

While the project involved practice in over 2500 classrooms, geographic distribution of classrooms was not even across Europe which could suggest that iTEC results are more appropriate to some countries, and less appropriate to others. With 20 pilot countries, it is perhaps not surprising that there are differences in approach that, arguably, should be further explored. Structures and systems, capacity for innovation and change, pre-existing relationships between students and teachers, and attitudes toward professional development all contribute to the differences in results between countries. Timing might also be considered important, with each country at a different stage in the cycle of reform, and travelling in quite different directions. A finding here is that resistance is often *not* caused by scepticism and *can* be mitigated by better contextualising the use of tools and approaches, such as in iTEC, in terms of readiness for classroom innovation.

Suggesting the Results of iTEC Are Influenced by Classroom Self-selection

It could be suggested that projects introducing emerging ICT only work in schools with teachers who are already innovative and enthusiastic. As a result, it could be proposed that scaling may not be possible because the precondition of innovative and enthusiastic teachers may not be in place. However, the first counter argument should perhaps be developing the conditions in which enthusiastic innovative teachers become the norm rather than the exception. Top down imposition is seldom an answer. Further evidence of the limitations of a top down approach comes from a group of teachers who participated in an Education Fast Forward[9] debate. The teachers reported that authorities were introducing a requirement for them to be collaborative. Their reaction was to withdraw their labour, an unintended outcome from a top down instruction.

However, the experience in iTEC was that self-selection meant that the teachers who did participate were effectively teacher leaders. There is evidence within the project that such teachers actively spread iTEC practices and messages to other teachers, in a way that was most acceptable to them (rather than a top down approach). That bottom up, organic approach, often associated with creation of movements, may ultimately be more powerful. In these circumstances, advanced, innovative and enthusiastic teachers are empowered to take a lead within their profession and to act as ambassadors.

Cost of Scaling Up Teacher Training

The cost of scaling teacher training is dependent on local or national circumstances. The OECD (2014) publication indicates some of the factors that influence participation in professional development activities. It should be noted that it is based on direct feedback from teachers. “TALIS[10] finds that, across participating countries and economies, teachers most often cite conflicts with their work schedule (51 % of teachers) and a lack of incentives (48 %) as barriers to participating in professional development activities”.[11] In comparison, evidence from the Survey of Schools : ICT in Education[12] shows that, as regards ICT, there is much self-directed, ad hoc, CPD in teachers’ own time: across the EU 74 % of grade 8 students are in schools where this is the case, demonstrating a high level of willingness to learn about ICT. The Survey suggests that this learning is in isolation however: only 28 % of grade 11 general students are in schools where teachers have taken part in online communities of fellow educators. This suggested an untapped opportunity to develop online social CPD offerings. We therefore argue that when teachers are suitably motivated, and training resources are of sufficient quality and availability, teachers can effectively engage in valuable CPD at low cost and at scale online. This evidence has led to further development in online flexible training programmes which many of the iTEC partners have produced as, a direct consequence of iTEC. A prominent example is the European Schoolnet Academy[13] that started to offer free online courses lasting 6–8 weeks for teachers’ professional development.

[9] http://www.effdebate.org/

[10] Teaching and Learning International Survey

[11] OECD (2014, p. 13)

[12] European Commission (2013, p. 75)

[13] http://www.europeanschoolnetacademy.eu/

Getting the Message and Language Correct for the Diverse Political Contexts of Europe

A central challenge was that there was no uniform way of promoting iTEC effectively and efficiently that would work across all countries and their contexts, owing to the significant differences in policy, culture, language, perceptions of education and its structures, etc. Strengths and positive outputs of projects such as iTEC play differently within different government philosophies and priorities. As a result, messages should be tailored for each circumstance in order to ensure a good fit with local and national policy. In the case of iTEC, the project has benefited from direct links to policy priorities across many countries, thanks to the involvement of Ministries of Education. Consequently, in some areas iTEC developments have gained near universal acceptance (e.g., influencing initial teacher education); there is unanimous agreement on the need for iTEC to seriously impact on ITE but this remains a challenge. Also here the right message and language must be used as ITE institutions operate quite independently in terms of their curriculum.

Similar consideration needs to be given to language used to promote iTEC's outputs. Terminology such as "21st Century Skills" and "Future Classroom" can invite cynicism and suspicion in some circumstances, but are persuasive in others. For example, "future" may give a sense of unobtainable fantasy to some, while to others it can be entirely appropriate. It is clearly important to understand the particular vocabulary of policy-makers and to avoid those commonly used terms and clichés that can lead to negative reactions.

Investment in Prototypes

While the iTEC process has proven itself, within the context of the project, the resulting toolkit was described by one member of the High Level Group of senior advisors as a "train without a rail network". This description was intended to highlight that the toolkit is a valuable resource, but appropriate infrastructure needs to be in place for it to show its true value. Funding tends to be drawn towards small-scale research projects, or infrastructure initiatives that rapidly provide more visibly concrete outputs, rather than long term initiatives that can impact working practices more subtly and more fundamentally.

Linked to this, is evidence of impact on learner achievement. This was outside the iTEC project's scope, but may present an additional challenge for acceptance and adoption of iTEC outcomes, particularly if further investment is required. While the evaluation results give very good evidence of the benefits in terms of motivation and engagement by learners together with improvements in twenty-first century skills, many policy makers are fundamentally concerned with evidence of learners achieving improved results in exams.

Strengths Supporting Implementation

The High Level Group of senior advisors identified strengths of iTEC, which are seen as offering the most compelling arguments to attract support and investment from policy makers and to enable wider impact of iTEC's outputs. The identified strengths were important for iTEC, but are in general worthwhile for any Technology Enhanced Learning project.

Engagement of Teachers at Low Cost

It can be universally appreciated, that any action that can positively motivate and inspire teachers is worthy of consideration. If such motivation is clearly cost effective then adoption is even more compelling. This is perhaps the key component of iTEC's work. There is good evidence to show that teachers were engaged, enthusiastic and motivated by iTEC, even though teachers were not paid to participate and effectively encountered additional burdens and challenges. The enthusiasm to participate was reinforced by involvement of several additional countries and regions in iTEC. These countries played active roles in the project without receiving any funding for doing so. The countries included Spain, Finland and the Czech Republic.

Innovation in Practice Involving a Large Number of Teachers

With over 2500 classrooms participating in the project, iTEC stands out for its size. It should also be emphasised that this project is not based on theory and research alone, but has demonstrated the possibility to bring change in practice at scale. Large-scale validation projects involving (the practice of) thousands of teachers, such as iTEC, help raise a project's profile and validity.

Promoting Teacher Community Collaboration

iTEC, through both its technical and pedagogical activities, has exploited the trend of social networking to encourage teaching professionals to use such tools and share resources, ideas and practices at low cost and high scale. iTEC has shown that when teachers work in collaboration, and collaborate together in communities, many benefits can result. Collaboration and community-based action have the potential to reduce costs of administration and to encourage development and change, appropriate to local groups, individuals and organizations. Technology is often seen as being at the core of this change.

Focus on Learning and Teaching, Cross-Curriculum and Cross Age Group

The principles and practices established as a part of iTEC can be applied in any subject area or age group. Policy makers can therefore engage these principles and practices for a wide range of policy initiatives, and thereby be helped in policy formulation and implementation. In addition, it should be noted that iTEC's processes are not driven by technology, but instead by pedagogy. It is widely suggested that, too often, projects and initiatives focus on a technology as the main driving force, while fundamental learning aims are forgotten and pedagogy underserved. Evidence from teachers in iTEC highlights changing and positive relationships developed within classrooms, and a positive impact on learning. Teachers' digital competencies and pedagogy were enhanced, and teachers became more enthusiastic about their pedagogical practices.

Conclusions

Based on extensive testing within the iTEC project, the Future Classroom Toolkit proved to have great potential in achieving wide scale innovation. The toolkit was made available in seven languages (English, French, Portuguese, German, Norwegian, Italian and Spanish) under an open licence allowing use and adaptation, including commercial use.

The scenario development process, elaborated in iTEC, provides a professional approach to developing, documenting and disseminating innovative practices. The process supports an approach to rethinking pedagogy with technology that is not technology-led but pedagogically-led.

It also encourages teachers to consider themselves **learning designers**, to vary the range of activities and to focus on what students (not the teacher) are doing. It brings a wider range of stakeholders together, enables a focus on local priorities and provides a standardised approach. The outcomes of the scenarios, the Learning Stories and Learning Activities, are perceived to offer a structured approach for introducing new technologies into classroom practices. These resources are seen by many to be innovative for teachers and important enablers of change because they provide concrete and well-structured examples, emphasise innovation and offer flexibility whilst being easy to use.

Experience shows that the iTEC process will not be "transferred" and adopted by the majority of schools simply as a result of exhortation or advocacy or showcasing these large-scale pilots at national level. For example, the European Commission[14] states that: "Campaigns aimed at school heads and teachers to convince them of the relevance and positive impact of ICT use are no longer of value". Centrally driven

[14] European Commission (2013, p. 121)

dissemination campaigns may also struggle to be effective unless practitioners, and those involved in teacher professional development and initial teacher education organisations are provided with new tools for rethinking teaching and learning and which support change management. It is increasingly clear from work in iTEC that the mainstreaming gap concerning ICT use in schools needs bottom-up as well as top-down actions, and particularly requires each school to be able to innovate with ICT and develop a sustainable change management process on its own terms and at its own pace.

References

Bradley G (2010) Benefits realisation management, 2nd edn. Gower, Surrey

Ellis W (2014) Exploitation plan of the iTEC project. http://itec.eun.org/web/guest/deliverables

European Commission (2013) Survey of schools: ICT in education. https://ec.europa.eu/digital-agenda/node/51275

Hevner A, Chatterjee S (2010) Design research in information systems: theory and practice. Springer, New York

Luckin R, Bligh B, Manches A, Ainsworth S, Crook C, Noss R (2012) Decoding learning: the proof, promise and potential of digital education, NESTA report. http://www.nesta.org.uk/sites/default/files/decoding_learning_report.pdf

OECD (2014) A teachers' guide to TALIS 2013: teaching and learning international survey, TALIS. OECD, Paris

Peffers K, Tuunanen T, Rothenberger MA, Chatterjee S (2007) A design science research methodology for information systems research. J Manag Inf Syst 24:45–77

Van Assche F (ed) (1998) Using the World Wide Web in secondary schools. ACCO, Leuven

References

Chapter 2
Development of the Future Classroom Toolkit

Sue Cranmer and Mary Ulicsak

Abstract Key to iTEC was the need to empower teachers to facilitate positive and sustainable innovative classroom practices enhanced by digital technologies. Initially it was envisaged that experts would create challenging yet feasible scenarios that would be refined by stakeholders. From these scenarios, Learning Activities would be developed that would lead to innovation either pedagogically or technologically. Nevertheless, the complexity of defining innovation and the challenge of innovating within different contexts had been somewhat underestimated. As the nature of the project work became better understood, it became clear that stakeholders—particularly teachers—needed to be responsible for scenario creation in order to be able to assimilate innovative approaches into current practice. This chapter explains the evolution of this process from the creation of scenarios to the development of the Future Classroom Toolkit. Within this, it focuses on the role of maturity models to enable stakeholders to assess their current context and practice in terms of the level of innovation. In addition, it shows how the Future Classroom Toolkit can support and encourage stakeholders to take ownership of and augment their own innovative practices using digital technologies for the benefit of learners.

Keywords Scenarios • Digital technologies • ICT • Innovation • Future classroom toolkit

Introduction

This chapter focuses on the challenges of innovation; specifically how the Future Classroom Toolkit was designed to encourage innovation through the development of educational scenarios and, in turn, within classrooms. To achieve this, it considers the evolution of the three key outputs from Work Package 2: scenarios, the Maturity Model and the Future Classroom Toolkit.

S. Cranmer (✉)
Department of Educational Research, Lancaster University, Lancaster, UK
e-mail: s.cranmer@lancaster.ac.uk

M. Ulicsak
JISC, Bristol, UK
e-mail: mary.ulicsak@jisc.ac.uk

F. Van Assche et al. (eds.), *Re-engineering the Uptake of ICT in Schools*,
DOI 10.1007/978-3-319-19366-3_2

The Challenge to Innovate

The concept of innovation is difficult to define and this provided a key challenge throughout the iTEC project. Innovation is a matter of perception, not an absolute (Rogers 1995). It is dependent on subjectivity and context. As Somekh (2007) points out, 'the difficulty in understanding the process of innovation is that we see it necessarily from our own standpoint'. Concepts like 'new' and 'better' are based on subjective assessments of the value of an innovation (Moyle 2010); and as (Kozma 2003) found in the international Second Information Technology in Education Study (SITES), 'innovation often depends on the cultural… context within which it is observed'. Therefore, recognising and accounting for the context where the innovation is introduced is critical.

Educational innovation must be a change that creates positive value, not simply something new. OECD/CERI (2010) define innovation as '… any dynamic change intended to add value to the educational process and resulting in measurable outcomes, be that in terms of stakeholder satisfaction or educational performance' (p. 14). Innovation is typically considered to be deliberate, designed to be of benefit, about change, dynamic and potentially unpredictable and 'occurs in a specific political, sociocultural, economic, technological, and organisational context that influences its development, diffusion, and use' (Kampylis et al. 2012, p. 6).

The level of innovation can also be defined in various ways. Kampylis and colleagues (2012) refer to incremental (progressive change involving a few new elements); and radical (involving a number of new elements) and disruptive innovation 'a profound and comprehensive change' (p. 9). However, Christensen et al. (2008) define two different trajectories: 'sustaining': building on and improving existing thinking, products, processes, organisations or social systems; or 'disruptive': which changes the core of what already exists.

A further challenge exists in the need to scale and sustain innovative and effective projects (Brecko et al. 2014; Bocconi et al. 2013; Kozma 2003). Dede (2010) argues that scaling up demands adaptable innovations, irrespective of context and particular circumstance. Others argue that it is essential to identify mechanisms to support system wide change (Brecko et al. 2014). Kampylis et al. contend that there is no single approach to scaling up innovation but instead there is a need for scaling up strategies to support 'multiple pathways and ecological diversity in innovation' (Kampylis et al. 2013, p. 133). Rogers' (1995) 'diffusion' model of innovation demonstrates how individual, small-scale (incremental) changes can support and lead to a broader set of local innovations. Moreover, Kampylis et al. note that 'more disruptive innovations are more difficult to scale up' (Kampylis et al. 2013, pp. 131–132). Therefore, innovation is best seen as a process of incremental steps, the most common approach in educational contexts (Kampylis et al. 2013).

In the context of the challenges outlined previously in relation to defining, scaling and sustaining innovation, iTEC's aim was to drive innovation by developing and trialling new approaches to teaching and learning enabled by technology. Specifically, iTEC's activities were intended to help teachers respond to the day-to-day and systemic challenges they face by providing them with pedagogical and technological solutions. The project also took account of research showing that innovations led and managed by teachers are more effective than initiatives from external forces (Von Hippe 2005; Sutch et al. 2008).

The issue of how innovative the interventions were remained an enduring challenge throughout the project and required partners to develop a clearer idea of how innovation should be evaluated within the project. It was agreed that innovation in iTEC could be either technological or pedagogical, or both. Nevertheless, this has its complexities. Technological innovation refers to widespread use of an invention or a technology regardless of its use or possible innovative practices with it (Béchard 2001). For example, it is possible that interactive whiteboards, a technology that is no longer new, could be used to either reinforce traditional teacher-centred practices or facilitate innovative learning approaches. The SITES project for instance found that many of the 174 case studies of innovative practice it gathered used 'ordinary technology' to do innovative things (Kozma 2003).

Pedagogical innovation exists only when approaches in teaching and learning are modified; this could be the introduction of a totally new approach or a novel combination of existing approaches. Consequently this could require a major change in educational values and organisation (both pedagogical and administrative—structures, functions, roles, communication). Given these conditions, it can be difficult therefore to pinpoint specific pedagogical practices and to recognise these as innovative. Such changes can be qualitative (e.g., depth) or quantitative (e.g., frequency, duration). The same analysis can be made of relationships between teacher and student (teacher or student locus, peer learning, etc.). In all cases, it is important to document qualitative and measure quantitative aspects, with and without the technology, and the wider effects (e.g., motivation, confidence in working with others). Gathering such evidence is also needed to scale up a pedagogical innovation but that is not possible through the development of a simple formula or step-by-step guide applicable in any context. What really makes an innovation scalable is that it can be adapted to any new environment (recombining, adjusting, etc.)—while retaining its essence (Tobin 2005)—in order for other teachers and learners truly to own it.

Furthermore, the iTEC project was firmly focused on delivering sustainable mechanisms for wide scale adoption of innovation that had deep and lasting impact. This aim was underpinned by belief that incremental change (Kampylis et al. 2012) is as important as disruptive innovation. And this is supported by Rogers' (1995) 'diffusion' model of innovation which demonstrates how individual, small-scale changes can support and lead to a broader set of local innovations by other 'end-users'. Similarly, Fierro-Evan's research (OECD 2008) identified: 'While micro-level innovations might seem to have "limited relevance", paradoxically, they are usually the most permanent and make the deepest impact on practice' (p. 19).

From this, in the iTEC project, an innovation in education is defined as a change that brings about a positive result in teaching and learning but which is context specific. This is because an innovation in one country or school is not necessarily considered innovative in another. Moreover, innovations are often found to be most effective when they bring about incremental change building on existing practice as these can be easily scaled and lead to local innovations by others.

Keeping this in mind, the next section will define scenarios, one of the key drivers of innovation and outputs of the iTEC project, and the rationale for their use. Specifically it will look at how scenarios sought to stimulate innovation and how the evolution of the development process refined the understanding of innovation within the project.

Overview of Scenarios, and Scenario Development and Monitoring Process

Scenarios have been used in multiple projects as a tool to consider the possible future of education. They have been recognised for stimulating 'new, visionary thinking' and helping to motivate educators to get 'unstuck' (Ogilvy 2006). The Future Classroom Scenarios were defined as narrative descriptions of teaching and learning that provided a vision for innovation and advanced pedagogical practice, making effective use of ICT. Scenarios were key to the success of iTEC in enabling stakeholders (including school leaders and teachers, advisers at a regional or national level, and technology providers) to recognise the needs of students, *and* inspire teachers to change their own practices. The three predominant aims of scenarios in education can be summarised as:

- Explore and illustrate the potential interactions of the many factors such as technology, pedagogy and policy that seem likely to shape the future and how this will impact on the classroom.
- Be appropriated by those involved in education to develop and evaluate their own visions while avoiding undesirable futures.
- Provide tools to allow those with differing backgrounds, such as policy makers, educators and academics, to engage in strategic dialogue around the direction of policy and practice.

Future Classroom Scenarios were structured around specific trends and challenges that affect and are affected by education. These could be economic, social or technological factors that were either recognised as important and/or could influence the context. The trends identified during the project were viewed as having long-term impact. For example, the introduction of twenty-first century skills such as problem solving, collaboration and negotiation, vertical teaching or mixed-age classes, or that assessment would become more personalised. Trends could take account of technology developments outside the education environment. They included physical devices such as 3D printers, an increased use of web 2.0 collaborative tools to enable peer-learning; technology which could automatically adapt to the ability of users—already a feature of many electronic games; the inclusion of repositories on the web where contents were well-organised, and checked for quality and reliability.

Future Classroom Scenarios were designed to have five elements which were considered to be key:

- Activities and tasks (what happens in the scenario);
- Environment (where the scenario is happening);
- Roles (who is involved in the scenario);
- Interactions between the other elements (how the scenario happens);
- Resources (what is required to support the scenario).

Future Classroom Scenarios are **not** lesson plans; they are designed to be inspirational and flexible in order to be adapted by teachers according to the local context.

The Theoretical Basis for the iTEC Scenario Development Method

The iTEC scenario development process was adapted from a range of scenario development techniques and consensus building tools such as the Delphi method (Rowe and Wright 1999; Scheele 1975). It also drew on methods developed to support futures-facing prototype development such as the Beyond Current Horizons programme (www.beyondcurrenthorizons.org.uk).

The resulting Future Classroom Scenarios provided a means of thinking about the needs of future students and provided inspiration for teachers. The scenarios were intended to be grounded in current realities as opposed to more 'blue sky' visions of the future where schools have been set aside (e.g., the IPTS project described by Ducatel et al. 2001).

Future Classroom Scenarios were based on trends and challenges considered to be important by the scenario designers *within their context* rather than setting a scenario in a broad futuristic environment. The theoretical principle behind this approach to trends' analysis is that, whilst the future is unknown, it is dependent upon current actions. Therefore, whilst accurate predictions of the future are impossible, there are possible realistic alternatives based upon changes or factors that can be envisaged or are known now. These alternatives constitute the 'evidence' as they refer to events and developments that can be observed empirically as they unfold in the present. This approach has been explored by a number of authors and thinkers (e.g., Bussey and Inayatullah 2008; Bell 2003; Slaughter 2002).

The generic trends and challenges were identified from a range of sources. Desk research identified factors from other projects that looked at education in the future.[1] In addition, to ensure that a wider set of perspectives about trends and drivers were included, iTEC partners were asked to also highlight trends in education and/or

[1] For example: Beyond Current Horizons programme (Facer 2009); The Future of Learning: European Teachers' Visions Report (Ala-Mutka et al. 2010); New Assessment Scenarios (Perrotta and Wright 2010); The Horizon Reports (New Media Consortium NMC 2009, 2010).

technology that they were particularly familiar with or interested in. Given the number of potential trends, they were classified according to themes. These were:

- Changing roles of teachers and learners
- Curriculum and assessment
- Knowledge and skills
- Learning spaces
- Technology

These trends were presented to teachers and other stakeholders across the EU in focus groups and through online surveys to obtain feedback on content and to identify those that they believed to be particularly important.

As the project evolved, participants were encouraged to identify for themselves the types of changes that would impact education in their context from relevant organisations (e.g., OECD, Pew Research, Eurydice) or by their stakeholders. They were also encouraged to consider how technology, again in their own context, would impact on learning. For instance, at the time of the project, a growing trend was the increasing number of student-owned mobile devices being brought into schools.

The Evolution of the Scenario Development Process

The scenario development method consisted of five cycles of development and monitoring which are summarised next. In this cyclical, iterative approach, both the process of development and the content of scenarios themselves were fine-tuned during the process to incorporate feedback and reflection from completed cycles. This practice improved the development process, helped strengthen the rationale for and use of scenarios, and importantly, increased the involvement of teachers and learners.

In all five iTEC cycles, the process was designed to be a collaborative approach to exploring how emerging trends in teaching and learning, technology and society can support institutional self-review and transformation.

Cycles 1 and 2

The first and second cycles had a similar structure. Initially in both there was a 2-day workshop attended by experts representing technology, pedagogy and industry. Participants were briefed on the trends as identified through the method detailed previously and provided with summary presentations of the results of a specially commissioned European teacher survey, focus groups, and the students' views.

A template setting out the elements of the scenario was provided for workshop participants to generate up to 20 mini-scenarios. The template was designed to encourage participants to brainstorm what were considered to be the key aspects needed for the scenario: activities and tasks; environments; roles; interactions and resources (as outlined above).

The activities to create scenarios were undertaken in groups, mixing pedagogical and technical partners.

After the initial workshop, in both cycles, the scenarios were then published online and iTEC partners, invited experts in technology and education, and other stakeholders assessed and ranked the mini-scenarios using the online survey tool Survey Monkey. In both cycles respondents were asked to assess desirability (how much they liked the scenario) and probability/timescale (how long it would take for the content of the mini scenario to become common practice in schools without the influence of the iTEC intervention). Once the feedback had been collated, the top eight scenarios were further developed in a second workshop attended by members of the project team.

Similar activities were carried out to those in the first workshops, that is, summary presentations were given of the trends, findings from the teachers' survey and Power League. Again, a template was provided to ensure standardisation of the content of the scenario.

Refinements in the second cycle added criticality and addressed lessons learned in Cycle 1. For instance, many of the first cycle scenarios were seen to be rather too similar in their focus on collaboration, peer teaching and problem-based learning. Steps taken to address this included presentation of feedback about the Cycle 1 scenarios, evaluation criteria and prompts designed to interrogate and challenge each scenario. Partners with a stronger pedagogical background were given prompts to challenge and criticise each scenario from a pedagogical perspective and partners with a stronger technological background were given prompts to challenge and criticise the technological content of the scenario.

Also, to ensure the inclusion of teacher and learner opinions, each group in Cycle 2 were given a list of headlines from the teacher survey and learners to incorporate.

Cycle 3

In this third cycle the need to include more learners, teachers, subject and pedagogical experts in the scenario development process was addressed and the number of invites expanded.

In relation to young people's input, half-day workshops for learners that gathered their ideas and suggestions for scenarios were organised. Five workshops were held in four countries (Portugal, Italy, Norway and UK), and all materials were translated and then locally adapted to suit the situation and requirements of the participating students. Workshop activities began with exploratory activities that asked students to imagine and discuss what schools could be like or should be like. In groups, the youngsters then outlined what they would like learning and education to be like. They responded to this question in relation to four categories (People, Space, Activities, and Technology and Resources) that aligned with the iTEC taxonomy of teaching and learning used in the scenario development workshops with professionals.

The method for scenario development was also modified in Cycle 3 in order to try to increase innovation further. Project partners were asked to research and submit ideas that they considered to be innovative before the workshop. Workshops with teachers and pedagogical experts from Finland, France, Spain and the UK were then held to evaluate and develop these ideas rather than to co-author them from scratch. The intention was that preparation and research beforehand could lead to more innovative scenarios and also allow people to contribute who were not able to attend the workshops. Again, at the workshops activities were designed to facilitate this process, which included a synopsis of 'Pedagogical Approaches' and results from the young people's workshop.

At the workshop, participants were asked to challenge and suggest improvements to the scenario in relationship to the following criteria:

- How inspiring is this scenario?
- How well are young people's views represented or included in this scenario?
- How innovative is this scenario?
- How pedagogically feasible is this scenario?

Participants were asked to carefully capture their discussions on a template so that enhancements and recommendations could be incorporated for each mini-scenario before they were put online for feedback from iTEC partners.

The workshop participants then ordered the scenarios in terms of preference and innovation according to the criteria previously outlined. After the scenarios had been ranked in the workshop they were published and again Survey Monkey was used to elicit feedback on the positions as ranked at the workshop. The request was distributed to all iTEC partners who were asked to indicate whether they agreed or disagreed with the scoring; and to add comments if they wished.

Cycle 4

By Cycle 4 it was clear that scenarios created by teachers were most popular with other teachers: which was important for ownership and localisation. Thus a one day workshop with 46 teachers took place which produced six draft scenarios that reflected their particular interests and challenges.

There was also a shift to integrate scenarios and research from existing EU projects and a separate 1-day workshop with iTEC academic and industry partners was held that focused on ensuring that the technical vision and capabilities provided by industry were used to enhance the Cycle 4 scenarios. After the face-to-face session the teachers were invited to continue collaborating online in a purpose built community.

Unlike the previous cycles, the scenarios were reviewed against fixed assessment criteria which were developed by project partners to ensure that a range of innovations in pedagogy and technology were represented (for a complete description of the areas see Le Boniec et al. 2012, pp. 29–38).

The reflection questions alongside the areas of focus are given below:

- Is the scenario sufficiently innovative for the future classroom? (Match identified trends and challenges.)
- Does the scenario have the potential to support teacher competency acquisition? (Feasibility of pedagogical implementation.)
- Is the scenario innovative in its potential use of technology? (Feasibility of technological implementation.)
- Does the scenario address recognized focus areas for educational reform? (Innovative/transformational character.)
- Is the scenario currently feasible and sufficiently scalability for potentially large scale impact? (Prospects of impacting at scale, if validated successfully.)

The feedback against these indicators was incorporated into the scenarios before they were taken forward.

Throughout the scenario development process, it was clear that a major challenge was to ensure that the scenarios were innovative. For this purpose, both paper-based or electronic materials were used to develop scenarios. For example, Fig. 2.1 shows a Futurelab facilitator using an interactive whiteboard displaying a scenario template to capture and develop ideas generated by iTEC partners at a workshop in Paris. The process for the creation of innovative scenarios led to the development of

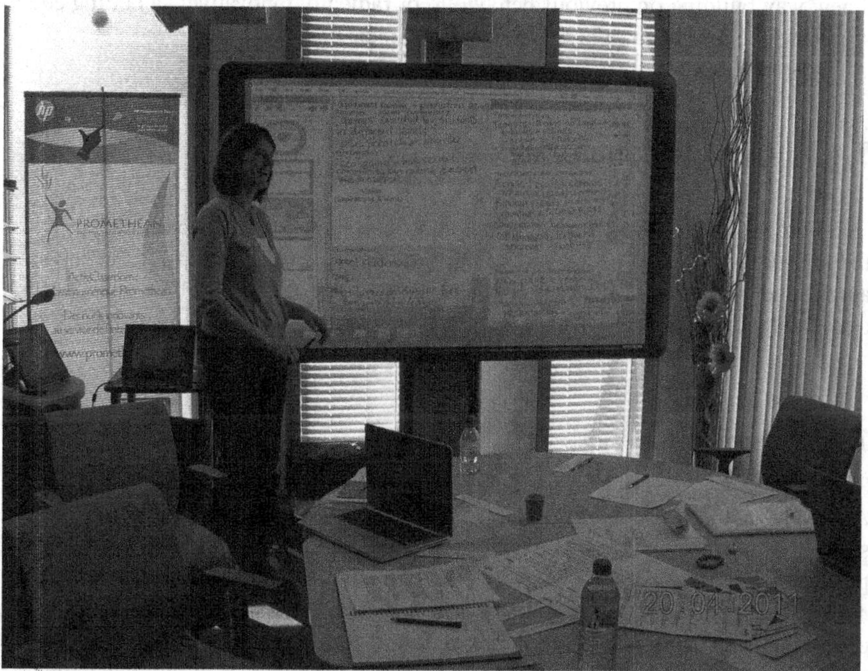

Fig. 2.1 A Futurelab facilitator capturing ideas on a whiteboard at a scenario creation workshop in Paris

the Future Classroom Maturity Model discussed in the next section. This allowed stakeholders to assess not only the overall innovation but also the relative levels of innovation in each of the key areas of the scenario.

Cycle 5

This cycle departed from all previous cycles as teachers took on the role of creating scenarios using a toolkit developed to create bespoke scenarios for their own contexts. The toolkit is further discussed in section "The Future Classroom Toolkit" but in brief, it allowed teachers to identify and consider factors that would impact on their classroom, to create meaningful scenarios for their students.

The scenarios were then reviewed as in Cycle 4, that is, the same reflection questions and feedback questions were used, and again the Maturity Model was used to assess the levels of innovation.

The Future Classroom Maturity Model was key to Cycle 5 in stimulating scenario production. Teachers were encouraged to assess the current level of innovation in their own situations and then to assess their proposed scenario in order to develop or adapt it to be more innovative. In this case, the maturity model enabled stakeholders to identify whether or not a scenario was innovative in a given context. And whether this innovation was incremental—that is, used tools or pedagogies in a new way building on previous behaviour, or radically innovative—a cutting edge scenario (even if not straight forward to implement).

The Future Classroom Toolkit

The Future Classroom Maturity Model and Future Classroom Toolkit encapsulate the final development process; and, in line with the scenarios, were aimed at encouraging innovation. Firstly, the process and not just the output will be considered in terms of innovation.

The Maturity Model

An analysis of the scenarios selected for further development by stakeholders showed a discrepancy in what experts viewed as innovation—either in process or product—and what was innovative to teachers and other stakeholders. Thus scenarios which included the introduction of interactive whiteboards, the validity of online data and using maths as a language to integrate students who have the native tongue as a second language, were not viewed as innovative by all stakeholders because of local differences. For instance, in some European classrooms, these scenarios had already occurred.

To tackle this challenge the working definition of innovation was further refined to enable the application of two characteristics.

- '**Relatively innovative**' was ascribed to scenarios considered by some to be new and more advanced in terms of outcome, process or by its use of technology in a specific context. This is regardless of the fact it may be common practice in other contexts.
- '**Absolutely innovative**' was ascribed to scenarios that result in an outcome that all stakeholders believed to be new, or used a process or technology that all considered cutting edge.

There was also a need to discern sustainable more incremental change and disruptive more radical innovation. For example, was there an incremental change in the use of technology or was the script being totally rewritten? This led to the introduction of maturity model theory in the project.

Maturity models have been used in a variety of fields but fundamentally they set out the stages in an organisation's development of its capacity and capability to exploit new opportunities afforded by, for example, technology, in pursuit of its objectives. In this sense, maturity refers to the co-occurrence of systemic, economic and individual factors that enable a certain innovation or a cluster of innovations to become established, in the words of James Utterback (1994) to form the 'dominant design'.

Following this line of thought, it could be argued that maturity—or "e-maturity" in the context of ICTs for education—depends on a similar combination of factors: the presence of 'dominant designs', which are yet to emerge in educational technology. As noted by Zemsky and Massy (2004), these include the presence of an adequate infrastructure (e.g., bandwidth, connectivity, support and even technical training), positive attitudes and adequate levels of technical knowledge within the teacher community.

'E-maturity' has been used in the past to describe the conditions that might support the uptake of ICTs in education—most notably by the former agency for ICT in the UK, Becta (Bradbrook et al. 2008)—and this made it particularly suited to iTEC. According to Becta, e-maturity refers to the capacity to make strategic and effective use of technology to improve educational outcomes, and is understood to be an additional stage of development beyond 'e-confidence'. The latter embodies high levels of ICT knowledge and skills, and a readiness to apply these to existing situations and new challenges. E-maturity can be observed when professionals apply ICT in strategic and discriminating ways.

The model could be used:

1. As an assessment tool for relative innovation if the prior and current state were ranked;
2. As an assessment tool for absolute innovation by looking at the scenario against the top level (although, it should be noted that the content of each level is constantly evolving in order to take account of future developments);
3. As a design tool to highlight factors that the scenario should contain to ensure that innovation occurred.

The potential of Future Classroom Scenarios to drive technology-based innovation in European education systems is influenced by the degree to which such conditions of maturity are present in different countries.

At the same time, there is widespread agreement that access to technology cannot increase the degree of maturity by itself. Even the best-equipped schools will fail to become 'e-Mature' unless teachers have the competences, vision, training, support and time required in order to harness ICT to support innovative teaching and learning. Pupils are also unlikely to be motivated to learn if they are not engaged by the technology they are using. Moreover, there are important cultural and legal contexts influencing the adoption of a scenario. These include: attitudes to risk; curriculum rigidity; various national and even local policies and regulations that dictate how digital technologies can be accessed and used in schools—not least health and safety regulations determining the circumstances in which technology use is acceptable; the restrictions placed on certain types of content; and the modalities in which teachers can interact with students through digital and networking technologies. For example, it is not uncommon for schools to explicitly advise teachers against using digital media to communicate with students outside of school hours (Vasager and Williams 2012).

This implies that the underpinning technology should only be one dimension of the model; in the model it is called 'Tools and resources'. From section "The Challenge to Innovate", pedagogy also needs to be considered, but this is pedagogy in context—which can be subdivided into: Learner's role, Teacher's role, and Learning objectives and assessment. Finally, there is the overall context, which is the category: School capacity to support innovation in the classroom.

Moreover, unlike maturity models already in existence which focus on the stages of implementing and realising the benefits of technology, this one uses the stages of innovation itself as the core organising principle. The model is represented in Table 2.1 with level 5 being more aligned to the notion of disruptive innovation.

It is important to remember that maturity models are constantly evolving. What is currently empowering (at level 5) may be extended in the future as technology progresses. They also need to be adapted according to circumstance. This may be merely changing the labels—feedback showed that the terms enrich and enhance are not distinct when translated—but it may also involve revising content as new ways of learners working together emerge.

Rationale for the Development of the Future Classroom Toolkit

The Future Classroom Toolkit was not part of the original project proposal. It was developed in response to the need to provide an innovative approach to the scenario development process that could be carried out by schools autonomously. This would sustain the process developed within iTEC of creating contextually appropriate innovative scenarios. This need was identified earlier in the project when the original scenarios were trialled across schools throughout the EU.

Table 2.1 Overview of the future classroom maturity model

	Learner's role	Teacher's role	Learning objective and assessment	School capacity to support innovation in the classroom	Tools and resources
5—Empower The capacity to extend teaching and learning through ongoing whole school innovation, with teachers and learners empowered to adapt and adopt new approaches and tools					
4—Extend Connected technology and progress data extends learning and allows learners greater control on how, what and where they learn					
3—Enhance The learner is able to learn more independently and be creative, supported by technology providing new ways to learn through collaboration					
2—Enrich The learner becomes the user of digital technology, which improves teaching and learning practices					
1—Exchange Isolation of teaching and learning, with technology used as a substitute for traditional methods					

At the level of individual schools, school leaders need a framework for developing curriculum delivery, classroom design and practice, for example, when a school is considering investment in technology, or when a school is making changes to the curriculum or school layout. Looking at the regional and national level there was also a need for countries to support policy change, particularly involving deployment of technology. In each case, the fundamental principles of creating a shared and reliable vision of the future education situation needed to be consistent—and this can be in the form of a shared scenario generated through the toolkit.

The second reason was that teachers had been selecting Learning Activities, concrete descriptions of discrete actions (derived from the scenarios), which were easy to understand and fitted in with their curriculum. Learning Stories present a package of Learning Activities and exemplify how they might work together (see Chap. 3 on Learning Design). By devolving scenario development to stakeholders, supported by the toolkit, the scenarios would be more relevant to their context and curriculum. The resulting Learning Activities derived would therefore also be more diverse and provide appropriate innovation for the future needs of the school or region.

Finally, the Future Classroom Toolkit encourages those creating scenarios to work with wider groups of stakeholders, for example, teachers, suppliers, experts, policy makers, those in the local community or TEL researchers, to develop scenarios that address trends and issues that impact their schools at a local or national level. To achieve this the toolkit contains tools to suggest, identify and record possible relevant stakeholders and methods for collaboration. These tools are generic and can be used across the various EU member states.

Future Classroom Toolkit

The Future Classroom Toolkit enables participants to create scenarios from scratch by identifying stakeholders and trends, the current context—locally or nationally through maturity modelling, and then creating or adapting a scenario structured by completion of a template. It then goes on to briefly explain about designing innovative learning activities and concludes with methods to evaluate the innovation.

Training courses incorporating this toolkit have been developed to ensure that stakeholders outside the project can replicate the iTEC scenario development process at national, local and community levels. In addition, the toolkit resources are available on the web[2] so that teachers and other stakeholders can create scenarios independently.

The toolkit encourages whole school use of ICT by:

- Creating an educational vision that is ambitious but achievable;
- Involving all key stakeholders involved in designing a schools' curriculum;
- Focusing on advanced pedagogical practices and change management.

The Future Classroom Toolkit Development Method

The Future Classroom Toolkit provides a structure for the process of scenario creation. The toolkit was designed to be used during the iTEC project but also afterwards hence the need to make it flexible and standalone. It was designed to have a

[2] See the website: http://fcl.eun.org/toolkit

facilitator who co-ordinates and drives the activities. As the toolkit is modular facilitators can decide which tools are useful, who needs to be involved, the timescale, and where necessary collate and publish any input, for example, trends and challenges identified, or the results of assessing the current context using the Maturity Model.

To deploy the Future Classroom Toolkit, the facilitator selects partners and other stakeholders to develop scenarios tailored to the needs of specific communities and organisations at a national, local or community level. Bringing together partners and stakeholders in this way is the first example of innovation; rather than merely being consulted on curriculum changes, partners and stakeholders take an active role in helping the school shape its priorities.

Next, the toolkit structure enables stakeholders to fully understand the end-to-end process and all key features within a scenario. This flexibility means that it can be adapted to local needs and contexts. For example, a school may seek to visualise the impact of a new library or policy makers in central government may explore what would happen if the curriculum was modified. In turn, this will support long term exploitation of the process.

Many of the activities within the toolkit are adaptations of the process facilitated prior to and within earlier cycles, for example, the initial identification of trends, a review of emerging technologies, the Future Classroom Maturity Model, the completion of a template to ensure relevant areas are considered, etc. However, the toolkit contains new activities to support stakeholders to structure their trends and review the existing and identified descriptors and prioritise them against a number of factors (including timescale, concerns and aims of education).

Innovation with Respect to the Toolkit Process

As discussed in section "The Challenge to Innovate", innovation within a scenario is not merely dependent on the technology employed but is a combination of technology and pedagogy. For example, the result of implementing a scenario might be students doing a presentation to illustrate their understanding of biodiversity. A presentation is not particularly innovative, but if the students were responsible for identifying the research questions, designing interview schedules, collaborating to devise and run experiments, etc. the process might be highly innovative. In contrast, placing QR codes around a historical part of town describing the importance of the buildings might have an innovative outcome, but if in previous years the same information appeared on a paper map, the process is not innovative. However, there is more to iTEC than the production of innovative scenarios, importantly there is also the process of creating scenarios.

The act of measuring technological innovation can be found in the 'Oslo Manual' (OECD 1997). This makes a helpful distinction between technological product and technological process innovations that can be transferred to the context of education. The product is the desired learning outcome as expressed as a teaching objective,

Table 2.2 Process and output innovation summary

	Process innovation	Product (scenario content) innovation
Planning	Curriculum planning based on future needs and opportunities identified within trends and challenges	Scenarios for future teaching and learning
Teaching and learning	Greater personalisation through considering how to seamlessly integrate new technologies and approaches	Learners developing new knowledge and capabilities, including twenty-first century skills

such as the teaching of new subject content and new skills, or content and skills that have to date been beyond those expected of a particular group of students. Innovation in educational processes includes changes in pedagogy, the learners' role and how learning is managed and assessed—see Table 2.2 for a summary of how it was developed by iTEC to apply to the Future Classroom Maturity Model.

To summarise, the toolkit does not only lead to innovative scenarios, but the act of creation is in itself innovative.

Overcoming the Barriers to Innovation Within iTEC

As set out above, the scenario development process is in itself innovative. Nevertheless, there were other stages which occurred during the project where barriers to innovation were identified and the process was refined to overcome these. This section discusses examples of this. For example, it was known that there were different levels of innovation and e-maturity across European schools, where great variation could be found between and within countries, regions, districts, *and* even between and within individual schools. See, for example the findings of the schools ICT in Education survey (European Schoolnet 2013). In response to this challenge, it was decided to develop scenarios which allowed for openness in interpretation and could therefore be adapted to different conditions, including variations in technological access, differences in skills and knowledge, different attitudes and perceptions and so forth.

The scenarios were also designed to be non-prescriptive so that they could be implemented according to the individual teacher's ability, creativity and willingness to make the most of the scenario's potential in any of the cycles. The aim was to allow teachers to adapt the scenarios so they could be used by the mainstream while still being innovative. For example, several of the scenarios developed included the collection and analysis of real-world data. The scenarios make suggestions as to how such analyses could be carried out, but they never "lock" teachers into one solution or another. So, for instance, it is entirely possible that the same scenario might be based, in one classroom, on basic uses of the spreadsheet application Excel to analyse certain forms of environmental data; in another classroom, a teacher might decide to use different educational modelling software to develop visualisations. This idea of flexibility according to context also fits in with the underlying principles of maturity models.

There were other issues encountered during the earlier cycles of iTEC which required a rethink and subsequent re-design to overcome. For example, in the initial plan, scenarios were to be created by a project team with expertise in the areas of learning, technology and policy to create preferable and appropriate responses to challenges and trends identified by research, experts, and surveys of teachers across the EU. These were then to be reviewed by stakeholders (school leaders and teachers, policy advisors, partner organisations, and technology providers) across the EU to ensure consensus in which scenarios should be taken forwards. Approximately 8–10 scenarios were to be deemed most desirable **and** most feasible to be extended and used in the next stage. Unfortunately, this method led to less innovative scenarios being selected as teachers and other stakeholders selected those which could realistically be incorporated to support current curricula. Also, it became clear that some of the scenarios created by experts in the first four of the five cycles were not relevant to stakeholders across Europe. Teachers had been selecting Learning Activities (based on the scenarios) which were easy to understand, fitted in with their curriculum and could be the easiest to implement (see Chap. 3 on Learning Design). It was important therefore that there was a shift from scenarios produced by experts (as described in the original proposal) to scenarios produced by the stakeholders that were not only innovative but appropriate to individual context to be feasible and to provide greater choice.

Alongside this concern from project partners, external reviewers emphasised the need to develop and therefore investigate the potential to introduce 'radical scenarios', to test the assertion made in some quarters that the limits of reform in the system may have been reached (OECD 2010). Therefore, indicators were developed by iTEC partners to further define the characteristics of more 'radically' innovative scenarios.

- There is no or very little evidence of the scenario currently in use in European Schools, other than in specific research projects.
- There are clear barriers to up-scaling resulting in very low probability of mainstreaming in the near future e.g., policy barriers (e.g., preventing the use of personal technologies in educational contexts), technical barriers such as limited technical infrastructure and current pedagogical constraints of curriculum and assessment.
- Technologies rarely seen in schools are used (e.g., very new technology, expensive technology, or technology not perceived to have a place in education).
- The innovation concerns a theme of current TEL research (e.g., cloud computing; mobile learning; 3D printing; augmented reality; serious games and gamification; personalised learning; and virtual laboratories or remote labs).

Scenarios that are only relatively innovative are not ignored as the degree of innovation is context dependent. For example, in one of the cycles, scenarios building on the introduction of interactive whiteboards were shortlisted by stakeholders. However, as they were already regularly used in some classrooms they were not considered to be a radical innovation but rather relative, reflecting the differing contexts across the 17 countries and over 2500 classrooms involved in the project.

Whilst the piloting of radical scenarios involving emerging technologies may provide evidence for their future potential if, and once, such tools become established within educational contexts, project partners decided that, in terms of facilitating up-scaling and mainstreaming, the promotion of radical scenarios could be counterproductive. Rather, scenarios that support incremental innovation are much more likely to lead to pedagogical change and wide-scale uptake as discussed in section "The Challenge to Innovate".

Teachers participating in iTEC pilots have reported changes in technology-supported pedagogy (see Chap. 9 on Evaluation). The nature of these changes varied from individual to individual. The filtering processes adopted at European, national, regional and local levels in relation to the selection, presentation and uptake of Learning Activities have led to the majority of teachers making incremental rather than radical changes. This is not surprising given the nature of education and the risks and challenges involved in relation to radical change. It also reflects the ethos adopted throughout iTEC: that the resources provided should be a source of inspiration for teachers, introducing them to new pedagogical approaches and new technologies, and not a prescriptive lesson plan.

A Reflection on the Scenario Development Process

This chapter has described the evolution of the scenario development process within iTEC. It has discussed what is meant by scenarios, the challenges and trends upon which they are based, the Future Classroom Maturity Model that defines how innovation can be assessed—for the current context as well as the proposed scenario. It has also described the toolkit itself—used by stakeholders to design a narrative for innovating practice, supported by information on the who, what, when, where and how, that addresses the concerns specific to that classroom, school, or national context. In addition, it discussed the activities within the five cycles that led to the creation of the toolkit and the reflective process that ensured that scenarios addressed concerns and minimized any risks or issues. As explained in this chapter, innovation within iTEC is more than the actual production process for creation of scenarios; the process for scenario creation is itself an innovation, providing as it does a structured way of thinking about the future.

In this final section the outputs from this work package are considered in the wider context of the iTEC project. It reflects on the various goals of iTEC discussed in Chap. 1 and the tangible and intangible benefits to stakeholders from using the scenario design process.

Scenario Development in the Context of iTEC Goals

Scenarios underpin the impetus for changes in the classroom; they are the basis for the Learning Activities implemented in classes across Europe and from which the descriptions for the technical products evolved. As a consequence, scenarios underpin the goal of iTEC to improve the uptake of ICT in schools. For example, they address the mainstreaming gap, by which we mean the discrepancy between rapidly changing technology and the slower pace of change in some classrooms. The scenarios can be adapted according to the technology available. Furthermore, the systematic review process is designed to address risks, issues and barriers in advance so that each scenario is less likely to fail when implemented.

Another goal is to connect with the concerns and current practice of learners, teachers, head-teachers and policy makers. This is achieved by emphasising that *all* stakeholders need to be involved in the scenario development process. At the level of individual schools, school leaders need a framework for deciding on how to develop curriculum delivery and classroom design and practice, for example, when a school is considering investment in technology, or when a school is making changes to the curriculum or school layout. As a change management process, it includes an effective methodology to ensure that key stakeholders are consulted and their support secured. As part of this, stakeholders (not just the head and teachers but advisers at a regional or national level, and technology providers) have to recognise the needs of students in this environment of tomorrow. Furthermore, the analysis needs to inspire all teachers to change their own practices appropriately. Looking at the regional and national level, there is a need for countries to support policy change, particularly involving deployment of technology. In each case the fundamental principles of creating a shared and reliable vision of the future education situation is consistent—and this can be in the form of a shared scenario which can be at a classroom, regional or national level.

The scenarios build on the engaging potential of emerging technologies; scenarios can incorporate the potential distractions that multimedia and the digitally driven world of today offer. ICT provides the capacity to link the physical spaces where learning takes place (school, home, library, museums, community, etc.)—and scenarios incorporate these. The Maturity Model makes explicit the importance of incorporating emerging technologies without necessarily defining them.

Finally, and most importantly, the scenario design process was designed to lead to systemic change—that is, rather than focus on incorporating a new technology which may be obsolete in a few years, it is the process of reflecting on current trends and challenges and once a need has been identified, generating a scenario to address it. The scenario design process encourages reflection on incorporating new technologies—and this is supported by the toolkit which can be used by all to innovate as set out earlier.

The Tangible and Intangible Benefits of the Scenario Development Process

As well as addressing the wider goals of iTEC, the scenario development process that was created can be seen to have tangible and intangible benefits for the various stakeholders that use it. As discussed in previous sections, key outputs in relation to the development process are:

- **Future Classroom Scenarios**—narrative descriptions of teaching and learning that provide a vision for innovation and advanced pedagogical practice, making effective use of ICT.
- The **Future Classroom Maturity Model**—a tool to assess current and desired practice based on the idea of innovation, in particular relative and absolute innovation.
- The **Future Classroom Toolkit**—a modular collection of tools and processes to support the scenario-led design process including the identification of trends, the development of scenarios, and the development of Learning Activities and Learning Stories.

These three outputs are clearly tangible benefits. Scenarios can be used or adapted by any of the stakeholders. They provide a 'realistic' inspiration for teachers. From scenarios, specific Learning Activities can be derived which leads to a change in practice (see Chap. 3 on Learning Design). Moreover, by having a narrative that relates to desired practice it is easy for all stakeholders to comprehend the scenario and analyse and refine it collaboratively. At a national level the scenarios can relate to educational policy in the real world and allow for an exchange and comparison of approaches.

The Future Classroom Maturity Model is also of tangible benefit. It enables stakeholders to reflect in a structured manner on the current levels of innovation within schools, local and national contexts. This is important because shared understanding allows stakeholders to identify what needs to be done to actually innovate practice. It also leads to discussion around terminology allowing stakeholders to define what is required and analyse the current situation. Thus stakeholders can be explicit about current status and develop a shared vocabulary.

Similarly the Future Classroom Toolkit itself is of tangible benefit. It provides a structure for the creation of scenarios, and a way of thinking about practice embodied in the modules. The process enables the stakeholders to reflect on who are required to input to the scenario, what issues need to be addressed, what technology will be used, etc. The toolkit is a forum for the exchange of ideas—stakeholders will have differing views on what is important to them, as well as ideas around what factors will be influential that have not necessarily been identified previously.

In addition to the tangible products there are generic intangible benefits for stakeholders: the first being an appreciation for individuals of the potential of scenarios and their role in changing education. Also, there is a growing understanding that innovation is relative to the context and that it is equally important that practice advances incrementally rather than just aiming at radical innovation. The Maturity Model approach highlights that it is often better to move up one level at a time rather than introducing new technologies and practices for teachers and students without the experience and knowledge to use them effectively. The model also acknowledges that many factors lead to innovative practices, and technology is only one aspect.

A second intangible benefit is the creation of a relationship between the stakeholders. Through the process of scenario creation, stakeholders learn to share their viewpoints and engage in strategic dialogue around the direction of policy and practice.

The process allows them to form relationships and appreciate the differing perspectives which come from their varying roles.

Conclusion

The feedback towards the scenarios and their development process was positive. Stakeholders felt that the process of evaluating their own current levels of innovation and designing scenarios that increased the level of innovation in at least one dimension was a useful exercise. The maturity model framework allowed them to establish a shared vocabulary and a means of analysing their own understanding and expectations. The process gives the opportunity to be creative, and to think laterally about how technology can be used. Furthermore, the introduction of the idea of trends, an abstract concept, made stakeholders more aware of context. Having scenarios allowed a way of sharing best practice.

Some participants recommended that the toolkit be incorporated into teacher training in order that stakeholders would become familiar with reflecting on context and practice in this structured way. It could also be integrated within national professional development structures. Facilitators and trainers mediating the process would benefit from targeted support on the use of the toolkit and should be supported to use the toolkit in their own practice.

In relation to lessons learned, the scenarios which were selected show the importance of ownership. A greater range of scenarios are implemented if the stakeholders—particularly teachers—are responsible for their creation. The process also shows how stakeholders need support to recognise and integrate trends and challenges into their practice but that these need not be abstract and can address issues affecting them not only at a national level but also in the classroom. The resulting scenarios must not be rigid either. They are intended to be inspirational and must allow flexibility in implementation according to the context and the resources available.

Finally, there are implications for policy and practice; the toolkit has been designed to be used at national, regional and school levels—pulling in all relevant stakeholders in a structured manner. The methodology allows relationships to be established with industry, research and policy makers. As discussed by those who used the toolkit in Cycle 5 the Future Classroom Toolkit would be especially applicable in countries where the toolkit clearly supports current policy directions.

Acknowledgements The success of our work was highly dependent upon participation by stakeholders, European Schoolnet as co-ordinators and the project partners of iTEC. We would also like to give particular thanks to Roger Blamire at European Schoolnet for acting as a 'critical friend' to our work throughout the project. Equally, we would like to thank the young people, teachers, policymakers and other practitioners who took part in this work and helped to make it a success. Also, our colleagues at Futurelab and Futurelab@NFER who worked on this project, specifically Niel Maclean, Alison Oldfield, Sarah Maughan, Sarah Payton, Carlo Perrotta and David Sims.

References

Ala-Mutka K, Redecker C, Punie Y, Ferrari A, Cachia R, Centeno C (2010) The future of learning: European teachers' visions report. Report on a foresight consultation at the 2010 eTwinning conference, Sevilla, 5–7 February 2010. http://ipts.jrc.ec.europa.eu/publications/pub.cfm?id=3679. Accessed June 2014

Béchard J-P (2001) L'enseignement supérieur et les innovations pédagogiques: une recension des écrits. Rev Sci Educ XXVII(2):257–281

Bell W (2003) Foundations of futures studies, vol 1, History, purposes and knowledge. Transaction, New Brunswick

Bocconi S, Kampylis P, Punie Y (2013) Framing ICT-enabled Innovation for Learning: the case of one-to-one learning initiatives in Europe. Eur J Educ 48(1):113–130

Bradbrook G, Alvi I, Fisher J, Lloyd H, Moore R, Thompson V, Brake D, Helsper E, Livingstone S (2008) Meeting their potential: the role of education and technology in overcoming disadvantage and disaffection in young people [online]. http://eprints.lse.ac.uk/4063/1/Meeting_their_potential.pdf. Accessed June 2014

Brecko BN, Kampylis P, Punie Y (2014) Mainstreaming ICT-enabled innovation in education and training in Europe: policy actions for sustainability, scalability and impact at system level. JRC scientific and policy reports. JRC-IPTS, Seville. doi:10.2788/52088

Bussey M, Inayatullah S (2008) Pathways: alternative educational futures. In: Bussey M, Inayatullah S, Milojevic I (eds) Alternative educational futures, pedagogies for emergent worlds. Sense, Rotterdam, pp 1–9

Christensen MC, Horn MB, Johnson CW (2008) Disrupting class: how disruptive innovation will change the way the world learns. McGraw Hill, New York

Dede C (2010) Comparing frameworks for 21st century skills. In: Bellanca J, Brandt R (eds) 21st century skills: rethinking how students learn. Solution Tree Press, Bloomington, pp 51–76

Ducatel K, Bogdanowicz M, Scapolo F, Leijten J, Burgelman JC (2001) Scenarios for ambient intelligence in 2010. A report by the IST Advisory Group (ISTAG) to the EU, DG INFSO. IPTS, Seville, Spain. ftp://ftp.cordis.europa.eu/pub/ist/docs/istagscenarios2010.pdf. Accessed June 2014

European Schoolnet (2013) Survey of schools: ICT in education [online]. http://essie.eun.org. Accessed June 2014

Facer K (2009) Beyond current horizons. DCSF/Futurelab, Bristol. http://www.beyondcurrenthorizons.org.uk. Accessed June 2014

Kampylis P, Bocconi S, Punie Y (2012) Towards a mapping framework of ICT-enabled innovation for learning. Publications Office of the European Union, Luxembourg. EUR 25445 EN. http://tinyurl.com/d5wn6lb. Accessed June 2014

Kampylis P, Law N, Punie Y, Bocconi S, Brečko B, Han S, Looi C-K, Miyake N (2013) ICT-enabled innovation for learning in Europe and Asia: exploring conditions for sustainability, scalability and impact at system level. Publications Office of the European Union, Luxembourg. doi:10.2791/25303

Kozma RB (ed) (2003) Technology, innovation and educational change: a global perspective. International Association for Technology in Education, Eugene

Le Boniec M, Muñoz King P, Ellis W (2012) Deliverable 4.3: second validation report on large-scale piloting. http://itec.eun.org

Moyle K (2010) Building innovation: learning with technologies (Australian education review no. 56). ACER, Melbourne

New Media Consortium (NMC) (2009, 2010 editions) The horizon report. NMC, Austin. http://www.nmc.org/publication-type/horizon-report/. Accessed June 2014

OECD (1997) OSLO manual: the measurement of scientific and technological activities, proposed guidelines for collecting and interpreting technological innovation data, Paris. http://www.oecd.org/science/inno/2367580.pdf. Accessed June 2014

OECD (2008) Innovating to learn, learning to innovate. OECD, Paris

OECD (2010) The nature of learning: using research to inspire practice. http://www.oecd.org/edu/ceri/50300814.pdf. Accessed June 2014

OECD/CERI (2010) Inspired by technology, driven by pedagogy: a systemic approach to technology-based school innovations, educational research and innovation. OECD, Paris

Ogilvy J (2006) Education in the information age: scenarios, equity and equality. In: Think scenarios, rethink education. OECD. http://www.oecd.org/document/27/0,3746,en_2649_39263301_36507370_1_1_1_1,00.html. Accessed June 2014

Perrotta C, Wright M (2010) New assessment scenarios. Futurelab, Bristol. http://futurelab.org.uk/sites/default/files/New_assessment_scenarios.pdf. Accessed June 2014

Rogers EM (1995) Diffusion of innovations. Free Press, New York

Rowe G, Wright G (1999) The Delphi technique as a forecasting tool: issues and analysis. Int J Forecast 15:353–375

Scheele DS (1975) Reality construction as a product of Delphi interaction. In: Linstone HA, Turoff M (eds) The Delphi method: techniques and applications. Addison-Wesley, Reading, pp 35–67

Slaughter R (2002) Futures studies as an intellectual and applied discipline. In: Dator JA (ed) Advancing futures: futures studies in higher education. Praeger, Westport, pp 91–107

Somekh B (2007) Pedagogy and learning with ICT: researching the art of innovation. Routledge, London

Sutch D, Rudd T, Facer K (2008) Promoting transformative innovation in schools. A futurelab handbook. Futurelab, Bristol. http://www.futurelab.org.uk/sites/default/files/Promoting_Transformative_Innovation_handbook.pdf. Accessed June 2014

Tobin K (2005) Exchanging the baton: exploring the co in co-teaching. In: Roth WM, Tobin K (eds) Teaching together, learning together. Peter Lang, New York, pp 141–1161

Utterback JM (1994) Mastering the dynamics of innovation. Harvard Business School Press, Boston

Vasager J, Williams M (2012) Teachers warned over befriending pupils on Facebook [online]. *The Guardian*, 23 January. http://www.theguardian.com/education/2012/jan/23/teacher-misconduct-cases-facebook. Accessed June 2014

Von Hippe E (2005) Democratizing innovation. MIT Press, Cambridge

Zemsky R, Massy WF (2004) Thwarted innovation: what happened to e-learning and why [online]. The Learning Alliance, University of Pennsylvania, Philadelphia. http://www.immagic.com/eLibrary/ARCHIVES/GENERAL/UPENN_US/P040600Z.pdf. Accessed June 2014

Chapter 3
Designing Edukata, a Participatory Design Model for Creating Learning Activities

Tarmo Toikkanen, Anna Keune, and Teemu Leinonen

Abstract Closing gaps between visionary ideas and classroom practice was the key achievement of the design research and work of the iTEC project. The design activities were based on the traditions of Scandinavian participatory design, activity theory, service design, artistry, and a specific view on learning design. Within iTEC, the design research and work brought forward the concept of Learning Activities as a useful mode of communicating new ideas to teachers that provided both challenges and support for overcoming those challenges. Evaluation results showed that Learning Activities were extremely successful. This success led to the need to ensure the continuation of Learning Activity design and production beyond the project. The design approach for creating the Learning Activities was captured for educators in the Edukata toolkit. Radical simplification yielded a model that seems to be valuable for teachers even with small amounts of training. However, the full impact of this model and its applicability in the diverse school learning settings across Europe remains to be validated. In this article we present the design research process and one of its main results: the Edukata toolkit for teachers to design their own Learning Activities to bridge the gap between tie visionary ideas and classroom practice.

Keywords Participatory design • Design • Learning activity • Prototyping • Change management • Teaching • Learning

Introduction: Design and Pedagogical Research

Curricular requirements in European classrooms are handed to teachers top down, although educators are often invited to take part in the process of defining them. The top down model is an obvious hindrance to teacher-led innovation. From our experiences in Finland, where teachers have much autonomy on classroom activities, we see teacher-led innovation as a crucial part of developing school practices and culture. Teachers often know their students and their needs, understand the subject matter and can make well-informed calls about how to design their classroom activities.

T. Toikkanen (✉) • A. Keune • T. Leinonen
Aalto University, Espoo, Finland
e-mail: tarmo.toikkanen@aalto.fi; anna.keune@aalto.fi; teemu.leinonen@aalto.fi

F. Van Assche et al. (eds.), *Re-engineering the Uptake of ICT in Schools*,
DOI 10.1007/978-3-319-19366-3_3

In the iTEC project Lewin and McNicol (2014) have found empirical evidence that well designed Learning Activities following a certain template are valuable tools for teachers to challenge their own established practices and to try out new methods and tools. The results demonstrate that the experiments by teachers offer significant improvements in the students' working culture, engagement, motivation, and ultimately, learning outcomes. Evaluations from over 2500 classroom pilots have indicated that the Learning Activities designed in the iTEC project are effective at enthusing teachers and students, affecting change in classroom practices, and prompting other teachers to adopt similar practices. They also encouraged teachers and students to start using novel ICT tools and services, and to use the tools in the way the educational designer intended for them to be used so that they benefit the learning process. Furthermore, when teachers are supported to design their own Learning Activities with proper facilitation and guidance, results are even better (Lewin and McNicol 2014).

Our design research question was:

What kind of support, training, materials, and experience is needed for teachers to create their own Learning Activities that integrate visionary ideas into classroom teaching and learning?

Our hypothesis is Edukata, a set of guidelines targeted towards teachers, which are intended to enable them to better design and reformulate their teaching practices in collaboration with students and other expert educators. Edukata is based on the group's design-research approach called "Research-based design with prototypes", described in Leinonen et al. (2008).

This design-research approach has been used and developed by the research group since 1997 and is continually being developed (see Fig. 3.1). The group is multi-disciplinary, consisting of designers, educators, engineers, psychologists and cognitive scientists. The method has been used to design and implement software prototypes for reflection, knowledge building, and Open Educational Resource (OER) authoring, as well as physical environments, future scenarios,

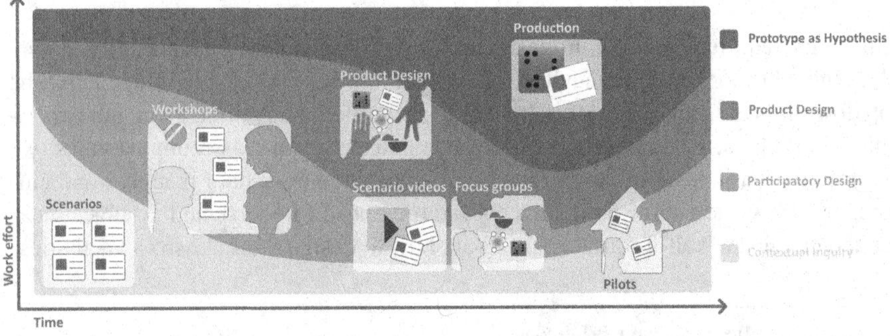

Fig. 3.1 An overview of the research-based design methodology and the design methods, as adapted for the iTEC project and called "Research-based design with prototypes". All four modes of work proceed in parallel, with the focus of work shifting between them as time passes. Concrete design and research activities from cycle 1 are overlaid

and educational practices (see e.g., Leinonen et al. 2003; Ford and Leinonen 2009; Keune and Leinonen 2013; Durall and Toikkanen 2013). The approach is constructed of, and builds on, four design approaches: tool design, educational design, participatory design and learning design.

Our philosophy on **tool design** draws on Engeström's (1987, 1999) emphasis that a tool may provide subjects with new abilities to act with objects around them, as well as being part of the larger socio-cultural context that is conditioned with various constraints. Similarly to the idea of a tertiary artefact, which can impact the way in which a person may see, interact with, and shape the world (e.g., Cole 1996), in the best case, this means that the tools created by a designer affect the socio-cultural system within which the tool is situated, and are affected and modified by the same (Leinonen 2010).

Our philosophy on **design** in and for education draws from Rittel's (1972) view that each challenge can have multiple solutions, and that attempts to solve challenges often construct new, potentially even more complex challenges. To differentiate from problem-based approaches, we value the idea of the designer as someone who creates desired additions to the present state, as opposed to merely reactively solving problems as they emerge. We acknowledge Schön's (1987) view on *artistry*, meaning the way designers combine their domain understanding and design expertise with intuition, often leading to surprising results, which might not be logically tracked back to the starting point. We also agree with Nelson and Stolterman (2003) in that the designer's actions are intentional contributions to the situation and the designer is an active participant in the change process. Nelson and Stolterman (2003) schematize the designer's intentions in relation to (1) **helping** (fixing, assisting, patronizing), (2) **art** (persuading, influencing, manipulating, proselytizing), (3) **science** (describing, explaining, predicting, controlling), and (4) **service** (serving, conspiring, emphatizing). Of these four designer intentions, our group's methodological approach focuses strongly on service intentions (Leinonen 2010).

Our way of utilizing **participatory design** is based on the Scandinavian approach to systems design, which considers it important for those stakeholders who might be affected by the new tools to genuinely participate in the design. Following Ehn and Kyng (1987), we see the people for, and with whom, design is practiced and created as primary drivers for realistic and working innovation. For this to work, the designer needs to spend time with the people in question and learn about their everyday life situations, in place of doing laboratory experiments (Leinonen 2010). We fully acknowledge that design challenges and their solutions are highly context-specific (Muller and Kuhn 1993).

In terms of **learning (and teaching) design**, we see that it is challenging to present and build on the complexity and messiness of teaching and learning (see e.g., Conole 2010). The attempt to downplay this messiness often leads to schematic representations of teaching, rather than empowering teachers to design their work practices. Our research method, and indeed Edukata, steer away from connections to such patterns, leaving many details open for teachers to complete as they see best. We acknowledge that this makes exact comparison and benchmarking rather difficult with the huge variety of approaches and results, but feel this space for innovation is critical.

Designing Learning Activities for Piloting

Edukata has been developed as part of the Innovative Technologies for an Engaging Classroom project (iTEC), a 4-year pan-European project. The workflow of iTEC was planned to be a straightforward 5-phase iterative process, in which each phase was intended to include four parts: (1) create Learning Scenarios, (2) design software and learning design prototypes based on the scenarios, (3) pre-pilot and pilot the prototypes in classrooms across Europe, and (4) evaluate the pilots. As the plans were implemented they needed to be adapted and changed.

The five piloting cycles gave project partners opportunities to learn from past cycles and to better serve the overall aim of the project. The first cycle was smaller than the later ones, both in scale of piloting activities and scope of challenges. Specifically, organizational challenges (such as combining two classes into a single course) were excluded from the first cycle, so teachers would not have to face challenges that they alone cannot overcome. The following cycles were each larger in scale. Significantly more schools, teachers and classrooms were involved, and the level of technical and pedagogical challenges increased, this time including any and all challenges that were raised in the design work.

The Design Process

During each of the five piloting cycles, the following design activities took place. A more detailed description can be found in the project's deliverable D3.1 (Keune et al. 2011).

- Each cycle's design work began with scenario analysis using the wall method (see Fig. 3.2). All scenarios were printed and placed on a wall. The team spent several sessions going through the scenarios, highlighting interesting passages, noting similarities, and comparing the scenarios to the state-of-the-art.
- Distributed participatory design workshops took place in most piloting countries. The scenarios were divided among the pilot countries so each had 2–3 scenarios to analyse. The national coordinators translated the scenarios and presented them to a group of teachers, following the guidelines developed by our team. The facilitators were encouraged to adapt the guidelines to their particular facilitation context, for example in relation to the location for facilitating the workshops (e.g., in schools or in ministry facilities). The ensuing conversations were recorded, and the coordinators wrote English summaries of the conversations, which they sent back to us. These summaries allowed us to understand differences in teaching practice and culture in various countries, and to see which aspects of the scenarios were appealing and which challenges teachers foresaw.
- The English summaries were added to the wall. We received 2–4 summaries for each scenario. Another round of analysis ensued, where we had to make hard design decisions on what seemed to be important; which challenges we should

Fig. 3.2 A central but low-tech mode of work is the wall method, where all pertinent information is placed on walls, so they are constantly visible. During design sessions, even a large group can see everything, it is easy to point to individual items, and notes can be added using sticky notes, pens, and highlighters

try to address or circumvent; and what kinds of support teachers would eventually receive from the project were they to try to implement essential segments of these scenarios.

- Prototyping work followed, where both technical prototypes (i.e., software tools with partially functional interfaces) and teacher guidelines for using the software prototypes in relation to the scenarios were designed and developed.
- Focus groups and interviews with teachers and headmasters were held periodically to gauge both the level of innovation and amount of support being built to the prototypes. Focus groups were formed openly from the network of teachers involved in the project. Invitations were sent via national coordinators, social media channels, partner community sites, and so on. Some focus groups were organized partly online and offline to allow more people to join and share experiences.
- Pre-pilots were organized in most piloting countries, in which one or two teachers from each country participated. These were teachers who were confident users of Information Communication Technology (ICT) and had advanced pedagogical skills, so they could work with rough prototypes (i.e., software that is not fully developed and may have parts that do not function fluently at all times), and report back to us any problems they experienced.

- For us, each project cycle, which marked an iteration, ended with product design, where we took all the feedback we had; decided (as a project consortium), which pre-piloted prototypes should be scaled up to full scale pilots; and polished those prototypes sufficiently to allow average teachers to make use of them.

This general process was followed in all piloting cycles. The details and guidelines evolved as we gained more experience with working with the national coordinators, who were responsible for managing the project in each piloting country, and with the teachers who participated in pre-pilots and pilots. The guidelines and practices were also shaped by the feedback of the teachers and national coordinators. In later cycles we started doing participatory design workshops with pupils, organized online focus groups, and varied the process to maximise its usefulness.

An Example of a Surprising Design Outcome: TeamUp

The design process outlined earlier takes a great deal of resources and time. To illustrate the concrete benefits of such an involved process, we will describe just one design outcome from the very first piloting cycle.

Twenty mini-scenarios were developed by iTEC partners across Europe during a scenario development workshop, organised by the iTEC partner organisation Futurelab (see Chap. 2). Of the 20 mini-scenarios, the nine most convincing and desirable ones were identified using a prioritisation protocol devised by iTEC partners. These were then fleshed out by Futurelab into detailed scenarios. These detailed scenarios presented the basis of the first cycle design process.

Six of the nine scenarios described the pupils working in small teams. Teamwork was taken for granted, and just mentioned in passing, as can be seen in the example scenario in Fig. 3.3. None of the expert pedagogues nor our design team, who participated in the scenario development workshops considered that this might be a challenge.

When analysing the participatory design workshop summaries from various countries, it became obvious that in most European countries, having pupils work in small teams was not a common practice, and was seen as a real challenge. Teachers from several countries pointed out that they normally do not facilitate teamwork exercises; that following all of the teams and guiding them is a lot of extra work for which the teachers do not have time; and that teams are often dysfunctional, with free-riders or friendship cliques making productive teamwork difficult.

This surprising finding lead us to reconsider the content for the first piloting cycle. Pedagogical experts agreed that teamwork is a useful form of learning without recognizing the challenges it may pose in practice, whereas teachers, by and large, saw teamwork as a foreign, time-consuming and problematic mode of working. No teacher denied the benefits of teamwork, but the practical challenges they saw were a clear showstopper.

"Ms Rossi, a science teacher, has been liaising with the geography teacher and they have noticed that their students need to develop a more in depth understanding of the local natural environment and wildlife. Ms Rossi has also noticed that although her class works well as individuals, they would benefit from more group learning. She decides to get the group to work collaboratively on a problem-based activity to do with nature and the local environment. When deciding on a specific activity for the class she liaises with the geography teacher to ensure the chosen activity could also support learning in geography. She sets her class the challenge of finding out why the population of ladybirds has decreased in the school grounds over the last year.

Carmen, a student, goes outside with her group to collect real data to help the class's investigation. Each group member has a different role and a different instrument to capture authentic data. Carmen uses her mobile phone to capture images of the areas where most ladybirds live, whilst others in the group record the temperature and survey habitats. Ms Rossi lets the students work together in groups so she can take the role of observer and coach. This helps her understand what skills the students need to practise. She notes down what skills the students need to develop to help her design future learning activities. She realises the group need more training on using instruments without disturbing wildlife, and also how to set specific group goals.

After gathering a series of photos Carmen comes back to class with her group and they share their data and findings with each other. They get some specific support from Ms Rossi on how to use a software package to draw conclusions from the group's numerical data. Having drawn their conclusions, the group choose to create a short film from their photos and data to share their findings with other students in the class. They work together using laptops and a web tool to create a short digital film explaining what they found. Carmen and another student upload their photos while the rest of the group write a script to present their findings. They each record a part of the presentation script and use the automatic editing software on the web tool to create the film. This film is posted on the school's learning platform for the class to view for homework, and also for students in a geography class, who are doing similar work, to comment on. The group also decide to post it on the public area of the learning platform so they can show their parents/carers when they get home."

Fig. 3.3 Example scenario narrative from the first cycle of iTEC, titled "Outdoor study project", written by iTEC partner organization FutureLab in the UK

We had to convene our entire research group to ponder this situation. Finally, we decided that making teamwork a key feature of cycle one's piloting, and providing explicit support for forming teams and for following the teams' study progress would be of most value to the piloting work and for the project.

We drew inspiration from the collaborative progressive inquiry framework (Hakkarainen 2003) and included its ideas on maximizing student motivation by forming interest-based teams to work on specific topics. We also tried to tackle teachers' objections over the time they need to spend following each team's progress with their study projects. The concept became a technological prototype, and finally a fully functional product called TeamUp (see Fig. 3.4).

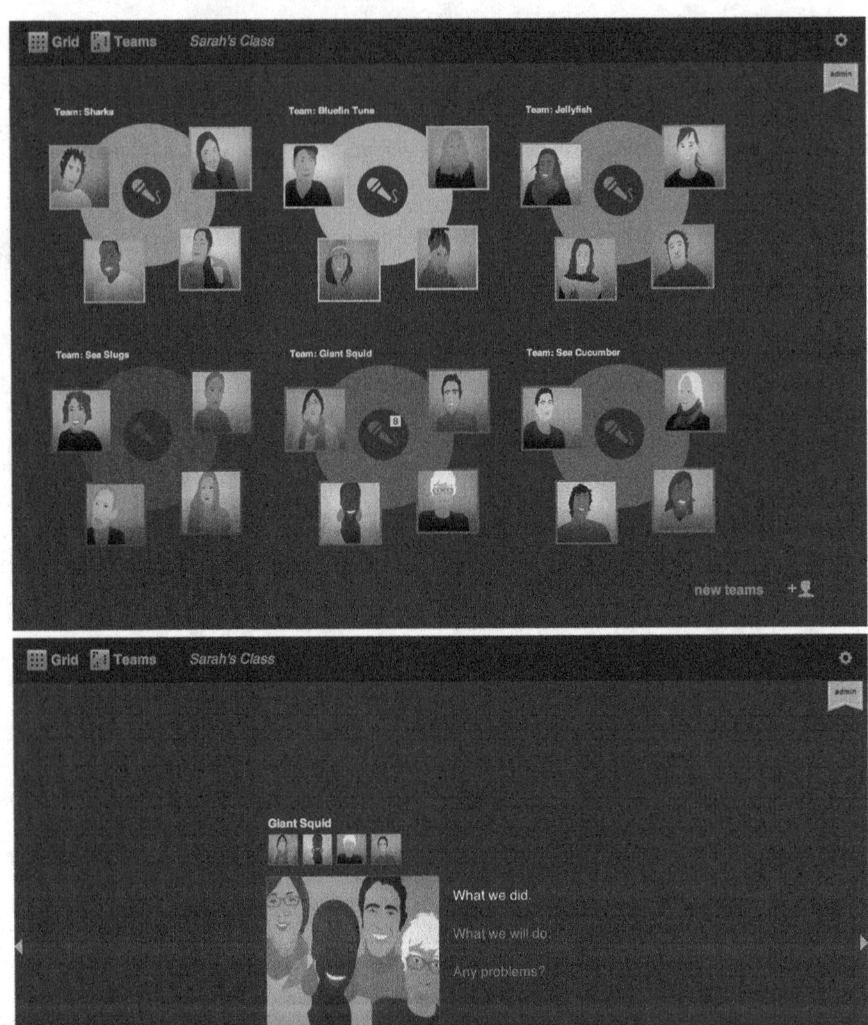

Fig. 3.4 Screen shots from the TeamUp tool with fictional, drawn characters. In real use, photos of students would be used. On the *top* is the team view, where the teacher and the students can see the team compositions. On the *bottom* is the view of a single team, with the controls to create new status updates, and to listen to existing ones

TeamUp is a web-based application that uses a complex algorithm to form heterogeneous, interest-based teams. Additionally, the application includes a feature for teams to record and share audio-visual updates of their work, the challenges they encountered, how these may have been overcome, and what they are planning on doing next (which follows agile stand-up meeting practices). The recordings can be no longer than 60 s. This time limit was intentional. We intended to support students to focus their summaries of their work, and aimed to ensure that a teacher with a class of, say, seven teams needs to spend no more than 7 min between lessons to get an update on the teams' progress. TeamUp also became the first tool to support student reflection, which became a major trend in the following iTEC pilot cycles. TeamUp is further described in both Keune et al. (2011) and Leinonen et al. (2014).

Although the design of TeamUp was intended to address challenges related to forming and following learning teams' progress, during the piloting we noticed that forming teams was not a universal challenge for all teachers. Especially experienced teachers mentioned that they are able to form functional teams without the support provided by TeamUp. However, the possibility to follow the teams' progress and the possibility to surface students' voices for reflection was highlighted as empowering by teachers and students. Therefore, in further developing TeamUp, the feature for forming teams was backgrounded and the feature for sharing team recordings was foregrounded in the interface. These changes made to the tool are examples of the research-based design approach's flexibility and on how the prototypes and tools created in the research work are partly communicating the research results.

Creating the Concept of Learning Activities

We faced our first challenge with the research in the spring of 2011, during the first cycle. While the scenarios were inspiring and challenging, and had started the creation of several technical prototype ideas (such as TeamUp, ReFlex, Ambire, Plates; see more details in Leinonen et al. (2014), we faced a problem not foreseen during the project-planning phase. What exactly would the piloting teachers be provided with so that they would be challenged as well as supported during their pilots?

With the diverse challenges mentioned by teachers in relation to the scenarios including questions on how to implement them (see D3.1: Keune et al. 2011), the scenarios on their own did not seem sufficiently supporting. The scenarios highlighted visionary ideas in a general narrative structure without mentioning many practical details or challenges that would support teachers in their attempts to implement the visionary ideas. The scenario in Fig. 3.3 is an example of a good quality scenario, conveying the idea of learning and teaching science content outside through narrative devices. However, the scenario skims over the details and practical advice, generalizing the context specific nature of teaching and learning across diverse European settings. Participatory design work with teachers highlighted many issues and challenges teachers saw with implementing the scenarios, some of which were even surprises to the experts who had created the scenarios (see previous section for an example).

The first idea was to rewrite the scenarios into Learning Stories, which would be more concrete, contain tips, notices, good practices, scheduling information, options for various tools and technologies, and so on. Drafting the first cycle's Learning Stories revealed that they would be too unwieldy. As each scenario contained many challenging elements, rewriting all of them in more detail would create very long stories, with lots of details obfuscating the visionary ideas. Moreover, as the scenarios shared elements (for example, most scenarios had students working in small teams), each story would end up containing many of the same details.

A workable solution emerged when the details were separated into modules. Each story was constructed with a story arc to present a narrative approach to the ideas, and to exemplify an implementation of particular ideas. All the details for various challenging elements were packed into separate modules, which the stories shared (examples: Reflection, Design brief, Ad-hoc collaboration, Working with outside experts). The term Learning Activity was deemed a good title for the modules, as existing uses of that term did not tie it to divergent preconceived notions, and teachers' intuitive understanding of the term was close enough to its use in this context.

When writing the first cycle's Learning Activities, the design team was very conscious of the tone and method of addressing teachers. While we as designers might have a broad view of the changing educational sector and may have good ideas for teachers to try out, we were aware that it is the teachers who are the experts of their profession and practice, their students, and know what may or may not work. Instead of telling teachers what to do in the pilots and pre-pilots, we decided to rely on their expertise as designers of their own teaching and learning, and merely provide them with new ideas, support, reassurance, and advice, packaged into the Learning Activities. In working with the Learning Activities, e.g., how to interpret them in practice, we gave them the freedom to choose which ones to try and how without strict limitations. This approach made detailed analysis of pilot activities challenging, but was essential in unleashing the creative potential of the teachers, empowering them to decide what to do, and in turn pass that empowerment on to their students.

Another aspect of Learning Activities had to do with their wide audience. We intended the Learning Activities to be used in classroom pilots in 12–16 European countries by teachers with very different didactic methods, technology experiences, and pedagogical approaches. Each Learning Activity had to be written in a way that it would be challenging for experts without fending off beginners by being too challenging. Any single activity, for example students keeping a learning diary in blogs, may be routine for some teachers, and completely new to others. The Learning Activity presenting this concept needed to provide an entry-point for the novices, as well as additional depth and challenges for those already experienced with similar activities. The example in Fig. 3.5 contains many aspects of a Learning Activity that a teacher may choose to include in their own teaching. A teacher not familiar with teamwork might simply split the students into teams and follow their progress, while a more experienced teacher would use the more advanced suggestions in creating motivation-optimized heterogeneous teams.

You divide the class into small teams of 4-5 learners that are optimal for collaboration. Each team has their own topic of inquiry that is related to the theme of the course. You let the learners suggest topics they are interested in and use the TeamUp tool to match learners and topics, using information stored in mental notes.

- *Preparation*
  Set up the TeamUp tool for your class by adding names, portraits and mental notes of learners. See TeamUp tool manual, part 1 'Add and edit learners' for more information.
  Your learners will be working in teams of 4, each team with a specific topic. Plan your course (or part of it) accordingly.
  Decide whether you grade teams or individuals.
- *Introduction*
  Present the theme of the course in a way that gives students some basic information, but leaves open many questions.
  Ask learners to think about what they would like to study in this theme.
- *Activity*
  Team work usually spans multiple lessons, often an entire course.
  Ask students to suggest topics for inquiry. Use your judgment to rephrase, alter or reject suggestions.
  Collect topics in the TeamUp tool.
  Let learners vote for their favourite topic and create the teams. See TeamUp tool manual, part 2 'Forming teams'.
  Ask learners to start their teamwork.
  Starting each lesson, show the TeamUp team view to remind everyone of the teams and their topics.
- *Assessment*
  Include contributions to teamwork into your assessment.
  You may brainstorm assessment criteria with the learners.

Fig. 3.5 Example Learning Activity narrative from iTEC cycle 1, called "Teamwork"

Title
Summary
Learning outcomes
Motivation: teacher, student
Reasons for using technology
Guidelines (including required time, preparation, assessment)
Technology support
Technical details

Fig. 3.6 Learning Activity template for cycle 1. Items in *italics* changed as work progressed through the cycles

The Learning Activity in Fig. 3.5 includes a short introductory paragraph, presenting the general frame of the activity, a section for preparing the activity before class, and one for introducing the activity to the class, the main activity description, and, finally, ideas for assessment. Figure 3.6 presents additional aspects that were included in the descriptions of Learning Activities, such as potential learning

Title Summary Motivation: teacher, student Ideas for using technology Guidelines (prepare, inspire, coach, assess)

Fig. 3.7 Learning Activity template for cycle 5 and Edukata

outcomes, motivations for teachers and students to perform the activity, and reasons for using technology.

The template for a Learning Activity changed as the cycles of piloting progressed. While the main elements remained throughout the process, the wording and explanations for them did change to avoid misunderstandings. Figures 3.6 and 3.7 show the template for cycle 1 and for cycle 5 respectively. Many details related to technologies and tools were removed as they were found to be not that important. For example, instead of providing reasons for using technology, we included a section with ideas for using technology. The motivational tips were retained as they were seen as very helpful, and the actual guidelines were structured differently from the first cycle.

Evaluation Results

Evaluation results from the pilot cycles show significant changes and gains in the piloting classrooms. The results are based on teacher surveys, interviews, and diaries, as well as student surveys. A quantitative analysis and comparison of pilot activities is not possible, since no two teachers did exactly the same thing. This was a design decision made early on in the project.

Focus groups and pre-pilots during cycle 1 confirmed that indeed the Learning Activities were a functional way to communicate to teachers what we hoped they would accomplish during their pilots. The granularity of a Learning Activity seemed to be suitable for teachers so they could look at each of the activities, understand them, incorporate some of them into their upcoming course plan, and use the tips and suggestions from the Learning Activities to create a course plan that challenged them to try new methods and tools.

The Learning Activities and their implementations by the teachers enabled their students to:

- engage in active and independent learning (84 %);
- express their ideas in new ways (89 %);
- communicate with each other in new ways (85 %);
- communicate with their teacher in new ways (81 %);
- use digital tools to support collaboration (91 %). (Lewin and McNicol 2014)

The teachers, in turn, reported increased

- engagement in exciting new practices (86 %);
- uptake of ICT (84 %);
- enthusiasm for teaching (73 %). (Lewin and McNicol 2014)

The library of Learning Activities was considered a valuable asset, and when national policies were aligned, the approach was seen to be likely adopted and to influence future practices (Lewin and McNicol 2014). Evaluation results of iTEC are more fully discussed in Chap. 9 of this book.

Packaging the Design-Based Research Method for Teachers

After three of the five piloting cycles, it was evident that the design process that provided each pilot cycle with Learning Activities was valuable. This was underlined by the annual review, which wanted to see this design process continue after the project. Thus, the process for the final piloting cycle was changed. Instead of repeating the same process, including the piloting of designer-created learning activities, project partners decided to create toolkits for teachers to create their own scenarios and Learning Activities. The toolkit for creating scenarios was named Eduvista, and the toolkit for designing Learning Activities was named Edukata. At the end of the project, both were combined into the Future Classroom Toolkit, although Edukata remains a separate, independent design model for teachers to use.

The challenge for the design team became how to package a complex professional design research methodology into a product that teachers could use independently with good results. Here are the main features that needed to change. Some of them were seen as challenges, while others were considered opportunities that made the process easier.

- Instead of professional designers, psychologists, cognitive scientists, graphical artists, and educators, the team includes mainly educators, and possibly students and educational policy makers.
- Instead of having a thorough understanding and practical experience of the design process, participants need to able to work with as little training as possible.
- Instead of working on design full time, the work needs to be done while working as educator (student, and educational policy maker).
- Instead of scheduling design work to span 2–3 months, the work needs to be completed in a shorter timeframe.
- Instead of working on 6–10 scenarios simultaneously, only one or two need to be sufficient.
- Instead of addressing challenges of all European teachers, the scope needs to be local.

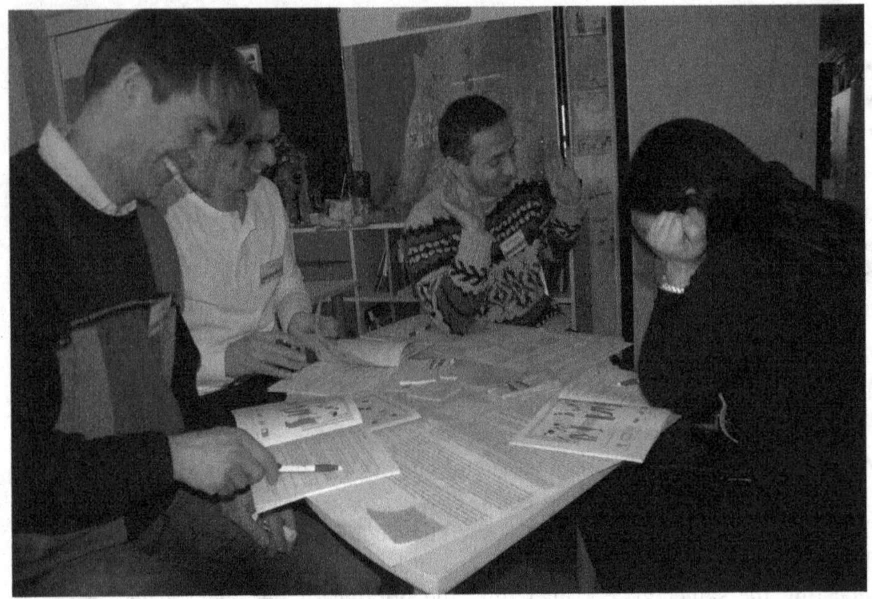

Fig. 3.8 A team of four teachers engaged in Learning Activity design in March 2013 in the iTEC Winter School. Each has the first prototype of the toolkit as a book in front of them

Much of the packaging of the design process was about simplification. Our concern was that essential parts and nuances of the process may be lost in pruning, and initially we were not sure this process would even be possible without an experienced designer facilitating the work.

We organized a 3-day workshop in the winter of 2013 in Finland, inviting 40 teachers from around Europe to attend (see Fig. 3.8). With them, we piloted the first prototype of the design toolkit. Based on observations and feedback, we continued our work, rewriting sections and simplifying them further. By the summer of 2013 a new version of the guidebook was available, and we named it Edukata.

During each cycle, national coordinators had organized workshops for their piloting teachers where the pilot materials were presented and worked through. The plan was that in cycle 5, at the end of 2013, national coordinators would train piloting teachers to facilitate the Edukata process, and each trained teacher would organize an Edukata design workshop with their colleagues. After these design workshops, teachers would use the Learning Activities they designed to plan their spring 2014 classroom pilots.

During this pilot, most national coordinators organized an Edukata design workshop with their teachers. In these design workshops, the coordinators acted as facilitators, instead of the teachers. Evaluation data showed that Learning Activities designed by the teachers themselves seemed to provide even better results than the ones in previous cycles. This was perhaps mostly due to the added freedom the teachers had, and the ability to address locally relevant challenges.

The suitability of Edukata facilitator materials in allowing teachers to act as design facilitators, however, was not shown, as the national coordinators enacted that role. What was evident from the results, and from workshops our design team organized independently, was that the Edukata facilitator guidebook required an additional complete rewrite, to further clarify some aspects of the process, remove design jargon, and structure the process more clearly. We needed to strike a fine balance in describing the fluid structure of the process, so that the end result suggests an open process without appearing to be without structure.

Additionally, as design researchers, we were concerned that calling Edukata a 'participatory design model' was not any more warranted, as the continual simplification of the model had reduced the role of participants to that of commenting on the work in progress. So in the final iteration, with consultation from other participatory design professionals, we provided more depth to the participation aspect of the model. While we still allowed simple commenting, we encouraged teachers to involve others in more meaningful ways, as co-designers. We presented the various participation levels as a spectrum, where the facilitator may move, depending on the circumstances.

The final rewrite was finished in May of 2014, and the final, version 1.0 Edukata facilitator guidebook was published in June 2014 and translated to various European languages during the following months.

Conclusion: Edukata

All educational institutions are changing, as new technologies bring new ways of acquiring, assimilating, and adapting information. Rather than reacting at the last possible moment, all schools can proactively look into the potential futures and take steps to incorporate new possibilities and challenges into their everyday practice.

Participatory design, or co-design, is a method for crafting design ideas that may be more likely to be adopted by the people they are designed for, because of their involvement in the design process, shaping and forming the artefact and tool into use. The outstanding evaluation results of the iTEC project show that thorough participatory design situations, when teachers and students are active contributors and designers of their own working environment, may produce lasting, significant improvements in the working cultures and practices of schools.

Our research question was:

What kind of support, training, materials, and experience is needed for teachers to create their own Learning Activities that produce beneficial results in their classrooms and those of their peers?

Edukata, the participatory design model, is our best hypothesis for answering this question (see Fig. 3.9). Edukata is a flexible and attractive model for approaching change management by utilising participatory design practices. The model consists of an iterative sequence of design workshops, which are prepared and organized

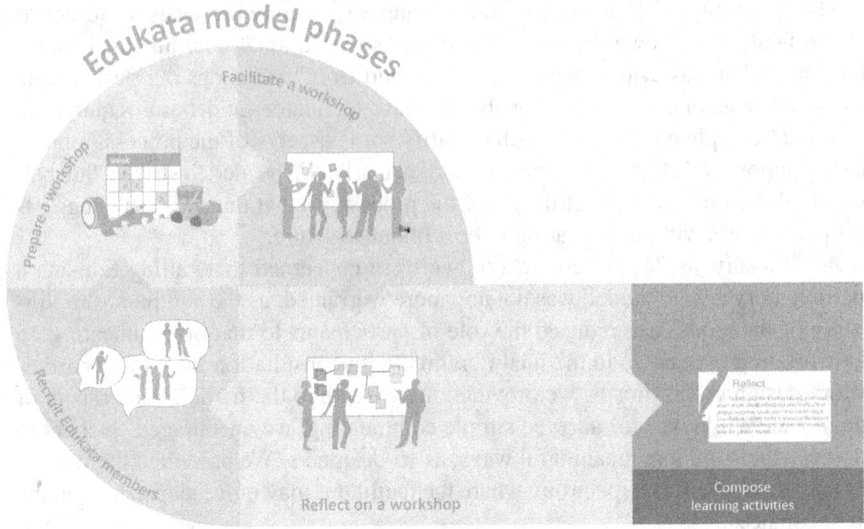

Fig. 3.9 The design process according to the Edukata model. Iterative progression of several workshops ends with writing new Learning Activities. Each workshop may involve partly different participants, so recruitment precedes other preparations. Each workshop is followed by a reflection session

by a trained facilitator. The process produces Learning Activities and learning stories, and as intermediate results, design challenges and design solutions related to the local context of the participants.

The Edukata model is described in a facilitator guidebook, which highlights aspects of each workshop phase (see Fig. 3.9), including how to recruit participants and how to engage everyone in an iterative design process. To ensure the quality of the design processes and their results, a tiered accreditation system has been set up, where people attending a facilitator workshop (see Fig. 3.10) and then facilitating a design workshop will be publicly recognized as Edukata facilitators. Several partners of the iTEC project have started their own national programmes related to teachers' continual professional development and teacher training that is including the Edukata model. Our hope is that by training more teachers to be proficient design facilitators, through these professional development opportunities, our own training workshops as well as Future Classroom training through the European Schoolnet, the contextual and adaptive aspects of Edukata will sustain without turning into a rigorous planning phase that precedes course planning.

When national policies call for renewed school practices, Edukata is a practice that can be used to turn those new policies into concrete activity ideas for teachers. When policy is defining the principles and direction, Edukata can be a way for teachers to help make them real in a school and classroom level.

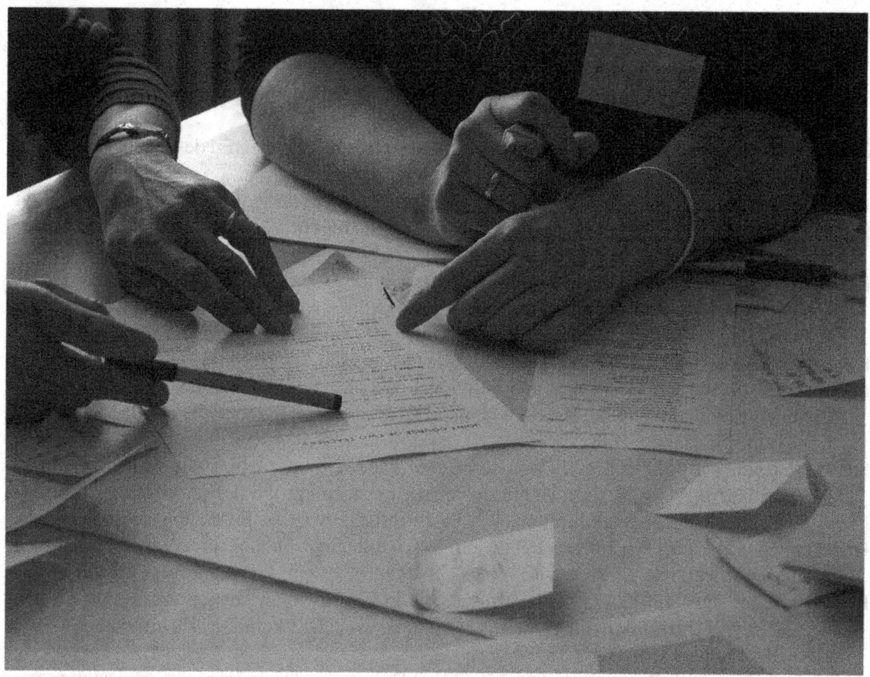

Fig. 3.10 Danish teachers working in an Edukata facilitator workshop in March 2014. The workshop consists of various exercises, including scenario analysis, simulated participatory design, challenge and solution design, and Learning Activity authoring. In this picture, teachers are evaluating an example to gain an understanding of the features of a high quality Learning Activity

As iTEC has drawn to a close, the design work can still be carried out by designers and teachers. Edukata is the design model that has been crafted specifically for educators, so they can work with their colleagues in facing new challenges and opportunities in a structured, creative, and productive manner. Edukata is part of the European Schoolnet's Future Classroom Toolkit and training programme, and also an independent participatory design model that can be used with existing scenarios. The website edukata.fi contains the guide book in several European languages, a library of existing scenarios and Learning Activities, as well as a listing of accredited Edukata facilitators and service providers.

All materials are published under an open CC BY-SA license at http://edukata.fi.

References

Cole M (1996) Putting culture in the middle. Cultural psychology: a once and future discipline. Harvard University Press, Cambridge, pp 116–145

Conole G (2010) Learning design—making practice explicit. In: ConnectEd design conference, 28 June–2 July 2010, Sydney, Australia

Durall E, Toikkanen T (2013) Feeler: feel good and learn better: a tool for promoting reflection about learning and well-being. In: Proceedings of the 3rd workshop on awareness and reflection in technology-enhanced learning, pp 83–89

Ehn P, Kyng M (1987) The collective resource approach to systems design. In: Bjerknes G, Ehn P, Kyng M (eds) Computers and democracy: a Scandinavian challenge. Avebury, Aldershot, pp 17–57

Engeström Y (1987) Learning by expanding. Orienta-Konsultit Oy, Helsinki

Engeström Y (1999) Activity theory and individual and social transformation. In: Engeström R, Miettinen R, Punamäki-Gitai R-L (eds) Perspectives on activity theory. Cambridge University Press, Cambridge, pp 19–38

Ford M, Leinonen T (2009) MobilED—a mobile tools and services platform for formal and informal learning. In: Ally M (ed) Mobile learning: transforming the delivery of education and training. Issues in distance education. Athabasca University Press, Edmonton, pp 195–214

Hakkarainen KAI (2003) Emergence of progressive-inquiry culture in computer-supported collaborative learning. Learn Environ Res 6(2):199–220

Keune A, Leinonen T (2013) Square1 Prototype: build your own devices for collaborative learning. In: Tuovi 11: Interaktiivinen tekniikka koulutuksessa 2013-konferenssin tutkijatapaamisen artikkelit. Tampere University

Keune A, Toikkanen T, Purma J, Leinonen T (2011) Deliverable D3.1: 1st report on design prototypes and design challenges for education. http://itec.eun.org/c/document_library/get_file?p_l_id=10307&folderId=37321&name=DLFE-1641.pdf

Leinonen T (2010) Designing learning tools, methodological insights. Aalto University, Espoo

Leinonen T, Kligyte G, Toikkanen T, Pietarila J, Dean P (2003) Learning with collaborative software—a guide to fle3. University of Art and Design Helsinki, Helsinki

Leinonen T, Toikkanen T, Silfvast K (2008) Software as hypothesis: research-based design methodology. In: The proceedings of participatory design conference 2008. Presented at the participatory design conference, PDC 2008. ACM, Indiana University, Bloomington

Leinonen T, Keune A, Veermans M, Toikkanen T (2014) Mobile apps for reflection in learning: a design research in K-12 education. Br J Educ Technol. doi:10.1111/bjet.12224

Lewin C, McNicol S (2014) Creating the future classroom: evidence from the iTEC project. Manchester Metropolitan University, Manchester. ISBN 978-1-910029-01-5

Muller MJ, Kuhn S (1993) Participatory design. Commun ACM 36(6):24–28. doi:10.1145/153571.255960

Nelson H, Stolterman E (2003) The design way: intentional change in an unpredictable world: foundations and fundamentals of design competence. Educational Technology, Englewood Cliffs

Rittel H (1972) On the planning crisis: systems analysis of the "first and second generations". Bedrifts Okonomen 8:390–396

Schön D (1987) Educating the reflective practitioner: toward a new design for teaching and learning in the professions. Jossey-Bass, San Francisco

Chapter 4
The iTEC Technical Artefacts, Architecture and Educational Cloud

Frans Van Assche, Luis Anido-Rifón, Jean-Noël Colin, David Griffiths, and Bernd Simon

Abstract This chapter introduces the technical artefacts of the iTEC project in the context of a cloud architecture. The rationale for the technology developed in the iTEC project follows from its overall aim to re-engineer the uptake of ICT in schools. To that end, iTEC focused (a) on some important barriers for the uptake of ICT such the effort that teachers must make in redesigning their teaching and finding the right resources for that, and (b) on enablers for the uptake of ICT, such as providing engaging experiences both for the learner and teacher. The technical innovations are centred around three themes: innovations in the support of learning design, innovations by using a-typical resources, and innovations in the integration and management of learning services and resources. Next this chapter presents the cloud architecture adopted by all technology providers, including a shared user management and control system, the shared data models and interoperability solutions. The technical artefacts and then further elaborated in the ensuing chapters.

Keywords Uptake of ICT • Schools • Technical architecture • Authentication • Authorisation • Exchange protocols

---

F. Van Assche (✉)
Department of Computer Science, University of Leuven, Leuven, Belgium
e-mail: frans.van.assche@gmail.com

L. Anido-Rifón
Telematics Engineering Department, ETSI Telecommunication, University of Vigo, Vigo, Spain
e-mail: lanido@det.uvigo.es

J.-N. Colin
University of Namur, Namur, Belgium
e-mail: jean-noel.colin@unamur.be

D. Griffiths
Institute of Educational Cybernatics, University of Bolton, Bolton, UK
e-mail: D.E.Griffiths@bolton.ac.uk

B. Simon
Knowledge Markets Consulting G.m.b.H., Wien, Austria
e-mail: bernd.simon@km.co.at

F. Van Assche et al. (eds.), *Re-engineering the Uptake of ICT in Schools*,
DOI 10.1007/978-3-319-19366-3_4

Rationale for the Educational Cloud and Technical Artefacts

Whereas Chap. 1 elaborates the rationale for re-engineering the uptake of ICT in schools, this section introduces the choice of artefacts developed in iTEC, the architecture for these artefacts, and how these fit together in what we call the iTEC Educational Cloud (IEC).

Barriers to the mainstreaming of technologies have been studied since the beginning of TEL. For example the first large scale European project about TEL in schools (Van Assche 1998) reported already the limited time of teachers, teacher training, the curriculum, etc. Other research added lack of teacher confidence (teachers being scared and intimidated by their student's increasing knowledge about Internet and communication devices), lack of pedagogical teacher training; lack of suitable educational software, limited access to ICT; rigid structure of traditional education systems, etc.

However, as many practitioners will testify (e.g. see in Van Assche 1998; Van Assche et al. 2006), the barrier most mentioned is the burden to teachers (often expressed as lack of time) when they have to explore and absorb emerging technologies. This in turn seems to influence other cited problems. Therefore, iTEC decided to explore how teachers can be helped in the following three areas.

Firstly, we noted that teachers reported in earlier projects that they spend most of their time, apart from contact hours in the classroom, in lesson preparation and assessment. The introduction of new technologies increases the burden by requiring established lesson plans to be revised, and by introducing elements into the planning process whose implications for the classroom process are unknown to teachers. iTEC sought to alleviate this problem by providing support in carrying out lesson planning which involved new technologies. An investigation with Ministries of Education (MoE) revealed that many countries and regions have lively teacher communities that exchange lesson plans and ideas. For example the lektion.se community in Sweden alone has more than 220,000 members. However, the challenge is to share lesson plans and ideas across national and regional boundaries. Therefore, iTEC decided to explore how **de-contextualized learning designs** (including lesson plans)—in iTEC called scenarios—could make ideas and elaborated designs more shareable. In addition, de-contextualisation would facilitate the introduction of emerging technologies without the need to refer to specific products. This was achieved by providing requirements for a lesson plan in an intentional way instead of an extensional way,[1] which has the additional advantage of making the requirements more resilient to changing technologies. The intentional way means that for example the scenarios refer to kinds of resources in a descriptive way, while the lesson plan will typically refer to specific resources.

Secondly, iTEC investigated how **learning can be made more engaging** by providing non-traditional resources through the use of ICT. While, the ambient

[1] "Intension" indicates the internal content of a term or concept that constitutes its formal definition; and "extension" indicates its range of applicability by naming the particular objects that it denotes.

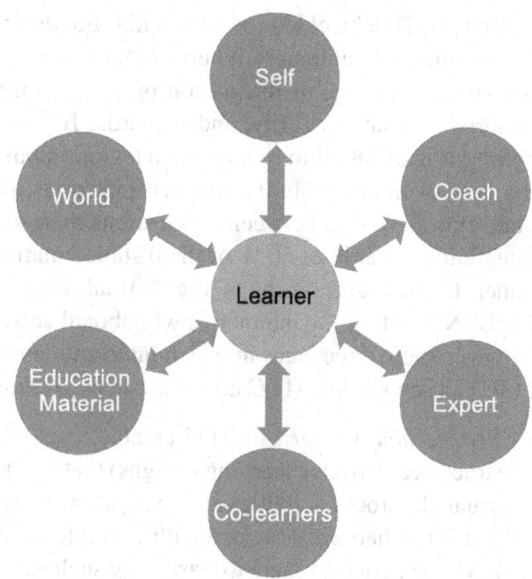

Fig. 4.1 Interactions of the learner

intelligent vision from 2001 (see Chap. 1) was unrealistic, it was indicative of a shift to different forms of more learner-centred, ICT-facilitated approaches including personal learning, individual learning, self-regulated learning, and ambient schooling (Van Assche 2004). Within such a learner-centred approach the levers for engagement come from interactions. The learning experience can only be influenced through interactions, and it is at these points of contact that we seek to identify the opportunities for creating and facilitating engagement. These opportunities are summarised in Fig. 4.1.

Typically a learner interacts with a coach (usually the teacher), a subject expert (usually the teacher), co-learners, education material, the world outside the closed educational environment, and with the traces of their own earlier activities. In this context of interactions, iTEC exploited the fact that ICT provides the means to go beyond the classroom setting. For example to be able to chat with an astronaut about space travel, participate in a distant experiment in CERN, get coaching support from a grandmother living a 100 km away, have access to simulation and serious games, and consult same-age learners abroad about how to pronounce a foreign language. As such, engagement can arise from the person, material, or environment one interacts with and/or the interaction conduit itself. Again from the early Web for Schools project up to recent TEL projects such as the Stellar project, research has pointed to the engaging potential of ICT.[2] iTEC therefore explores to what extent interactions other than the traditional classroom interactions can possibly enhance engagement.

[2] In the Stellar 'Big Meeting' of February 2012 there was only one factor mentioned by all business stakeholders: the engagement potential of TEL.

Thirdly, iTEC tackled the substantial **burden that comes with the integration** of emerging technologies. Whereas innovators and early adopters are prepared to put up with a range of integration problems, these are a real barrier for the early majority, the late majority, and laggards. If we want to cross the mainstreaming chasm, it is essential to reduce the integration burden. This burden originates from the lack of interoperability between platforms and applications running on these platforms as well as between applications themselves. iTEC aimed to provide easy integration for at least 50 % of the installed platforms for education including container technologies such as the Virtual Learning Environments Moodle[3] and DotLRN,[4] and for the interactive whiteboard software OpenSankoré.[5]

Given these three areas in which interventions can be made to improve the uptake of ICT in schools, the iTEC artefacts can be presented, together with their rationales:

- *Ready-made scenarios*: iTEC created a set of scenarios (i.e. de-contextualised structured narrative learning designs) that aim to help teachers to go beyond their usual classroom activities and to explore emerging technologies. iTEC proposes that if teachers are provided with examples of effective use of new technologies, it will be easier for them to start using such new technologies in their own classes. These scenarios are adapted by teachers to their own local context.
- *Ready-made learning activities*: Learning stories consist of learning activities and are further elaborations of scenarios as concrete instantiations whose purpose is to make the resource (material, people, events) requirements more concrete. By providing different levels of abstraction, teachers and learners can choose the appropriate level for their purpose.
- *A Future Classroom Scenario Method*: As iTEC was concerned with systemic change, it also created a method with procedures and techniques for developing such scenarios. An important part of this toolkit is the Future Classroom Maturity Model (see Chap. 2) that allows teachers, head-teachers, ICT co-ordinators, and MoE to assess where they are with respect to four innovation dimensions, and develop scenarios that facilitate taking the next step.
- *The Learning Activity Design Method*, that guides teachers in how to find and use an archive of Learning Stories and Learning Activities which are derived from iTEC scenarios. It is focused on enabling the adoption of advanced pedagogical approaches by teachers, supported by appropriate technologies and other resources. The Learning Activity Design Toolkit is used by individual teachers and collaborative communities.
- *A Widget Store*: The iTEC Widget Store provides access to a collection of small ready-to-use educational apps that can be deployed in a range of 'shells' which act as containers for widgets (see also later). The W3C specification for widgets was adopted in order to maximise interoperability, and support is provided for embedding widgets from the iTEC Store in Moodle, DotLrn, OpenSankoré, and even ordinary browsers.

---

[3] https://moodle.org/

[4] http://dotlrn.org/

[5] http://open-sankore.org/

- *A number of technical artefacts, including services and specifications*: These artefacts, elaborated in the next section, offer, inter alia, automated help in finding adequate resources, activities, and scenarios; automated support for localisation; finding more easily other types of resources such as people and events; play applications in the form of widgets; plug and play authentication and authorisation; support in establishing new collaborations, and last but not least the iTEC Educational Cloud (IEC).

All these iTEC artefacts have a **common characteristic**: facilitating the uptake of ICT in schools. However, the benefits are not restricted to this. For example some of the technical artefacts (see next section) are also beneficial to technology providers, standardization bodies, researchers, etc.

Technical Artefacts

In this section we focus on the *technical* artefacts. These artefacts primarily aim to support teachers in their learning design and assessment activities. A typical workflow is that the teacher selects an iTEC scenario, and then defines a number of learning activities based upon the scenario which together constitute a learning story. When the teacher finally puts the learning story into practice, the system assists in translating abstract requirements into concrete resources, that fit her pedagogical goals. While describing the technical artefacts, the innovations are highlighted.

Innovations in Support for Learning Design[6]

The aim of this iTEC technology is to support teachers in discovering the opportunities and limitations for the implementation of learning stories and activities within their technical contexts, and to assist them in the identifying learning stories and activities which are practicable given the technological resources available to them. In order to achieve this, iTEC created a Scenario Development Engine (SDE). This is a novel approach in this domain, as previous systems provided, at most, lesson plans that required a given collection of tools to be implemented. In other words, state-of-the-art systems did not provide assistance in discovering lesson plans that could be implemented with the tools available to the teacher. In addition to providing support in assessing feasibility, the SDE also provides recommendations on the three types of resources (people, events, and learning material) that can be used to implement learning stories and activities, namely technological tools including software applications, and events (see also next paragraph). The SDE offers the typical functionality of a traditional recommendation system (Ricci et al. 2011).

[6] Here the term 'learning design' is used as a generic term, not to be confused with IMS-Learning Design.

However, unlike typical recommendation systems, which base their operation on the computation of an estimated utility level for a given user, the SDE provides recommendations taking into account the technical and pedagogical context in which learning stories and activities will be developed. This approach is inherently more complex, as the 'suitability' of a resource in our case is more difficult to determine, because it cannot be computed according to the tastes or interests of a particular person, but rather depends on the assessments of a community of experts.

The SDE combines two state-of-the-art technologies. First, the SDE is based on multi-criteria recommendation techniques (Matsatsinis et al. 2007; Lakiotaki et al. 2008) that consider several factors (identified and ranked by the community of experts) to compute the relevance of resources. Second, like other recommendation systems (Peis et al. 2008), semantic technologies are used to represent the information managed by the system to improve the handling and integration of data from different sources, and above all, to update the underlying models. Note that these models have to be updated frequently, as new rules or resource types (e.g., new types of tools or events) may appear at any time.

Innovations in the Use of A-Typical Resources for Learning

Figure 4.1 describes five interactions that can be used as levers for engagement. For example be able to chat with an astronaut, seek help from a retired person willing to assist with mathematics, being able to participate to events organised by others. iTEC investigated whether new forms of interactions can be integrated in the classroom in an easier way and whether the approach can be scaled. While this may not be the first time that some of these interactions have been proposed, they are certainly not mainstream. The aim of iTEC was to identify the barriers to creating these interactions and to find ways to overcome them. By doing so, iTEC sought to facilitate the exploration of new ICT enabled scenarios, new roles, and new situations in the learning process.

The basic instrument is a People and Events repository that allows users to find People who are willing to contribute to a learning activity or Events organized by others and in which learners and/or teachers can participate. Whereas professional networks—such as LinkedIn—have already existed for some time, they are too generic for this purpose, and do not fulfil the requirements of the educational sector for professional networking. Similarly, the technology—a repository with faceted search—is not new, it is the application of this technology which is of interest. More specifically, iTEC investigated the following questions:

- To what extent is there an interest in sharing information on People and Events?
- Which types of People and Events are of interest?
- What information about People and Events should be gathered, using which vocabularies?
- What level of sharing is appropriate: in schools, region/country, or in Europe?

- To what extent do teachers make use of the opportunity to find people and events and/or recommendations for learning activities?
- What are the barriers and enablers?

Innovation in the Integration and Management of Learning Services and Resources

One of the main bottlenecks in mainstreaming technologies is the integration of technologies into the environment that the teacher is familiar with and/or which she is required to use. Innovative tools and services are often designed for a particular combination of operating system, hardware (PC, tablet, mobile phone, whiteboard), and software (e.g. Moodle, Blackboard, Facebook). Proprietary systems, also used elsewhere (Govaerts and Dahrendorf 2011), exist which resolve part of this problem, such as the Apple App Store and Google Gadgets, but they are restricted to particular platforms. Consequently, in order to facilitate the integration of new applications into as wide a range as possible of real-life classroom environments, iTEC chose to support the delivery of services through non-proprietary interoperability specifications and software. It was decided that the most effective and sustainable solution would be to use the W3C specification for Packaged Web Apps (Widgets), which is expected to facilitate the interoperability of a wider range of platforms.

Beyond the need to support this technical integration, it is also necessary to enable teachers and students to find and deploy the widgets which they would like to use. iTEC has developed a **Widget Store** to meet this need, which can be embedded in any web platform with a modest programming effort. This enables widgets to be described either formally, using the iTEC classification, or informally using tags. Paradata on the use of the widgets is cumulated across various instances of the store. The Widget Store has an API which provides access to this data, which can be processed by recommender engines (including, but not limited to, the SDE), or in learning analytics applications. The Widget Store and its underlying servers are all open source, and are built using Apache Wookie and the Edukapp server software. iTEC has been a leading contributor to both of these projects (Wilson et al. 2011; Griffiths et al. 2012).

This vision of making use of the W3C widget specification to deliver flexible services across platforms was set out in the iTEC project proposal, and has been realised in the Widget Store outlined above. The widget package is itself a rather simple structure, consisting of some HTML, some JavaScript and some image files. However, its very simplicity means that it can be used in a number of different ways, and as a consequence it may be misleading simply to state that iTEC makes use of widgets. It is more valuable to consider the approaches which can be taken to providing functionality with widgets. We may distinguish the following approaches:

- As a platform for delivery of single user applications (e.g. a task timer)
- As means of accessing services provided by the Wookie server which underlies the Widget Store. This manages user identity and enables applications to provide

threaded multi-user services which can be deployed over multiple platforms. These may be relatively simple (e.g. voting), or more complex
- As a simple way of accessing information tools (e.g. time servers, 'this day in history')
- As a means of integrating more complex external services (for example Etherpad)

In addition, part of the project vision for widgets was that tools would be provided which enabled teachers and learners to create their own widgets. The Widget Store supports using three principal approaches:

- As a way of delivering open content from the Internet, embedded into widgets
- As a way of publishing small websites created by teachers and students
- As an interoperability platform (e.g. uploading a Flash file and making it available as a widget)

The iTEC Technical Architecture

Even when the functionalities described earlier in this section are made available, it is still challenging for teachers and ICT coordinators to integrate such services. Therefore, iTEC has adopted the cloud approach—the iTEC Educational Cloud (IEC)—such that the described services are available without cumbersome installations by teachers, learners, or ICT coordinators.

The design of the IEC reported in this chapter has been guided by the following key design principles:

- Collaborative and social functionality
- Accelerated feature delivery
- Open integration protocols
- Serving multiple tenants, a tenant being a group of users (e.g. a school, region, or country) sharing the same view on the technology-enhanced learning environment providing ease-of-use in configuring and customizing such an environment

These principles are characteristic of cloud computing and more particular for Software as a Service (SAAS) models.

It is however not sufficient to develop the architecture according to the vogue of the time. The architecture should serve a relevant user community and follow a solid methodology. A number of efforts have been made to describe and guide construction-oriented research processes (Hevner 2007; Vaishnavi and Kuechler 2007; Takeda et al. 1990). iTEC opted to adopt design science research which is a research paradigm in which the researchers seek answers to their questions about the problem in focus through the creation of innovative artefacts (Hevner 2010; March and Smith 1995).

By making use of a design science research methodology, we ensured that the value of our solution to the general problem (i.e. a need to improve the uptake of ICT in schools) was evident to practitioners and researchers, in order to promote commitment to the solution and acceptance of the results. In the design process for the IEC we have identified the following stakeholder roles:

- *Learner*: A Learner is a person who is actively engaged in Learning Activities to enhance their knowledge, skills, and competences. A Learner interacts with the Resources provided to her via a Shell.
- *Teacher*: A Teacher is a learning facilitator who supports pupils in their Learning Activities. A Teacher administers a group of Learners via a Shell and stimulates learning by re-using Resources.
- *Learning Designer*: A Learning Designer is a role that can for example be adopted by advanced teachers, head masters, or faculty at universities. A Learning Designer inspires other teachers to adopt pedagogical innovation mediated by Learning Story and Activity Designs.
- *Technical Pedagogical Coordinator* (TPC): A TPC is in charge of inspiring the teachers in their organisation(s) to adopt pedagogical innovation mediated by Learning Stories and Activities. Coordinators are also in charge of administering and deploying the technical infrastructure that supports the facilitation of learning.

The IEC encompasses all the services that are made accessible to its user, whether directly or indirectly. It includes user-end services, back-end services and also some horizontal services that securely connect end-user technologies to form a single, homogeneous and consistent activity space. More specifically, the IEC consists of the following core services; for the sake of clarity not all them depicted in the Architecture Overview of Fig. 4.2:

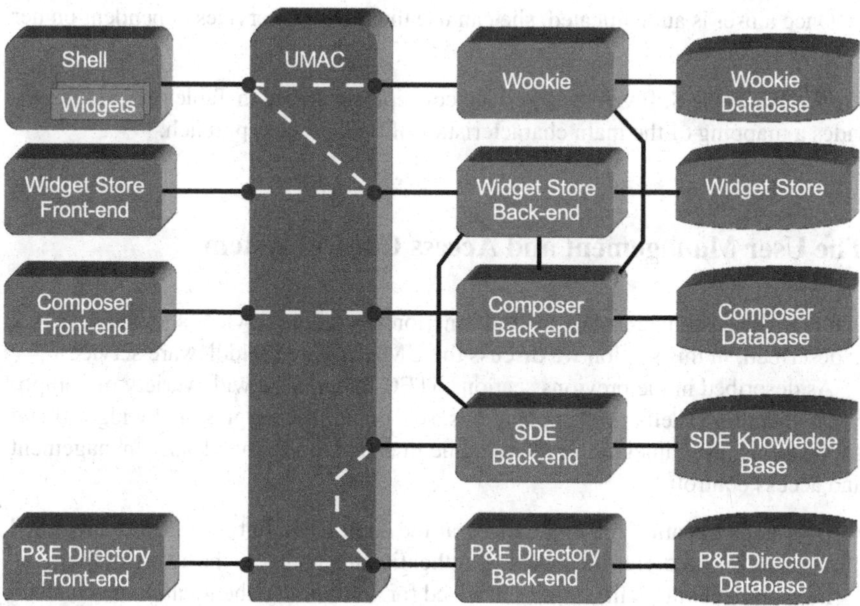

Fig. 4.2 The iTEC educational cloud architecture

- *Shell*: a configurable software container that (as the name suggests) acts as an empty shell allowing users to identify and add their own Resources and to integrate them in order to meet the educational objectives of a Learning Activity.
- *Composer*: an application that supports technical pedagogical coordinators as well as advanced teachers in accomplishing three main tasks: (1) composing Learning Activities and Learning Stories, (2) managing Learning Resources such as Content, and Tools, (3) administering Technical Settings of learning environments.
- *Scenario Development Engine* (SDE): a software component offering back-end services related to technical localisation, i.e., identifying which Learning Activities can be implemented in a school. The SDE also supports resource planning, providing recommendations on the best Learning Resources with which to fulfil the requirements included in a Learning Activity.
- *Widget*: a Web-technology based container for Resources that comes with a graphical user interface for displaying information arrangements and provides standardized methods for data manipulation. Widgets can run in a Shell (described above) supported by the Apache Wookie run-time environment.
- *Widget Store*: a software component that supports creation, upload, tagging, and searching for Learning Resources in the form of Widgets.
- *People & Events Directory*: a directory where users can find Contributors to a Learning Activity, and potentially useful Events.
- *User Management and Access Control* (UMAC): a set of components that supports user authentication and authorization throughout the IEC. It comprises three main modules: an authentication server, an authorization server and an authorization filter that controls access to the above mentioned components. Once a user is authenticated, she can use the different services dependent on her authorization.

Our use of the Software as a Service concept is clarified in Table 4.1, which provides a mapping of the main characteristics of SaaS to our approach.

The User Management and Access Control system

While in the ensuing chapters the full functionality of the services shown in Fig. 4.2 is described, in this section we discuss the UMAC shared middleware service.

As described in the previous sections, iTEC integrates a wide variety of components, including shells, web applications, self-contained widgets, and widget-based applications. This integration raises some questions in terms of user management and access control:

- User authentication may take place at the shell level, but also, some integrated services may require some form of authentication or at least be aware of the visiting user's identity. This implies the need for an central authentication mechanism that can span the range of components and provide consistent information about the user.

Table 4.1 Mapping of SaaS components to the IEC components

SaaS characteristic	Educational cloud components
Collaborative and social functionality	The three main subsystems: the composer, the people and events directory, and the widget store provide collaborative and social functionality. The composer supports the sharing of resources such as learning activities and learning stories; the P&E directory together with the Widget Store supports sharing of *people*, *events* and widgets, and also implements a full set of social metadata. In particular, the Widget Store, acts as a marketplace for learning resources, in content and tools targeting teachers and learners
Accelerated feature delivery	The IEC architecture combines various application service providers, allowing each to rapidly deliver new functionalities. In order to offer an integrated service, integration protocols (see below) are required
Open integration protocols	The IEC architecture combines the offerings of various application service providers, including the Composer, the P&E directory, the SDE, the Widget Store and UMAC. These are integrated using integration protocols. In Fig. 4.2, the communication between the components is shown as lines. This communication may or may not be controlled by UMAC. In the latter case, the service is itself responsible for the authorization handling of its API. In addition these protocols for integration are *open* for other applications to integrate with Examples of the open integration protocols are (a) the P&E API for updating and retrieving information about people and events, and (b) interfaces provided by the shell to be exploited by the widgets, for example Widget APIs and inter-widget communication capabilities Apart from the fact that each service comes with its own set of protocols, some protocols are common and are used by multiple IEC components; viz. the iTEC Protocol for Data Harvesting (iTEC-PDH) and the UMAC API for user management and access control
Serving multiple tenants	A *tenant* is a group of users sharing the same view on the technology-enhanced learning environment. Within the IEC multiple tenants (e.g. schools, regions, or countries) are served at the same time. One of the key features for achieving this is the provision of multilingual services based on shared multi-lingual vocabularies as well as customization and configuration features
Ease-of-use in configuring and customizing such an environment	Customization and configuration may be required for a context which includes multiple tenants, and it is certainly true in the present case. Therefore the IEC is built for easy configuration and customization through (a) its Shell that allows the IEC to be delivered with different application run-time environments such as Moodle and DotLRN, and (b) the widget engine that allows configuring one's own technology-enhanced learning environment

- Access control policies may be defined centrally, at the iTEC Cloud level, but these policies have to co-exist and be consistent with those defined at the shell level, or at the integrated services level, if any. Again, this requires an authorisation mechanism that integrates at the various levels of the architecture.

Because end-users are highly sensitive to authentication and authorisation mechanisms and difficulties they may encounter in using them, we ran a survey among iTEC teachers, and collected 269 responses from 17 European countries. One of the main conclusions of the study was that using iTEC services should not add extra authentication burden on users. Rather, iTEC will have to extend existing infrastructure and offer the possibility of re-using credentials that users may already possess with external identity providers. However, because some users are concerned that re-using credentials might constitute a security risk, it is important to propose a mixed approach.

Complete results of the survey are presented in Colin and Simon (2012).

Our goal was thus to design a system that meets the following requirements:

- Allow user authentication at the shell level, and convey the user information to sub-components (widgets and back-end services)
- Allow access policies to be defined globally to the IEC, based on a Role-Based Access Control (Ferraiolo et al. 2001) model
- From the global access rules, provision local policies to every iTEC sub-component
- Support interoperability with major service providers, like Google, Facebook, Yahoo…

Designed Solution

The interoperability requirements led us to focus on open standards and protocols to build authentication and authorisation mechanisms. We performed a thorough study, and identified candidate protocols like SAMLv2,[7] OpenID[8] and oAuth.[9] Due to their technological maturity, their relative simplicity, their support for web interactions, the availability of libraries and their wide adoption by main actors on the net, we selected oAuthv2 and OpenIDv2 as the basis for our solution. The fact that users are warned when an application wants to access protected data was also an element of choice.

OpenIDv2 (OpenID Foundation 2007) is an open and standard protocol for signing on to websites using one single set of credentials. The protocol has been developed for many years and adopted by major players on the Internet, like Google. It relies on the assumption that users have an identity defined with an Identity Provider (IdP), and want to use that identity to access various services offered by Service Providers (SP). The typical flow is a user visiting a Service Provider that requires authentication; SP prompts the user for her identity or that of her IdP. The user is then redirected to the IdP to authenticate, and if authentication succeeds, the user is sent back to the SP with the proof that successful authentication did take place. Optionally, the IdP may provide additional information about the user (this requires some protocol extensions).

[7] http://saml.xml.org/

[8] http://openid.net/

[9] http://oauth.net/2/

OAuthv2 (Hardt 2012) is a protocol for managing delegation of authorisation. Its main use case is a user (the resource owner) needing to give access to some of its resources hosted on a server (the resource server) to a client, typically another service. To avoid forcing the user to give her credentials to the client, oAuthv2 introduces a workflow where when the user is asked by the client to give access to a resource, she is sent back to an authorisation server where she authenticates and is then asked to grant or deny access. Upon success, the authorisation server issues an access token to the client that it will use to access the resource on behalf of the user. In this way, the user's credentials are never disclosed to the client. This is the protocol that Facebook or Yahoo use for granting access to their services to remote sites, after getting the agreement of the user. oAuthv2 supports various types of 'grants', to support different profiles of this protocol and accommodate different situations:

- **Authorisation Code Grant**: this is the most secure scenario, in which the client directs the resource owner to the authorisation server for authentication and access request; upon success, the authorisation server issues an authorisation code to the client, that the client then exchanges with the authorisation server for an access token, that is finally presented by the client to the resource server to get access to the resource. All interactions with the resource owner go through her user-agent (typically her browser). This scenario supports client authentication by the authorisation server before issuing an access token, and ensures that the access token never reaches the resource owner's user-agent, which could lead to token leakage.
- **Implicit Grant**: this is a simplified version of the previous scenario, in which instead of being issued an authentication code by the authorisation server, the client directly receives an access token. This scenario is targeted at clients implemented in a browser, typically in javascript. In this case, the authorisation server does not authenticate the client, and the access token is exposed to the resource owner or other applications with access to its user-agent.
- **Resource Owner Password Credentials Grant**: this scenario is built on the assumption that there exists a high degree of trust between the resource owner and the client. The resource owner provides the client with her credentials, and the client uses them to request an access token from the authorisation server. This scenario supports client authentication.
- **Client Credentials Grant**: in this scenario, the client is acting on its own behalf, not on behalf of the user. The client authenticates directly to the authorisation server and receives an access token.

It is worthwhile noting that oAuthv2 also supports extension grants that allow to extend the token request mechanism to support different types of credentials, like SAML assertions.

Because we chose to use oAuthv2 to secure widget access to back-end services, and because widgets usually involve client-side computing and get access to the user's environment, the implicit grant is the only option of choice. However, we also successfully implemented the client credentials grant to secure access to the SDE backend service. One of the drawbacks of the implicit grant is the absence of client authentication, but this can be explained by the nature of widgets, which are running client-side, making available any sensitive information to other components running in the user's environment (user-agent). It would thus not be possible to securely store client credentials at the widget level.

The User Management and Access Control (UMAC) sub-system glues together all IEC components with the above protocols, and comprises the following components:

- The *UMAC server* is responsible for user authentication, issuance of oAuth tokens, and management of user data and privileges; it plays the role of the OpenID's Identity Provider, the oAuth's authorisation server, and implements a back-end service to access, store and manage user data and privilege information.
- The *UMAC filter* is an authorisation guard that sits in front of back-end services; the back-end service represents the oAuth's Resource Server, and the UMAC filter is in charge of validating access tokens.
- The *UMAC management widgets* are a collection of widgets that allow to access and manage authentication and authorisation information in the iTEC Cloud. Those widgets allow to register a new user, to update a user's details, to create sets of users, and to assign iTEC roles.
- The *UMAC library* is a JavaScript library of tools to help the widget developer to easily integrate with the UMAC framework and not care about the various protocols' implementation.

These components are described in greater details in the next sections.

UMAC Server

The UMAC Server serves two main purposes: authenticating users and controlling access to back-end services.

To authenticate users, UMAC Server implements the OpenID Provider specification. It handles authentication requests from iTEC user-facing components (OpenId relying parties), typically shells or web applications, authenticates users, and responds to relying parties; UMAC Server supports SREGv1.0 and AXv1.0 OpenID extensions to provide basic information of logged in user (username, first and last names, email address, language, timezone, country). Authentication is checked against a local database of users.

One of the requirements drawn from the survey described above mandated that iTEC should allow users to login using third-party credentials, namely Google, Facebook or Yahoo. Thus the UMAC Server supports user authentication using any of those systems, by implementing an OpenID Relying Party (in the case of Google and Yahoo) and an oAuth client (in the case of Facebook).

Access control to iTEC services is handled by the UMAC Server. Access requests may come from widgets or web applications, in which case the oAuthv2 scenario implemented is the implicit grant, but requests may also come from standalone applications, which are run in a more controlled environment, and for which the selected scenario is the client credentials grant. Thus the UMAC Server implements the related sections of the oAuthv2 specification, and handles Authorisation Requests (for the implicit grant) and Access Token Requests (for the client credentials grant), issuing access tokens to widgets and controlled applications respectively.

In addition to the authentication and authorisation functionalities, the UMAC server is also used to store user information; this information is made accessible to UMAC widgets and some other IEC components through a REST API, protected by the oAuthv2 protocol, just like any other iTEC back-end service.

Finally, the UMAC server is used to manage user privileges; those privileges span all iTEC services, i.e. apply equally to shells, widgets or back-end services. Six levels of privileges are defined in a strictly hierarchical way: super-user, administrator, coordinator, teacher, student and guest. The level of privilege of a user is passed to the OpenID relying party upon authentication through SREG or AX extensions, where available, and they are checked by the token validation process between the UMAC filter and the UMAC server.

For a seamless user experience, UMAC authentication is propagated to the shell through a plugin mechanism which is dependent on the shell itself. In this way, once the user is authenticated, all shell components (typically widgets) can reuse the user information.

UMAC Filter

The UMAC filter is designed to be deployed in front of back-end services, and interacts with the UMAC server following the oAuthv2 protocol to control access to the services by ensuring that only authorised requests get served. The current implementation of the filter takes the form of a servlet filter, which makes it very easy to integrate and (de)activate and realises a separation of concerns by allowing the service developer to work independently from the access control mechanism.

In oAuthv2 terminology, the UMAC filter acts as the protection part of the resource server. It receives requests for access in the form of REST calls (basically http requests), and for each requests, it checks that a valid access token is provided. If no token is present, an error is returned, and it is up to the client to obtain one. If a token is present, its validity is checked by querying the UMAC server through a secure channel, and upon success, the lifetime of the token and the user id of the token owner are returned to the filter. Based on this information, the filter then checks the local access policy that defines the rules for accessing the service. These rules are expressed using the Apache Shiro[10] system. If the rules are evaluated positively, access is granted

[10] http://shiro.apache.org/

and the request is passed to the service. Otherwise, an error is returned. For efficiency reasons, the UMAC filter caches the validated tokens for a period of time to avoid unnecessary roundtrips with the UMAC server.

UMAC Library

The UMAC library is a Javascript library of functions that aims at facilitating the development of widgets and their integration with UMAC authentication service, more precisely, the oAuth authentication endpoint's service. It hides the complexity of the protocol by providing methods to manage the whole authentication process (request for token, redirect to authentication form, token transfer to requesting component and error handling).

Figure 4.3 presents the UMAC components (in gray) as well as the interactions with other iTEC systems. These components are a decomposition of the UMAC component depicted in Fig. 4.2. The UMAC Server is used for authentication (solid lines) either from a shell, widgets or web applications like the Composer or the Persons and Events Directory. This follows the OpenID protocol. Authentication may be local (using the User DB) or rely on third-party authenticators (right-most box). Regarding authorisation (fine dashed lines), UMAC widgets support registration or update of user information through the UMAC REST Web Service, which is protected by the UMAC filter. Similarly, any other iTEC component may access iTEC back-end services which are protected by the UMAC filter (see bottom of the diagram). The UMAC filter validates authorisation with the UMAC server (large dashed lines).

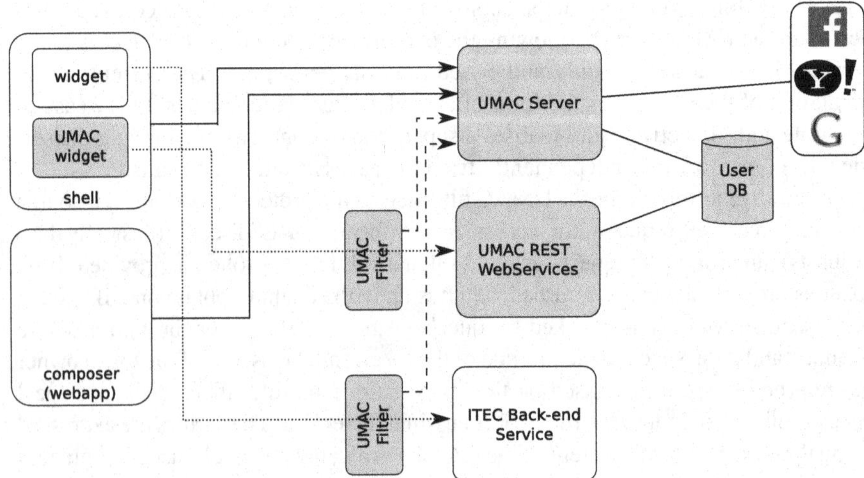

Fig. 4.3 Interactions of UMAC components with other iTEC systems: the example of the composer

Sharing Data

In iTEC, semantic interoperability was achieved by a shared data model for exchange between the iTEC systems and the multilingual vocabularies as described in the appendix of this book. The principle shared object types are:

- Event: a description of interesting Events, maintained in the Persons and Events directory
- Learning Activity: a description of iTEC Learning Activities as provided for example by teachers and maintained in the Composer
- Person: a description of a Person such as an expert, maintained in the Persons and Events directory
- Resource Guide: a description, maintained in the Composer, of resources used with LearningActivities
- Technical Setting: a description, maintained in the Composer, of the technical capabilities of a school or classroom
- Tools: a description of tools used in Learning Activities and Learning Stories, maintained in the composer
- Widget: a description of a widget as recorded in the Widget Store

In addition to the data models, iTEC also implemented a protocol for data harvesting (the iTEC-PDH). Within modern REST interfaces, JSON strings are currently preferred over XML technologies, because JSON facilitates rendering in user interfaces, especially browser-based user interfaces, e.g. W3C widgets. Consequently most REST interfaces in the iTEC architecture are based on JSON strings. The iTEC-PDH follows this approach while borrowing operational semantics from OAI-PMH.

iTEC-PDH request

A service implementing the iTEC-PDH must respond to an http GET request. The GET request has four parts:

- The first part refers to the service—i.e. the harvesting target, e.g. 'http://ariadne.cs.kuleuven.be/itec-directory/api/rest/'.
- The second part specifies the object type. In REST terms, it refers to the collection. For example 'Event'.
- The third part is the string '/harvest'.
- The fourth part is optional and is given as an http query string. It may contain the following elements: 'from=<date-time spec>' and 'until=<date-time spec>'. The <date-time spec> is following the date-time data type (see "Person" in Appendix). As customary the http query string parameters are joined together with an ampersand and follow a question mark. For example '?from=2012-09-15T00:00:00.000+02:00&until=2012-09-16T23:59:59.999+02:00'. As for OAI-PMH the

boundaries must be included in the search results. A service may also implement EPOCH time in milliseconds for these too parameters. For example '?from=135 8377200000&until=1358463599999'. The default value for the 'from' value is the beginning of the service. For practical reasons this may be taken as 0 in EPOCH time. The default value for the 'until' parameter is the time the request is received by the service.

iTEC-PDH Response

The response to an iTEC-PDH request is a regular http GET response with a JSON array as the payload. The JSON array contains the update elements as shown in Table 4.2. Each element has

- An identifier labelled "id" with a value following the 'identifier' data type described in "Person" in Appendix.
- A date of last modification labelled "last_mod" with a value following the 'date-time' data type described in "Person" in Appendix.
- The status of the last update, labelled "status" with a value from the value space {"created", "modified", "deleted"}.

In addition an element with the status "created" or "modified" must have an element labelled "entry" that gives the created or modified entry. The entry itself must follow the data model as specified in the data model as described in the appendix of this book. Note that vocabulary tokens are used if a data element of an entry is of the data type "VocabularyTerm".

It should be noted that an entry may contain an internal identifier such as shown in Table 4.2 "_id".

Conclusions

This chapter has reported on the iTEC architecture and artefacts addressing the most important choking points in the uptake of ICT in schools as well as building on the engaging potential of ICT in learning activities. We have focussed specifically on the innovations in the technical area, and provided and introduction to the Scenario Development Engine, the Widget Store, the People and Events directory, and the iTEC Education Cloud.

Dozens of classroom experiments have led to the identification of both successes and problems for each of the different technical artefacts, and also indicate that as a whole iTEC makes a significant contribution to re-engineering the uptake of ICT in education (See also Chap. 9: Evaluation). It is our belief that the realisation of the future classroom as envisaged by current research efforts can only succeed if sufficient progress is made in technology that will facilitate (and not hamper) the uptake of ICT in schools.

Table 4.2 Example harvesting result


```
[
  {
    "id": "http://itec-directory.eun.org/Person/2305",
    "last_mod": "2012-09-16T10:45:31.190+02:00",
    "status": "modified",
    "entry": {
      "_id": 2305,
      "givenName": "Otto ",
      "familyName": "Leskinen",
      "loginName": "Otto Leskinen",
      "mbox": "otto.leskinen@eduouka.fi",
      "gender": "1",
      "birthDate": null,
      "categories": [
        "teacher"
      ],
      "languageMotherTongue": "fi"
    }
  },
  {
    "id": "http://itec-directory.eun.org/Person/2405",
    "last_mod": "2012-09-07T12:26:15.984+02:00",
    "status": "created",
    "entry": {
      "givenName": "Frans",
      "familyName": "Van Assche",
      "loginName": "fvanassche",
      "gender": "1",
      "description": "Test",
      "birthDate": null,
      "_id": 2405
    }
  },
  {
    "id": "http://itec-directory.eun.org/Person/2605",
    "last_mod": "2012-09-12T18:32:29.884+02:00",
    "status": "deleted"
  }
]
```

Acknowledgement The authors wish to thank Elena Schulman for coordinating the work on the data models and vocabularies, and David Massart for his early work on the architecture.

References

Colin J-N, Simon B (2012) D7.2: second generation of iTEC shells and composer. Project deliverable 7.2, University of Namur

Ferraiolo DF, Sandhu R, Gavrila S, Kuhn DR, Chandramouli R (2001) Proposed NIST standard for role-based access control. ACM Trans Inf Syst Secur 4(3):224–274

Govaerts S, Dahrendorf D (2011) Deliverable D3.4 of the ROLE project, prototype implementation (2nd updated version)

Griffiths D, Johnson M, Popat K, Sharples P, Wilson S (2012) The Wookie Widget Server: a case study of piecemeal integration of tools and services. J Univ Comput Sci 18(11):1432–1453

Hardt D (ed) (2012) The OAuth 2.0 Authorization Framework. RFC 6749, RFC

Hevner AR (2007) A three cycle view of design science research. Scand J Inf Syst 19(2):87

Hevner A, Chatterjee S (2010) Design research in information systems: theory and practice. Springer, Berlin

Lakiotaki K, Tsafarakis S, Matsatsinis N (2008) UTA-Rec: a recommender system based on multiple criteria analysis. In: Proceedings of the 2008 ACM conference on recommender systems, Lausanne, Switzerland, 2008

March ST, Smith GF (1995) Design and natural science research on information technology. Decis Support Syst 15(4):251–266

Matsatsinis NF, Lakiotaki K, Delias P (2007) A system based on multiple criteria analysis for scientific paper recommendation. In: 11th Panhellenic conference in informatics, Patras, Greece, 2007

OpenID Foundation (2007) OpenID authentication specifications 2.0. Openid. http://openid.net/developers/specs/

Peis E, Morales-del-Castillo JM, Delgado-López JA (2008) Semantic recommender systems. Analysis of the state of the topic. Hipertext.net, no. 6

Ricci F, Rokach L, Shapira B, Kantor P (2011) Recommender systems handbook. Springer, New York

Takeda H, Veerkamp P, Tomiyama T, Yoshikawa H (1990) Modeling design processes. AI Mag 11(4):37–48

Vaishnavi VK, Kuechler W (2007) Design science research methods and patterns: innovating information and communication technology, 1st edn. Auerbach, Boca Raton

Van Assche F (ed) (1998) Using the world wide web in secondary schools. ACCO, Belgium

Van Assche F (2004) Towards ambient schooling. In: Delgado Kloos C, Pardo A (eds) EDUTECH: computer-aided design meets computer-aided learning. Kluwer Academic, Boston

Van Assche F et al (2006) iClass Project Educational Vision Statement, deliverable D3.1 of the iClass project, Aug 2006

Wilson S, Sharples P, Griffiths D, Popat K (2011) Augmenting the VLE using widget technologies. Int J Technol Enhanc Learn 3(1):4–20. doi:10.1504/ijtel.2011.039061

Chapter 5
The Composer: Creating, Sharing and Facilitating Learning Designs

Bernd Simon, Michael Aram, Frans Van Assche, Luis Anido-Rifón, and Manuel Caeiro-Rodríguez

Abstract Developing tools for sharing learning designs is a well-established, but still on-going endeavour in the technology-enhanced learning domain. However, to date tools supporting educational modelling languages have not achieved wide adoption in school practice. In this chapter we report on the design, implementation, and evaluation of a pedagogical tool referred to as the Composer. The Composer supports the composition of learning designs activities and has been developed according to design principles such as (a) interoperability between design-time and run-time systems based on the W3C Widget Standard, (b) inclusion of artefact types beyond content such as tools, people and events, (c) a user-friendly authoring environment. An evaluation of the proof-of-concept implementation suggests that the tool is easy-to-use and provides added value for teachers when it comes to reflecting about Learning Designs.

Keywords Learning design • Educational modelling • W3C widgets • Mashups • Wookie • Design science

B. Simon (✉) • M. Aram
Knowledge Markets Consulting G.m.b.H., Wien, Austria
e-mail: bernd.simon@km.co.at; michael.aram@km.co.at

F. Van Assche
Department of Computer Science, University of Leuven, Leuven, Belgium
e-mail: frans.van.assche@gmail.com

L. Anido-Rifón
Telematics Engineering Department, ETSI Telecommunication,
University of Vigo, Vigo, Spain
e-mail: luis.anido@det.uvigo.es

M. Caeiro-Rodríguez
University of Vigo, Pontevedra, Spain
e-mail: mcaeiro@det.uvigo.es

F. Van Assche et al. (eds.), *Re-engineering the Uptake of ICT in Schools*,
DOI 10.1007/978-3-319-19366-3_5

Motivation and Research Methodology

The primary role of any teacher, is to stimulate learning activities that will gradually result in the attainment of certain learning outcomes (Koper and Bennett 2008). As a consequence, the design of learning activities—in short learning design—has always been of a particular interest to the educational domain. The work of iTEC is no exception, and in this chapter we consider both the progress made by the project in furthering the state of the art in learning design, and the way in which learning design activities can be conducted within the infrastructure created by the project.

Attempts to provide computer-based support for this process have had some success, but have not been widely adopted by teachers. A number of projects have developed learning design authoring software that aims to simplify the design process, and the work described here can be situated in that context. An overview of related work is provided by Derntl et al. (2011), while Neumann and Oberhuemer (2009) describe a graphical user interface for designing learning activities based on IMS Learning Design. Evaluation of the latter revealed the disconnection between the design tool and the run-time system as one major problem with respect to user acceptance. To date tools supporting educational modelling languages have not reached wide adoption (see Derntl et al. 2011; Durand et al. 2010; Durand and Downes 2009). In the work reported here 'learning design' is understood as the preparation of a unit-of-learning (e.g. course, lesson) and includes the definition of learning outcomes, the selection of learning resources, and the sequencing of measures (see Koper and Bennett 2008; Durand 2010).

In our work we focused on blended learning environments in the school sector. This is because the infrastructure for information and communication technology (ICT) in schools remains weak, despite the evidence suggesting that ICT can have a positive impact on the expansion of learning opportunities (Core ICT Indicators 2010; ITU 2013). There is still a significant number of schools in Europe that lack sufficient ICT (ITU 2013), and at the same time the adoption of ICT also varies between subjects (OECD 2009). Consequently fully ICT driven approach is not feasible in the present school system (leaving on one side the question of whether such an approach would be desirable).

In line with the overall approach of the iTEC project (see Chap. 4), we addressed the need to support learning design activities by applying a design science research methodology (DSRM) to the problem. DSRM identifies six activities (Peffers et al. 2007), i.e. problem identification and motivation, objectives for a solution, design and development, demonstration, evaluation, and communication. Though the activities in the DSRM are represented sequentially and start with "identify problem …", one may start at any of the first four steps. The entry point depends on the nature of the problem and triggering factors. In our case we combined problem identification and the definition of the objectives of the solution in one phase and documented the results of both steps in section "Problem Identification and Requirements" of this chapter. Based on the requirements identified a solution was designed and developed that is documented in section "Implementation of a Widget-Based Solution". Finally, several evaluations were conducted. In section "Evaluation and Outlook" this chapter concludes with summing up the findings of these evaluations.

Problem Identification and Requirements

This section starts from an initial idea, and a typical user story, followed by the basic concepts and user roles derived from it, in order to come to functional and non-functional requirements, taking into account the school context.

From an Initial Idea to an Agreed User Story

The user requirements that the proposed solution needed to satisfy where initially described in the description of work of the grant agreement. We started off with the idea of allowing users to describe teaching situations and attach learning resources to those descriptions. A few internal meetings later the following user story was developed:

> *Livia is a Teacher in a secondary school in Izmir, Turkey. She is very enthusiastic about applying new teaching methods and tools. One day, Livia decides to investigate a tool called the Composer by starting to search for learning designs created to support collaborative learning. Since she needs to teach about air pollution in a couple of weeks she looks for learning stories that address this subject.*
>
> *She finds a very interesting one that combines the puzzle method with the participation of external experts and the attendance at events related to the subject being taught. The next step is to select all the learning resources needed to implement this Learning Story in Livia's school.*
>
> *The Composer proposes a list of tools that could be used from those available in Livia's school. The first recommendation to cope with file sharing is the file sharing functionality of Livia's learning management system. In terms of content the Composer provides a video on the effects of air pollution plus some online tests that she can use for a formative assessment of the intended learning outcomes. When it comes to searching for Events the Composer returns a list of eight events. The first one is an online event on 'All you need to know about air pollution'. This event is part of a series of webinars supported by a European project.*
>
> *Finally, she needs to select an external expert that she aims to bring in. This time she goes to the 'Recommend Contributors' option of the Composer. Unfortunately there are no experts on air pollution available that are fluent in Turkish. It seems that only English speaking contributors with the required knowledge on that topic are available. Well, the head of Livia's department is pushing his staff to progressively introduce English in their lectures. So, this could be a good opportunity for Livia's pupils to practice their English. She selects Dr. Knopfler, a professor from the Vienna University, Austria, who is an expert in air pollution and kindly offered himself to participate in such kind of activities.*
>
> *After having sufficiently prepared her personal Learning Design on teaching about air pollutions, she makes it available in her learning management system of choice. Now she feels ready to deliver high quality education on her chosen subject.*

Conceptual Foundations and User Roles

Driven by the user story mentioned above, we started to layout its conceptual foundations. Our proposed solution is centred on the design and facilitation of Learning Designs. These, and related key concepts describing our key artefacts are defined as follows:

- *Learning Activity Design*: describes a discrete session of Learner interactions, including potential Learning Resources to be used, in order to achieve a set of educational outcomes.
- *Learning Story Design*: Learning Activity Designs are "packaged together" to provide a description of a possible context for the delivery of several Learning Activities.
- *Learning Design*: refers to both Learning Activity Design and Learning Story Design.
- *Learning Resource*: We opt for a broad view of the term "Learning Resource" and distinguish the following types of Learning Resources:
  - *Content*: Any information resource that can be used for teaching and learning.
  - *Contributor*: is a person who agreed to make personal contact information available, so that a teacher is able to include her as a contributing participant in the context of a Learning Activity.
  - *Event*: something that takes place at a determinable place and time, and which can be used within a Learning Activity.
  - *Tool*: An *Application* (software) or *Device* (hardware) that can be used for educational purposes by end users.

Our approach assumes, that all artefacts that are meant to become part of the final learning experience are represented as—or delivered through—appropriate (or appropriately configured) widgets.

In line with the user story described above the stakeholder roles (see Chap. 4, section "The iTEC Technical Architecture") of *Learner*, *Teacher*, and *Learning Designer* are confirmed.

Schools as Educational Context

Our work focuses on learning environments of the school sector. Hence, we primarily assumed blended learning environments as the context for the uptake of technology. Although evidence suggests that ICT can have a positive impact on the expansion of learning opportunities (Core ICT Indicators 2010; ITU 2013), there is still a significant number of schools in Europe that lack sufficient computer equipment when it comes down to the student per computer ratio (ITU 2013). At the same time the adoption of ICT also varies between subjects: 26 % of students use computers in language lessons while only 16 % of OECD students use computers in mathematics lessons (OECD 2009). As a consequence we could not assume a learning environment that fully relies on the availability and usage of ICT when it comes to supporting the definition and exchange of learning activities.

Functional and Non-functional Requirements

Based on our user story as well as an analysis of the educational context led us to the identification of the following requirements. Although somewhat controversial (Glinz 2007), we distinguish them between functional and non-functional requirements.

The identified problem was translated into high-level functional requirements using the user story format (Cohn 2004): "As a <role>, I want <goal/desire> so that <benefit>":

- As a Learning Designer, I want to create new Learning Designs and publish these so that they can give inspiration to Teachers.
- As a Learning Designer or Teacher, I want to find innovative Learning Designs and create a personal copy so that I can edit them to suit my needs.
- As a Learning Designer, I want to publish Learning Designs I have adapted or created to a shared space so that I can share my best practices.
- As a Teacher, I want to easily find a Learning Activity Design and together with its required Learning Resources at a central place, so that I can make these Learning Resources available to my Learners when conducting the Learning Activity.
- As a Teacher, I want to take advantage of other Teacher's assessment of Learning Designs so that I can easier find highly relevant ones that actually work in practice.

Beyond the functional requirements the key non-functional requirement *Interoperability* was identified. In order to support the exchange of Learning Designs beyond system boundaries the systems involved need to be interoperable. Interoperability indicates the ability of two or more systems or components to exchange information and to use the information that has been exchanged (IEEE 1991). Interoperability research distinguishes between interoperability on the object, referring to a proper use of the information provided—and interoperability in the communication, referring to an agreed communication protocol between systems (Van Assche et al.). These two aspects of interoperability translated into the requirement to make learning designs—including their resources—re-useable in different technical contexts as well as the requirement to agree on communication protocols between the various system components.

Implementation of a Widget-Based Solution

When designing the Composer we opted for a widget-based approach that consists of the following components: A *Widget* is a packaged web application (W3C 2012) that is designed to be easily distributed and embedded within varying contexts (e.g. within a portal-style mashup, on a mobile phone, etc.). Widgets rely on open standards with respect to both their representation format and their communication protocols.

A *Widget-Based Authoring Environment* is used to create widgets. This supports our technical assumption that all artefacts that are meant to become part of the final learning experience are represented as, or delivered through, widgets. Hence, a Learning Design as well as the Learning Resources included are represented as Widgets.

The *Widget Store* is a software component that is built on the Apache Wookie and EDUKApp technologies (Griffiths et al. 2012). It supports the uploading, tagging, and searching for Learning Resources and learning designs in the form of Widgets. The *Composer* supports Learning Designers and Teachers in designing Learning Activities, and augmenting them with Learning Resources.

A *Widget Run-time Environment (RTE)* acts as the "entry point" for end users and is a configurable software container that provides an environment allowing users to identify and add their Widgets and to integrate them in order to meet the educational objectives of a Learning Activity. Typically, a Widget RTE connects to a Widget Store to provide users with an integrated experience when selecting and instantiating widgets (Soylu et al. 2012). Examples include mashup engines like Apache RAVE as well as Widget-enabled learning management systems like Moodle and DotLRN.

Representing Learning Designs via Widgets

We now describe our layered approach to representing Learning Designs, which follows the "web best practices" of progressive enhancement and the rule of least power (Soylu et al. 2012). Consequently, when entering a higher level, interoperability decreases, while functionality increases. At the lowest layer we render a Learning Design as HTML. Hence, the fundamental (narrative) information of such a guide is represented as a web document, thus can be viewed in any standard web browser, or processed otherwise by third-party applications.

Packaging this Learning Design as a W3C Widget represents the second layer, which gives teachers easier control of the Learning Design in various manners, e.g. by instantiating it in their Widget RTE, viewing it offline on a phone, or publishing it in a Widget Store. At these two levels the Learning Design already provides added value to the teacher, both when preparing the learning activity and when it takes place.

However, many useful Learning Designs will go beyond mere textual descriptions and will require particular resources to be used by teachers and learners (e.g. Applications, Content). Hence, the technology supports the Teacher in augmenting the (virtual) learning environment with these resources. We therefore progress further in functional enhancement by "transforming" the instantiated Learning Design Widget into a mashup. Technically, to this end our approach utilizes a client side cross-context communication channel-based on PMRPC[1] (Soylu et al. 2012). To transmit a description of the additional Learning Resources required. As we consider all resources to be delivered via Widgets, we represent the resources required by the Learning Design in the form of a mashup description based on the Open Mashup Description Language.[2] Finally, the RTE instantiates all the Widgets required for conducting the learning activity that is described by the Learning Design Widget.

[1] PMRPC is a HTML5 JavaScript library for RPC-style (remote procedure call) Inter-window and web workers communication.

[2] http://omdl.org/

Authoring Widget-Based Learning Designs with the Composer

From a user's point of view, the Composer is intended to provide Learning Designers and Teachers with the means to compose and re-use Learning Activities and augment them with Learning Resources. We interpreted this process as a Widget aggregation. A typical usage scenario of the Composer can be given alongside the "typical usage scenario for learning resources" (see Van Assche et al. 2006):

- *Discovering*: A Teacher who wants to create a Learning Design for use in the classroom uses the Composer to search for existing Learning Designs, which seem to fit the particular learning outcomes she has in mind. Having discovered an interesting Learning Design, she evaluates it both according to her personal criteria. Before Teacher begins with augmenting the Learning Design, she creates a personalized copy within the Composer.
- *Repurpose and Re-use*: This is the central step, where a Teacher modifies the Learning Design according to her personal needs. In doing so, the Teacher aggregates (references to) Widgets from the Widget Store. For example, the Teacher enriches the Learning Activity with concrete Learning Resources. The result of this mashup process is a personalized Learning Design that is augmented with concrete resources.
- *Publishing*: In case the Teacher decides to publish this Learning Design, the Composer makes it available to others in a public area, so that it can be reused in other "development cycles". Moreover, a Learning Design Widget—representing the interoperable output representation—is generated[3] and published into the Widget Store.

Technically, driven by the non-functional requirement for interoperability, the Composer was implemented as a highly embeddable web application. To this end, the Composer seamless integration via the emerging IMS Learning Tools Interoperability[4] (LTI) protocol and implements a responsive user interface.[5]

LTI enables a seamless integration into for example in the DotLrn learning management system as far as identity management is concerned. Hence, a DotLrn user can directly access the Composer via DotLrn using her DotLrn user account. Once logged into the Composer the user can start to compose a Learning Design. A user can start composing also by reusing other Learning Designs. This is supported by a browse functionality and a copy feature that allows her to copy an existing Learning Design into her personal workspace. At the personal workspace a user can create new and alter existing Learning Designs. Users are also encouraged to publish their private Learning Designs to the public space, where they can again be found by other users.

---

[3] For generating these learning activity design widget, we use the open source content packaging software "xocp", see http://wiki.tcl.tk/28538

[4] http://www.imsglobal.org/lti/

[5] We use the "Bootstrap" user interface library from Twitter for this purpose: "http://twitter.github.io/bootstrap/"

The metadata used for describing Learning Designs is limited to the a few elements in order to simplify the authoring process and include title, summary, and descriptions of the activities recommend to be carried out. Once the authoring of the Learning Design is finalised the Learning Design can be pushed to the Widget Store where it can be discovered and reused.

Sharing Learning Designs via the Widget Store

As explained above, Learning Resources are highly relevant during both the design-time and run-time of a Learning Design. In this context, we consider that an educational Widget Store plays a key role. On the one hand, it acts as a repository of Learning Resources, in particular Content and Applications. On the other hand, the Store also provides the user with means to "widgetize" arbitrary web resources. Hence, the Widget Store has the potential to evolve into a living, collaboratively curated repository of user-selected and user-generated Learning Resources. These Learning Resources can be added to a Learning Design during the authoring process mentioned above (see Fig. 5.1). In order to find appropriate Learning Resources the Scenario Development Environment was introduced as an additional system

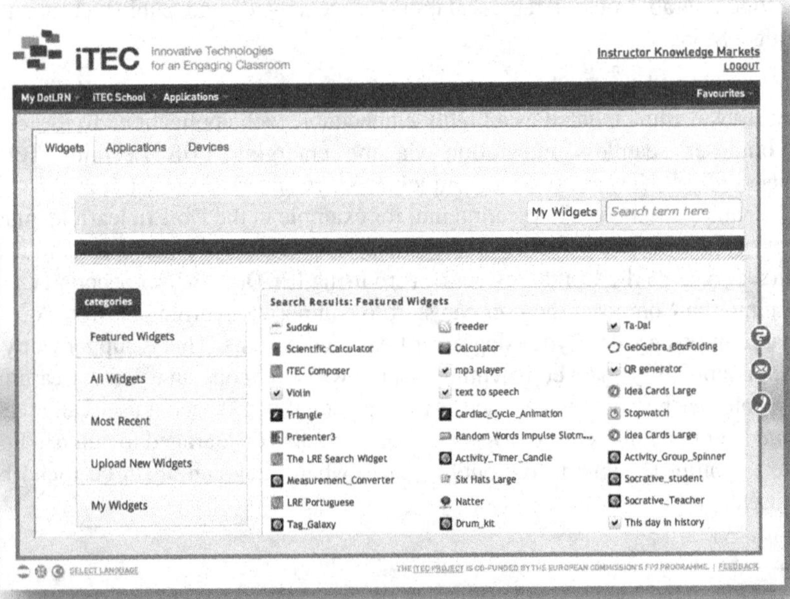

Fig. 5.1 The iTEC Widget Store as part of DotLrn

component providing recommendations for learning resources based on the user profile as well as the educational context of the author composing the Learning Design.

Technically, the Widget Store (see Chap. 8) consists of three layers. Firstly, it builds on the Apache Wookie server. Secondly, management of data relating to the description of Widgets and their use, is handled making use of the EDUKApp Educational Widget Store initiative (Griffiths et al. 2012). Thirdly, its front-end is delivered to the user as a Widget.

Facilitating Learning Designs with a Widget Run-Time Environment

The software component that acts as the "entry point" for the end user—in particular the Learner—is referred to as a Widget RTE. Examples include, but are not limited to, mashup engines such as Apache Rave[6] and Widget-enabled learning management systems such as Moodle[7] and DotLRN.[8]

In the DotLrn-instantiated Widget Store a Teacher can select her Widget of-choice, like for example a Widget represented a Learning Design for teaching children about air pollution (see Fig. 5.2). Once this Learning Design is identified in the Widget Store, the Teacher can simply configure the DotLrn by pressing an "Install" Button. As a next step the Teacher is asked to confirm the population of her DotLrn course with all the widgets required to conduct this Learning Activity. Once the Teacher has confirmed, additional widgets are added to the Teacher's course. Hereby the Widget RTE becomes ready to support the Learning Design about teaching "Air Pollution".

Evaluation and Outlook

At the end 19 small-scale evaluation activities of the proposed solution were carried out. Early evaluation activities mainly consisted of open expert interviews from which a better understanding of the problem definition was derived. At a later stage these activities were used to iteratively revise the requirements. The evaluation events mostly involved pedagogical experts. The evaluations were documented in the form of action logs resulting in concrete changes to requirements. In the case of the Composer the main findings relate to: (a) provide an even more simplified user

[6] Apache Rave Project Homepage—http://rave.apache.org/

[7] Moodle Project Homepage—http://moodle.org/

[8] DotLRN Project Homepage—http://www.dotlrn.org/

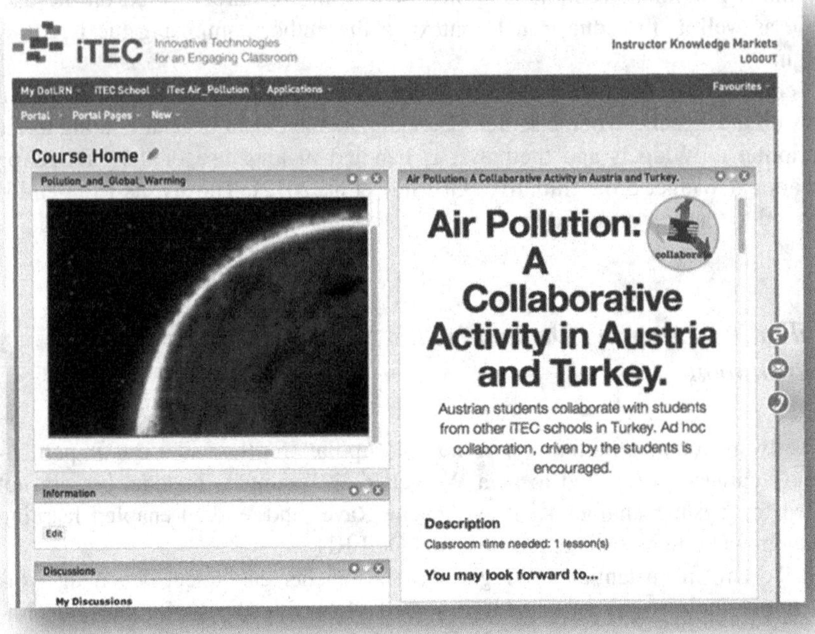

Fig. 5.2 DotLrn configured with Widgets of the Learning Design "Air Pollution"

interface, (b) support private areas within the collaborative, wiki-style tool, and (c) improve support of mobile devices like tablet computers.

Finally the Composer formed part of the Edukata process in two of the iTEC case study countries. When using the Composer in this deployment phase, teachers looked at existing Learning Designs for inspiration and used the Composer to 'present' the Learning Designs they had devised during the workshop. In the context of this evaluation activity the main improvement requests were related to enhancing the metadata model used for describing the Learning Desings. Extending the metadata model for example by suggested elements such as typical age range or level of difficulty would subsequently allow for an improved search mechanism.

Overall, we concluded from our evaluations and deployment experiences that the idea of the Composer was generally well received, but it looked like that the idea of sharing Learning Designs cannot create critical mass as a standalone component. As a consequence we transferred the ideas of the Composer to the learning management system DotLrn and introduced a new learning resource type called "teaching idea" there. Teaching ideas are Learning Designs created to inspire other teachers in use of technologies in the classroom. A project initiated by the Austrian ministry of education called "App-o-thek" was launched, where this new learning resource type is already used in order to provide teachers with hands-on guidance when it comes to using Apps in the context of their classroom teaching.

References

Cohn M (2004) User stories applied: for agile software development. Addison-Wesley Professional, Boston

Derntl M, Neumann S, Griffiths D, Oberhuemer P (2011) The conceptual structure of IMS learning design does not impede its use for authoring. IEEE Trans Learn Technol 5(1):74–86

Durand G, Downes S (2009) Toward simple learning design 2.0. In: Computer science & education, 2009. ICCSE'09. 4th International conference on, 2009, pp 894–897

Durand G, Belliveau L, Craig B (2010) Simple learning design 2.0. In: IEEE 10th international conference on advanced learning technologies (ICALT), 2010, pp 549–551

Durand G, Durand L, Belliveau, Craig B (2010) Simple Learning Design 2.0. In IEEE 10th International Conference on Advanced Learning Technologies (ICALT), 2010, pp 549–551

Glinz M (2007) On non-functional requirement. In: Proceedings of the 15th IEEE international requirements engineering conference, IEEE, 2007, pp 21–26

Griffiths D, Johnson M, Popat K, Sharples P, Wilson S (2012) The educational affordances of widgets and application stores. J Univers Comput Sci 18(16):2252–2273

IEEE (1991) IEEE standard computer dictionary. A compilation of IEEE standard computer glossaries, 1991

ITU (2010) Core ICT indicators 2010. International Telecommunication Union (ITU)

ITU (2013) Technology, broadband and education advancing the education for all agenda—a report by the broadband commission working group on education. International Telecommunication Union (ITU)

Koper R, Bennett S (2008) Learning design: concepts. In: Adelsberger PDHH, Kinshuk P, Pawlowski PDJM, Sampson PDG (eds) Handbook on information technologies for education and training. Springer, Berlin, pp 135–154

Neumann S, Oberhuemer P (2009) User evaluation of a graphical modeling tool for IMS learning design. In: Spaniol M, Li Q, Klamma R, Lau RWH (eds) Advances in web based learning—ICWL 2009. Springer, Berlin, pp 287–296

OECD (2009) PISA 2009 results: students on line digital technologies and performance. http://www.oecd.org/pisa/pisaproducts/pisa2009/48270093.pdf

Peffers K, Tuunanen T, Rothenberger MA, Chatterjee S (2007) A design science research methodology for information systems research. J Manag Inf Syst 24:45–77

Soylu A, Mödritscher F, Wild F, De Causmaecker P, Desmet P (2012) Mashups by orchestration and widget-based personal environments: key challenges, solution strategies, and an application. Prog Electron Libr Inf Syst 46(4):383–428

Van Assche F, Duval E, Massart D, Olmedilla D, Simon B, Sobernig S, Ternier S, Wild F (2006) Spinning interoperable applications for teaching & learning using the simple query interface. J Educ Technol Soc 9(2):51–67

W3C (2012) Packaged web apps (Widgets)—packaging and XML configuration, 2nd edn

Chapter 6
Recommender Systems

Luis Anido-Rifón, Juan Santos-Gago, Manuel Caeiro-Rodríguez, Manuel Fernández-Iglesias, Rubén Míguez-Pérez, Agustin Cañas-Rodríguez, Victor Alonso-Roris, Javier García-Alonso, Roberto Pérez-Rodríguez, Miguel Gómez-Carballa, Marcos Mouriño-García, Mario Manso-Vázquez, and Martín Llamas-Nistal

Abstract The purpose of this chapter is to describe a software system that allows for discovering non-traditional education resources such as software applications, events or people who may participate as experts in some Learning Activity. Selecting the more suitable educational resources to create learning activities in the classroom may be a challenging task for teachers in primary and secondary education because of the large amount of existing educational resources. The iTEC Scenario Development Environment (SDE), is a software application aimed at offering supporting services in the form of suggestions or recommendations oriented to assist teachers in their decision-making when selecting the most appropriate elements to deploy learning activities in a particular school. The recommender is based on an ontology that was developed in a collaborative way by a multi-disciplinary team of experts. Its data set is fed not only from entries that come from registrations made by human users—using tools from the iTEC Cloud—but also from software agents that perform web scraping, that is, automatic enrichment of the semantic data with additional information that come from web sources that are external to the project. Therefore, the recommender system takes into account contextual factors when calculating the relevance of every resource. The SDE defines an API that allows third-party clients to integrate its functionalities. This chapter presents two success stories that have benefited from the SDE to enhance educational authoring tools with semantic web-based recommendations.

L. Anido-Rifón (✉)
Telematics Engineering Department, ETSI Telecommunication, University of Vigo, Vigo, Spain
e-mail: lanido@det.uvigo.es

J. Santos-Gago • M. Caeiro-Rodríguez • M. Fernández-Iglesias • R. Míguez-Pérez
A. Cañas-Rodríguez • V. Alonso-Rorís • J. García-Alonso • R. Pérez-Rodríguez
M. Gómez-Carballa • M. Mouriño-García • M. Manso-Vázquez • M. Llamas-Nistal
University of Vigo (ES), Pontevedra, Spain
e-mail: jsgago@det.uvigo.es; mcaeiro@det.uvigo.es; manolo@det.uvigo.es; rmiguez@det.uvigo.es; agustincanas@det.uvigo.es; valonso@gist.uvigo.es; jgarcia@gist.uvigo.es; roberto.perez@gist.uvigo.es; miguelgomez@det.uvigo.es; marcosmourino@gmail.com; mario.manso@uvigo.es; martin@det.uvigo.es

F. Van Assche et al. (eds.), *Re-engineering the Uptake of ICT in Schools*,
DOI 10.1007/978-3-319-19366-3_6

Keywords Recommender systems • Multi-criteria decision analysis • Ontology • Information enrichment

Introduction

In the current panorama of educational practice in primary and secondary education across Europe we find that technology is increasingly present in the classroom. On the one hand, we have government programs that provide classrooms with a technological infrastructure. For instance, the Abalar[1] project, financed by the Galician Ministry of Education provides classrooms with an interactive digital whiteboard, Wi-Fi Internet connection, and a laptop per student, in which a Linux distribution comes already installed and ready to be used. On the other hand, students themselves, usually have mobile devices—such as smartphones and tablets—and carry them everywhere, including the classroom.

In addition to hardware resources, nowadays we find an enormous amount of free software resources, ready to be used in the educational practice. Besides standalone applications, we can use many applications in the cloud, both from personal computers and mobile devices. Complete suites as that of Google[2] are freely available with zero cost, ready to be used in educational practice (Herrick 2009; Patterson 2007).

But the resources that may be used in educational practice are not limited to hardware and software. Many everyday events, especially cultural events, may have an educational value. As Redding (1997) states:

> *Stimulating the child's desire to discover, to think through new situations and to vigorously exchange opinions, is fostered also by family visits to libraries, museums, zoos, historical sites and cultural events.*

We might think, for instance, of events such as theatre performance and lectures that may be very relevant to illustrate some points of the curriculum, and that can certainly be used in educational practice. If there is a free performance of Hamlet in our city, why do not use it as a resource for the subject of literature, especially if Shakespeare is in the curriculum? In a similar way, experts on particular topics are the best people to explain certain concepts. A doctoral student who is carrying out their Ph.D. in the area of genetic research might be very inspiring for secondary education students during their biology class.

This was the context for the work of the iTEC project which we report here. It contributed to the conception of the classroom of the future, in which technology is complemented with innovative pedagogical approaches, which entail a high degree of dynamism in educational practice. Thus, iTEC promotes an educational practice

[1] http://www.edu.xunta.es/espazoAbalar/

[2] http://www.google.com/enterprise/apps/education/

in which students interact in small projects which include participation in events, speeches with experts, with all of this seasoned by the use of technology.

In taking a step along the path toward iTEC's objective we were confronted by an initial difficulty: how do we select the technologies, events, and experts that will take part in an educational experience? Firstly, there is no central directory of technologies, events, and people at an European level, in such a way that a teacher may make searches in it. And, secondly, were it to exist, the difficulty of selecting between an enormous number of technologies, events, and experts would be very considerable.

In iTEC, a series of directories were developed in which technologies can be registered, as well as events and experts, which form part of the iTEC Cloud (see Chap. 4). Thus, the Composer (Simon et al. 2013) includes a directory for hardware and software technologies; the People and Events Directory (Van Assche 2012), as it name suggests, enables users to register educational events as well as experts in some knowledge area; and the Widget Store (Griffiths et al. 2012) is a repository of widgets ready to be used in the educational practice. Section "The iTEC cloud" briefly explains the components of the iTEC Cloud.

In order to solve the problem of selection from a large number of technologies, events, and experts, the iTEC project proposes the SDE, which is conceived as an artificial intelligence agent that uses Semantic Web data, and that has among its objectives to act as a recommender. Section "Background" provides some background about recommender systems. Thus, during their planning, a teacher may use the recommendations that come from the SDE in choosing the most appropriate technologies, events, and experts, as discussed in section "The SDE". In order to conceptualise the elements that contribute to educational practice an ontology was conceived, and its final version was the result of several iterations of revisions by Control Boards made up of experts in the domain and knowledge engineers. We present a brief overview of its main concepts.

The AI agent provides an API that enables client applications to integrate its recommendations. These client applications are editors that support teachers in designing their educational practice. So far, two client applications have successfully integrated recommendations from the SDE. These are: the Composer, which is part of the iTEC Cloud, see Chap. 4; and AREA see Caeiro-Rodríguez et al. (2013), which is part of a project that counts with public financing from Galician regional government. These two successful cases are discussed in section "Client Applications That Integrate SDE Recommendations".

To date, we have conducted three experiments to evaluate the SDE with teachers as end-users of this application. The first was on 6th June 2013 in Santiago de Compostela (Spain), with a focus group composed of teachers of primary and secondary education. The second took place on 18th June 2013 in Bolton (England), with end users. The third took place on 29th and 30th October 2013 in Oulu (Finland). Sections "Evaluation" and "Conclusions and Lessons Learned" discuss these experiments, and provide some conclusions and lessons learned.

Background

As Ricci et al. (2011) state:

> *Recommender Systems are software tools and techniques providing suggestions for items to be of use. The suggestions provided are aimed at supporting their users in various decision-making processes, such as what items to buy, what music to listen to, or what news to read.*

Traditionally, users of recommendation systems provide ratings for some of the items, and the system uses these ratings for the items not yet assessed (Resnick and Varian 1997). This approach is fairly flexible insofar as the output parameters are concerned, but is limited if we consider the input information available, as it does not consider, among other things, systems basing their recommendations on objective information about the items to be recommended. For our present concerns, we may apply the term *recommender* to any system offering personalized recommendations or guiding the user in a personalized way, selecting the most useful services from a variable-sized collection (Burke 2002).

Indeed, the main differences between a recommender and a search engine (or an information retrieval system) are related to the level of interest or utility of the retrieved items (recommendations). Recommendations had a clear social attractiveness even before the emergence of the information society, and they became basic building blocks of new online applications, mainly for electronic commerce and digital leisure services. Recommendation algorithms use techniques from Artificial Intelligence, Data Mining, Statistics or Marketing, among many others. Traditionally, according to the methods and algorithms used, recommendation systems are classified as: Content-based recommenders (Pazzani and Billsus 2007), Collaborative filtering recommenders (Schafer et al. 2007) and, combining both approaches, Hybrid recommender systems (Burke 2002). This classification is a very generic one and it is strongly tied to the interaction of a user with a recommender system, i.e. their preferences on the items to be recommended and their relationships to other users.

In spite of the above classification being the most frequent in the literature, it is for us preferable to focus on a classification which pays particular attention to the sources of data which the system relies on, as well as the use that the information receives. Following this approach, Burke (2002) distinguishes between five types of recommenders:

- Collaborative recommendation
  The most familiar, most widely implemented and most mature. These systems aggregate ratings or recommendations of objects, recognize commonalities between users on the basis of their ratings, and generate new recommendations based on inter-user comparisons.
- Demographic
  These recommenders categorize the user based on personal attributes and make recommendations based on demographic classes.
- Content-based
  These recommenders define their objects of interest by their associated features. These systems learn a profile of the user's interest based on the features present in objects the user has rated.

- Utility-based
  These recommenders make suggestions based on a computation of the utility of each object for the user. In these systems the central problem is how to create a utility function for each user.
- Knowledge-based
  These recommenders attempt to suggest objects based on inferences about a user's needs and preferences. Their approaches are distinguished in that they have functional knowledge: they have knowledge about how a particular item meets a particular user need, and can therefore reason about the relationship between a need and a possible recommendation.

Having established a definition and classification of recommender systems that is adequate for our proposal, we highlight three conceptual approaches that we have taken into account when developing our proposal: multi-criteria recommender systems, context-aware recommender systems and semantic recommenders. Those approaches are transversal to the types of recommenders previously presented and they try, respectively, to establish mechanisms for defining a utility function that takes into consideration several factors, to consider the context where a recommendation is produced, and to improve knowledge representation using semantic technologies. Below, we go deeper into each one of these.

Multi-criteria Recommender Systems

In traditional recommender systems, the utility function considers only one criteria, typically a global evaluation of resources or a valuation from the user. Depending on the systems under consideration, the utility function may be a valid approach though it is rather limited, since the utility of a given element for a particular user may depend on multiple factors. Taking this into consideration, in the past few years the study of multi-criteria recommender systems has increased (Lakiotaki et al. 2008, 2011; Plantié et al. 2005). Multiple Criteria Decision Analysis (MCDA) is a very mature and active research area (Figueira et al. 2005). It focuses on studying methods and management processes in systems with multiple conflicting criteria in order to identifying the best possible solution from a set of available alternatives. Starting from research and theories from that area, (Adomavicius and Tuzhilin 2010; Lakiotaki et al. 2011; Liu et al. 2011) propose approaching the problem of recommendations as one of MCDA, following the methodology that was developed by Roy (1996) for modelling these kinds of problems.

Semantic Recommender Systems

The term semantic recommender system is normally used when, in a traditional recommender, we use semantic web technologies in order to represent and process information of users and/or elements with high level descriptions. According to this definition, we might think of content or knowledge based systems; nevertheless, semantic technologies are also used for collaborative recommender systems (e.g. Martín-Vicente et al. 2012; Shambour and Lu 2011).

Context-Aware Recommender Systems

Context is a very broad concept that has been studied across different research disciplines, including computer science, cognitive science or organizational sciences, among others. Looking for a formal definition, it can be stated that context is a set of circumstances that form the setting for an event, statement or idea, and in terms of which it can be fully understood (Oxford English Dictionary 2014).

The iTEC Ontology

In order to develop a software system based on semantic techniques such as the SDE, it is necessary to define a Semantic Model which makes explicit the existing knowledge about the Universe of Discourse. This model, together with the information gathered by the system from the iTEC Back-end Registry and other possible external data sources, makes up the Knowledge Base of the SDE. The process of semantic modelling is a complex task that has led to different methodological approaches. Presently there is no standard methodology commonly used by knowledge engineers, although there are proposals with a relatively high degree of maturity.

In our case, we have adopted a methodological approach strongly based on Methontology (Fernández-López et al. 1997). We selected this methodology because it is one of the most mature and most widely used, and it is the best suited to our purpose. However, in order to adapt it to our specific needs taking into account our experience in software application development (Gago 2007), we decided to simplify and reshape some aspects of it taking into account aspects of other methodologies such as DILIGENT (Pinto et al. 2004; Uschold and King 1995; Noy and McGuinness 2001), and UPON (De Nicola et al. 2005).

One of the main advantages of semantic technologies is their support for knowledge reuse. Indeed, reuse of widely accepted terms and conceptualizations is included among the good practice guidelines for ontology design, extending or refining them when needed. Thus, in iTEC we followed this design principle by reusing those terms, properties and rules from conceptualizations that were strictly needed to capture knowledge about our universe of discourse. The objective of this approach is to have a manageable TBox, where only the knowledge strictly needed for the correct operation of the semantic applications to be developed is defined, in our case the iTEC SDE. With this approach we can guarantee the usability and efficiency of these applications. Besides, the clarity of the generated models is improved because only the terms, relations and rules from the base ontologies relevant to the terms and/or rules defined in our Semantic Model are taken into account. For example, we have reused and included in this model most of the FOAF (People characterization), VCard RDF (characterization of the contact information of an individual or institution) and Organization Vocabulary (characterization of groups and institutions, and the relations between an individual and a group) ontologies due to their overall relevance to our application domain, but we have omitted some concepts lacking the mentioned relevance.

The parts of the semantic model that deal with technologies, events, and experts are briefly described below. The Universe of Discourse is, obviously, much wider; and certain parts of the semantic model characterise learning activities, their requirements, the educational context (e.g. students' language, age range), and many other things.[3]

Tools Characterisation

The SDE also facilitates the technical localisation of a learning story for a given school. Taking into account the functional requirements of learning stories, the system assesses the degree of feasibility of the learning activities in a school according to the tools available there. Thus, the semantic model needs to characterize the set of technological tools available in a school, that is, its technical setting, together with the distinct features of these tools (e.g., technical specifications, functionalities, supported languages, etc.). This enables both technical localisation, and the generation of recommendations on tools during planning. This information group collects all concepts and relations needed to model tools and technical settings, enabling eventual recommendations on tools (applications and devices) by the SDE. Figure 6.1 shows the part of the semantic model that characterises tools.

Events Characterisation

Events were also considered by the iTEC project to be relevant resources for the schools of the future. An event represents something that takes place in a given location at a given date. It includes properties such as: target audience, cost, language, place (e.g. museum, zoo) and location. Workshops, seminars, conferences and virtual meetings are examples of events that may support novel learning activities to improve the educational practice in European schools. As events are also resources, the SDE should offer recommendations on the events that best adapt to the context of a given school. Thus, event conceptualisation should be targeted to model the most relevant features of events, like the type of participants, venue, relevant dates, audience, or specific tools needed to participate. Elements identified in this information group enable a complete characterization of events, and therefore eventual recommendations on events made by the SDE. Figure 6.2 shows a diagram of the semantic model of events.

[3] The latest version of the iTEC ontology is available at: http://itec.det.uvigo.es/itec/ontology/itec.rdf.

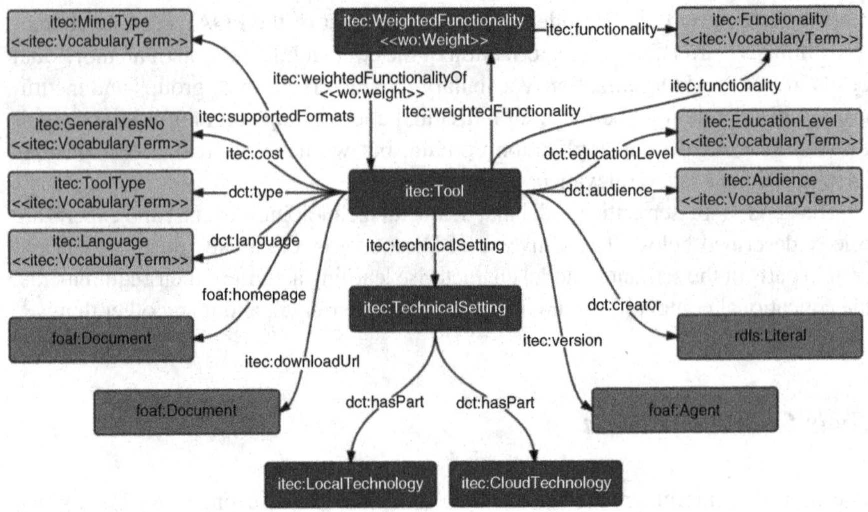

Fig. 6.1 Semantic model of tools

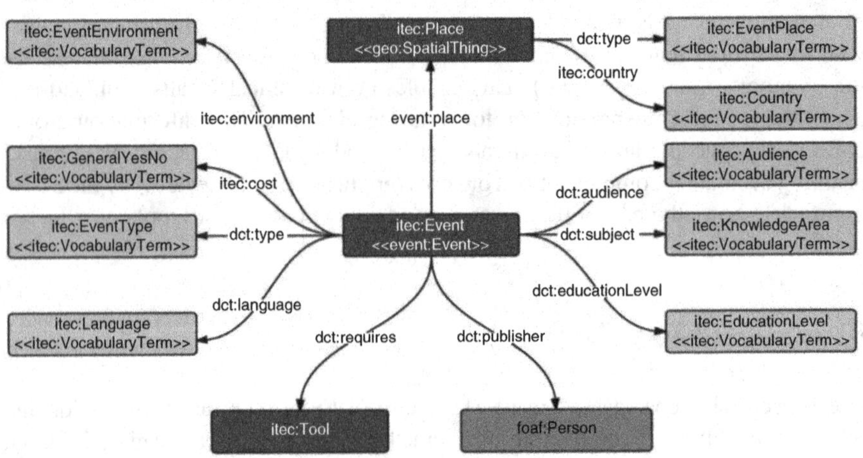

Fig. 6.2 Semantic model of an events

People Characterisation

One of the most notable innovations of the iTEC project is that people were considered to be resources that can be utilized in a classroom to provide added value to the learning process. Besides the teacher, pupils in future classrooms may have available a rich pool of experts in several areas to provide advice and support along learning activities. According to this new vision, where people are also considered resources available to configure learning processes, the SDE supports recommendations to

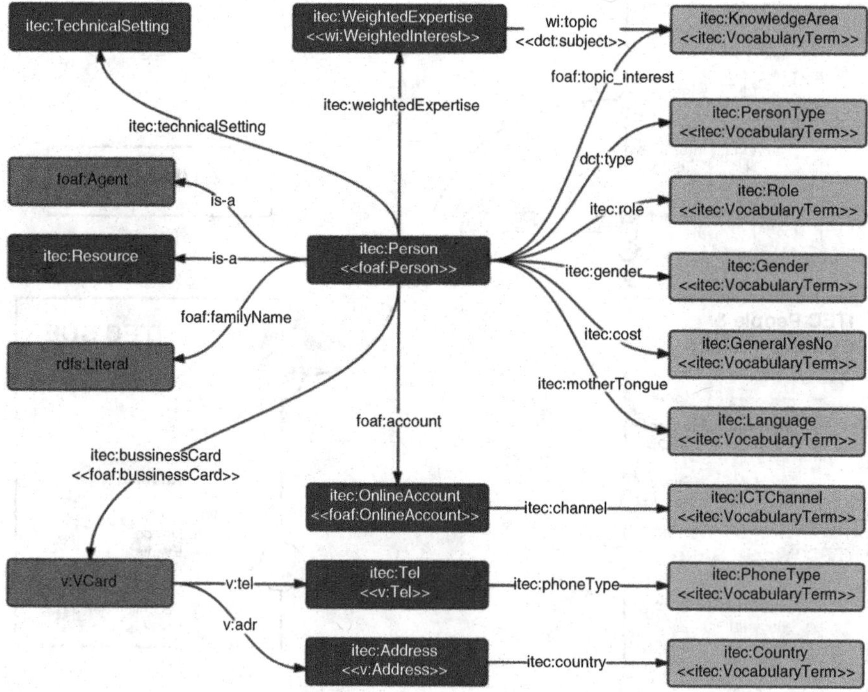

Fig. 6.3 Semantic model of a persons

teachers on the experts most suitable to enrich a given educational activity, taking into account the specific conditions at the school. Thus, the characterization of people goes beyond state-of-the-art people description, and includes all the skills, expertise and context relating to an individual relevant to educational scenarios (e.g., fluency in a given language, degree of knowledge of a particular subject, communication tools at his/her disposal, affiliation). This information group collects all the concepts and relations needed to enable the modelling of people in this context, and serves as the foundation for the recommendations that are eventually provided by the SDE. Figure 6.3 shows a diagram of the semantic model of a person.

The iTEC Cloud

The iTEC Educational Cloud (see Fig. 4.2) is defined as the collection of systems and applications, the SDE among them, offering the functionalities developed within the iTEC project. As it can be seen in Fig. 6.4 the iTEC SDE relates to the rest of the systems in the iTEC Cloud according to three different models:

- Information harvesting. The implementation of SDE functionalities relies on data provided by other systems in the iTEC Cloud. More specifically, data registered

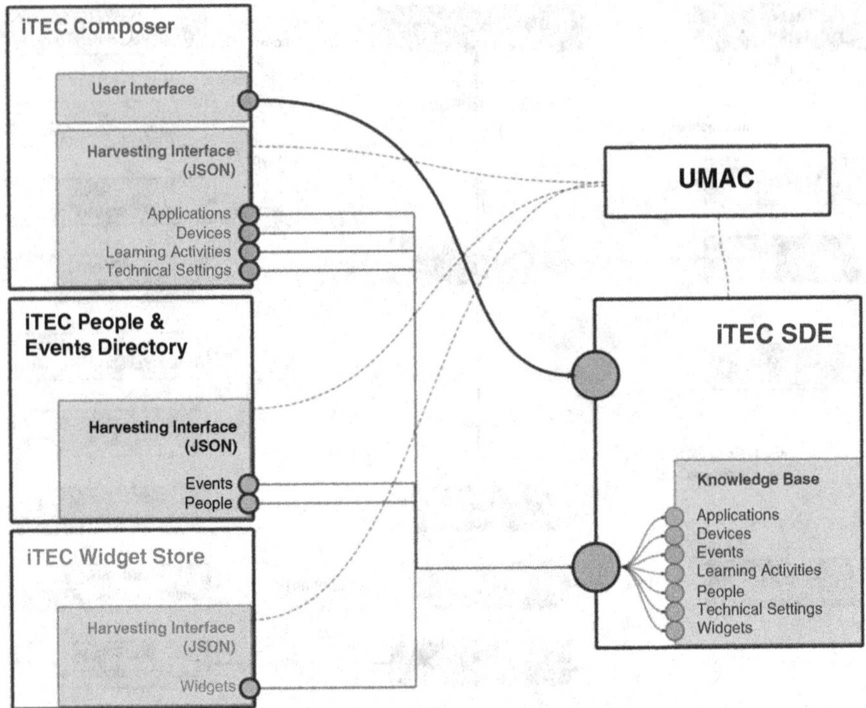

Fig. 6.4 The iTEC cloud architecture from an SDE perspective

with the iTEC Composer on tools (applications and devices), learning activities and technical settings, data stored in the iTEC P&E Directory on people and events, and data registered with the iTEC Wookie Widget Server on widget descriptions. The SDE needs to access these systems to collect data and keep its KB updated.

- Access to SDE functionalities. Access to the services offered by the SDE (technical localisation and resource planning services) is performed from the iTEC Composer through a specific Web Service API.[4]
- UMAC authentication. All interactions among the several systems in the iTEC Cloud, SDE's information harvesting and access to the services provided by the SDE from the Composer in particular, together with all user interactions, has to be authenticated and authorized by the UMAC.

[4] A digital version of a guide of the API is available at http://itec.det.uvigo.es/itec-sde/apidoc/index.html

The SDE

Traditional recommenders take into account two kinds of entities: users, and elements that make up the space of things to recommend. Context-aware recommenders follow a multi-dimensional model, instead of the traditional bi-dimensional model. The recommender integrated in iTEC does not consider the user as the main factor to take into account when generating recommendations, but rather takes the educational context as the most relevant factor. Thus, the utility function is defined in the following way:

$$f : Items \times Content \rightarrow Rating \quad (6.1)$$

In the *Items* dimension, we consider three kinds of elements—technologies, both hardware and software; events; and experts. Each one of these kinds of elements has different metadata: technologies are characterised, among other things, by their functionalities and languages of the user interface; events have space-time metadata, besides their topic; and experts are characterised, among other things, by their area of expertise. This diversity entails a multi-criteria approach, and the consideration of several factors. Each partial utility function follows a different approach—content-based, collaborative-based, or hybrid—that depends on the nature of those factors. Multiple Criteria Decision Analysis (MCDA) provides techniques and methods targeted to support the selection of the best alternative in systems where multiple criteria conflict and compete with each other. In recent years, contributions have been made in a number of different fields (Plantié et al. 2005; Lakiotaki et al. 2008; Matsatsinis et al. 2007; Manouselis and Matsatsinis 2001).

The Learning Context

The recommender builds on a semantic model designed by iTEC partners over several iterations of Control Board revisions, and captures knowledge of the domain. The learning context is one of the key abstractions in the domain, and it includes concepts such as: the technologies that are disposable in a particular classroom; the characteristics of the target students; and space-time considerations.

Recommendation Process

The recommendation process produces a list of recommended items—technologies, events, experts—that can be used during the performance of a learning activity in a particular context. Thus, taking the characterisation of a learning activity and its context as inputs, the recommender goes through the items in its Knowledge Base and fetches the fittest items. This process has three stages: pre-processing, filtering an ordering of results by their relevance. All the stages are important though the ordering algorithm (relevance calculation) is the one that has most impact on the results.

In the pre-processing stage, the requirements of a given activity—the generic description of the kind of resources needed—are composed with those from the context, thus forming an integrated set of factors that have to be taken into account when calculating the relevance of resources.

In the filtering stage, some candidates are selected from the Knowledge Base, thus restricting the final number of resources whose relevance is going to be calculated. Due to the impact of this stage in the results, there are three configurable running modes:

- Strict: only resources that comply strictly with the requirements of the learning activity are selected.
- Permissive: in addition to the resources selected in the point above, this mode includes those resources with incomplete/black properties. Thus, it does not discard those resources that are not perfectly defined.
- No filtering: in this mode there is no filtering stage. This mode is especially useful in testing/depuration, as well as in scenarios with a low number of available resources.

Once a subset of valid resources has been obtained, the next stage consists of calculating the degree of relevance for each resource, while taking into account the requirements of the activity and the context. The heterogeneous nature of the resources and its complex description forced us to follow a rigorous strategy in order to obtain a satisfactory utility function. We followed an approach inspired by multi criteria recommender systems, which uses analysis techniques from the field of MCDA. Specifically, we followed the general methodology proposed by Roy (1996). We set (6.2) as the mechanism for calculating the relevance of resources, where f_i represents the marginal utility function for a given factor and w_i the weight that such a factor will have in the final value of relevance.

$$\sum_{i=0}^{n} w_i \cdot f_i \qquad (6.2)$$

Below, we detail the process that we followed for selecting the factors and their associated weights. Rodríguez et al. (2013) go further into the decisions made in each of the stages of the followed methodology.

Selection and Weighting of Factors

Both the selection and weighting of factors that are taken into account in the recommendation process have been driven by iTEC Control Boards: a group of experts that collaborated in the project and that included people with technological and pedagogical expertise. Fifty-three experts from different institutions participated in this process.

- Selection: we generated a document including a description of the general recommendation strategy, as well as the data model of every type of resource, with a collection of all the factors that a priori might play a role in the recommendation process. For each factor, the document included a thorough description of its meaning. After a productive discussion, with more than 100 written commentaries on the idoneity of the factors, we obtained the set of selected factors.
- Weighting: the experts rated the impact that each one of the factors should have in the calculation of the relevance of resources. The following tables summarise the factors that were selected by the Control Boards with their associated weights. Rodríguez et al. (2013) describe the weighting of factors in further detail. Tables 6.1, 6.2 and 6.3 shows selected factors and their weighting.

Enrichment of Semantic Knowledge Base

The process of recommending educational resources depends on complete, thorough and up to date information being available on the knowledge base. In the end, the maintenance of information in the system is a responsibility of the community of system users. In the case of the iTEC Cloud, this community consisted primarily of teachers and technical and pedagogical coordinators registered on the platform. In many cases, these teachers lacked the appropriate knowledge and the time required to provide accurate and complete information on each of the resources catalogued (e.g., when teachers entered a new expert in the people directory, they were neither expected to be aware of all the areas of expertise of the individual

Table 6.1 Selected factors and associated weights for resources

Factor (f_i)	Description	Weight (w_i)
Functionality	Functionality offered by a tool to a given degree	0.1307
Language	Language(s) supported by the tool's user interface	0.1031
Type	Type of the tool (i.e. application or device)	0.1011
Shell	Ranks tools according to their running environment	0.0976
Age	Prioritizes tools having as their explicitly specified audience one of the audiences specified for the context	0.0976
Cost	Prioritizes tools having no usage cost within a specified school (or context)	0.0970
Rating	Community popularity	0.0916
Technology	Discriminates whether a school already has a given tool	0.0916
Competences	References the technical expertise of a teacher	0.0883
Education level	Prioritizes tools which are explicitly targeted at an educational level among those defined for the activity	0.0979

Table 6.2 Selected factors and associated weights for a resource of type person

Factor (f_i)	Description	Weight (w_i)
Language	Prioritizes people having as their mother tongue the language in which an activity is carried out	0.1359
Expertise	Reflects the expertise of a person in a given subject	0.1343
Experience	Considers previous experience of a person, according to the learning activities already carried out by this person	0.1238
Communication	Takes into account the communication tools a person participating in a learning activity has available	0.1186
Reliability	Indicates the degree of trust that the community, as a whole, has in the person to be selected	0.1119
Organization	Prioritizes persons belonging to the same organization as the learning activity creator	0.0998
Rating	Indicates the degree of popularity of a person	0.0984
Geographical	Indicates the degree of geographical proximity of the person to the location of the school	0.0915
Personal relations	Considers existing relations between the relations learning activity creator and the people who may participate in it	0.0856

Table 6.3 Selected factors and associated weights for a resource of type event activity

Factor (f_i)	Description	Weight (w_i)
Subject	Used to rate an event according to the event thematic area(s)	0.1574
Required tools	Identifies online events that can be accessed when using some of the available tools	0.1444
Cost	Prioritizes free events	0.1385
Geographical	Degree of geographical proximity of an event to the location of the school where the activity is performed	0.1238
Rating	Popularity	0.1186
Organization	Relevance of the event's organizer	0.1186
Audience	Prioritizes events having as their explicit audience one of the audiences specified for the context	0.0995
Education level	Prioritizes events being explicitly targeted at an educational level among those defined for the activity	0.0995

being included, nor had the time needed to try to find out what those areas might be). Any such shortcomings in the information held lead to reductions in the quality of the recommendations provided by the system.

To try to alleviate part of this burden to end users, when developing the SDE support was included to enrich the information available in the KB transparently to other iTEC systems by leveraging the information freely available on the Web. The enrichment of the information available on the KB is performed through an enrichment module that analyses external sources and extracts relevant information to complement descriptions of educational resources already on the KB, which in turn were obtained from the information available in the collection of repositories on the iTEC Cloud. Many sources of information are available on the Web in several

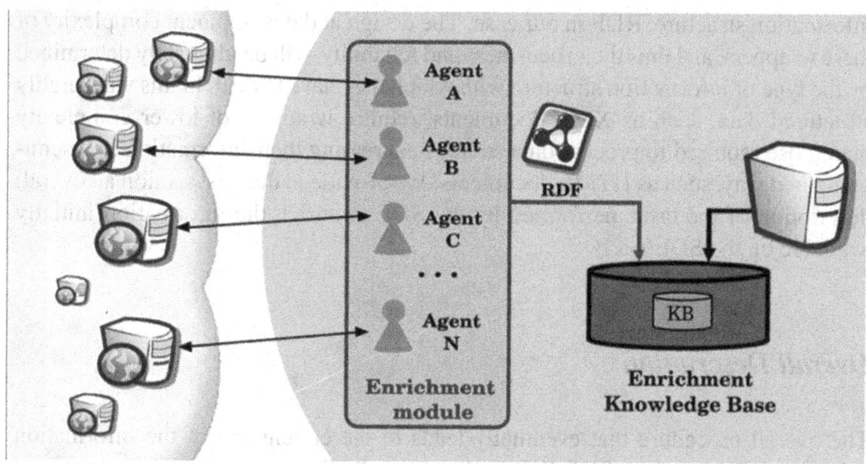

Fig. 6.5 The enrichment process

contexts that catalogue and describe in detail the information available for many entities and resources, including entities related to the resources handled in iTEC. For example, in the case of tools there are software application catalogues, which contain accurate descriptions developed by experts and endorsed by a large community of users.

In the case of the SDE, the enrichment process is carried out by a module composed of a set of smart independent agents that extract specific information from external sources (see Fig. 6.5), process it, and insert it into the KB in a way which is transparent to the rest of the system. Thus, the information available is eventually enhanced, and consequently users receive recommendations on educational resources of a better quality than those obtained solely from the information provided exclusively by the users themselves. It should be noted that in the early stages of deployment of a system lacking an enrichment module, when cataloguers have not yet entered enough information, the recommender is unable to provide quality recommendations. That is, it requires a significant initial effort from users to enter information on resources before appropriate recommendations can be offered. The extent of this effort may compromise the success of any platform. However, by the introduction of enrichment it is possible to mitigate this cold-start situation (Maltz and Ehrlich 1995) and provide available information on resources more quickly, thus considerably reducing the initial effort required from cataloguers.

Record Linkage (Winkler 1999) is one of the pillars of our enrichment algorithm. In the case of external sources publishing their information using RDF (i.e., semantic sources, as they use a form of information representation specifically targeted to preserve the meaning of statements) there are tools available (e.g., SILK (Volz et al. 2009)) that automate Record Linkage. In the case of non-semantic web sources, a specific wrapper agent has to be developed (Ferrara et al. 2011). A wrapper is an agent that extracts information from a source and transforms it to a particular information structure, RDF in our case. The design and development complexity of these wrappers, and thus their robustness and reliability, will be ultimately determined by the type of information structure with which they have to deal. In this way, highly structured data, such as XML documents, require wrappers of lower complexity than those required to process data sources expressing their information in a semi-structured way, such as HTML documents. We provide in the next section an overall description of the tasks performed by the SDE to enrich the information initially available on the SDE's KB.

Overall Description

The overall procedure that eventually leads to the enrichment of the information initially available on the SDE KB can be conceptually decomposed into a series of stages:

Source Localization and Definition of Information Extraction Patterns

The process is initiated by a domain expert who analyses the sources available in the Web to identify the most relevant ones. In other words, the sources sought are those containing useful information to complement the information available on the KB. Once the most appropriate sources have been identified, the corresponding extraction pattern is defined. This pattern is implemented by a wrapper. This piece of software determines which data and structures should be extracted, together with the operations required to extract that information and, if necessary, its transformation into RDF. The wrapper utilizes a different extraction mechanism depending on the language used to represent the information in each source (e.g., automated tools like SILK, GRDDL transformations (Connolly 2007)).

Record Linkage and Retrieval of Resource Descriptions

The next task consists of detecting the correspondence between data records in the external source and entities to be enriched, and on retrieving the information available in those records. In conceptual terms, to complete this task the following activities need to be performed:

- **Source location**: The location of relevant records in the external source can be performed directly in the case of sources providing internal searching mechanisms to final users (e.g., through SPARQL Endpoints (Prud'hommeaux and Seaborne 2008), API methods or Web content search support). These mechanisms are fairly common in most relevant sources, as these sources host large amounts of information that would be difficult to exploit without search support, and they reduce the overall complexity of the linkage process. Using the appropriate searching service, and by means of key-based queries, it is possible to retrieve the resources related to the entity to be enriched (e.g., using an individual's name, it is possible to recover the list of individuals registered with the external source having a similar name).

- **Extraction of characterization information**: From search results, and using the previously defined extraction pattern, information characterizing each record is retrieved. Records returned by the search process usually provide limited information, including only the details required to identify each object. In addition, they usually include a key or path to recover the complete description of each object. The information extracted is structured according to the language used by the source, so it has to be translated into RDF to be further processed by the wrapper. According to the granularity desired for the detection of false positives, two strategies are possible: (1) to recover at this point all the information available for each retrieved record to have as much information as possible for filtering; or (2) to perform filtering immediately (as described below) and, once duplicate records or false positives have been discarded, to recover all the information corresponding to the remaining valid records. The first strategy facilitates a more accurate filtering process as richer information is available, whereas the second strategy is more efficient, as the number of queries required and the amount of information managed can be dramatically reduced.
- **Filtering of false positives**: For information enrichment to be correct, we need record linkage to be exact, that is, resources deemed as equal should actually be representations of the same object. As a consequence, on some occasions it is necessary to internally filter out the resources retrieved after searching the external source to discard similar but not equal objects. For instance, when we look for a specific individual in a social network, we may obtain references to individuals with similar names (e.g., Mary Smith, Maria Smith). In these occasions, a syntactic comparison is launched on the list of retrieved resources, using in our case the Jaro heuristic (Jaro 1995). This is a simple record linkage mechanism.

In cases where the source does not provide a searching service, all records available will be considered candidate results. This implies that all descriptions will be extracted from the web to be further filtered for false positives. Thus, in a context where the only objective is to enrich the information available about a local resource, an external source not providing searching support would be of little use, as enrichment would be highly inefficient in terms of time and resources required. However, if the aim includes completing the knowledge base with new, previously non-existent records, this option can be considered.

Adaptation to the SDE Model

Data extracted follows a vocabulary defined by the managers of the external source. These vocabularies are not directly understandable by our system, which defines its own terminology through specific data models. As a consequence, extracted information cannot be directly utilized in the recommender's inference processes. Because of this, information obtained from external sources is adapted to the SDE's data model. This translation is specific for each source and each type of educational resource to be enriched.

Knowledge Base Insertion

Finally, processed information is entered in the KB to enrich the corresponding resources. This insertion process triggers several internal inference processes to obtain new information from the heuristic rules defined in the Semantic Model, and to pre-compute most of the factors needed for relevance estimation by the recommendation algorithms implemented by the SDE.

Wrappers developed according to the process described above may be periodically launched on the selected external sources. This facilitates the continuous availability of updated data without requiring additional efforts from the user community.

The generic processes described in this section are intended to enrich the information from the resource descriptions already stored on the SDE's KB. However, these same processes can be used to add new entities or non-existent records, such as new software applications that could be used in a Learning Activity that had not been yet registered by teachers because they do not belong to any technical setting in any school. That is, they also support the population of the KB with educational resources that have not been previously introduced by human cataloguers. This process will hereafter be referred as population. To do this, instead of searching for records at each external source that refer to the same resource in the KB, we will try to find all records that may serve as iTEC resources. For example, in the case of educational events, we will search events with agendas reflecting an educational or cultural event and use them to populate the KB.

This strategy is feasible for resources that, due to their characteristics and to their public nature, may be freely entered in the KB without the system detecting any difference between this automatically entered information and the resources manually inserted by cataloguers. In any case, it is always necessary to consider the treatment to be given to this data in relation to their private or public nature.

Experiments Using the Enrichment Module

We conducted experiments that dealt with the enrichment of technologies, events, and experts. For the sake of brevity, we detail here only the results of the enrichment of experts. You can see the results of enrichment events and technologies in Anido et al. (2013). The results obtained by applying the enrichment process to complete the descriptions of educational resources of type People are fairly satisfactory taking into account the initial data available. The SDE's KB included an initial list of

Table 6.4 Preliminary results of enriching the knowledge base of experts

Initial KB	# of experts	14
	Average RDF triples per expert	28
	Total RDF triples	389
Enriched KB	# of enriched experts	8
	Enrichment %	~57 %
	Average RDF triples per enriched expert	190
	# of new contact accounts	7
	# of new expert tags	112
	# of new localizations	7
	# of new languages	12
	# of new person-languages relations	3
	Total RDF triples (enriching)	1519

14 experts associated to the iTEC project. The descriptions of these experts were used as the input of the enrichment process described above. Eventually, we have established Record Linkage relations with eight records in external sources, which refer to exactly eight different experts (cf. Table 6.4). Therefore, almost 60 % of the initial records were enriched. Analysing in further detail the enrichment process, 1519 new RDF triplets were generated, corresponding to an average of 190 triplets per expert. Most of these triplets refer to articles and other publications. Regarding the most relevant properties to the recommender, we obtained: 7 new contact accounts to facilitate communication with the corresponding experts; 112 new tags enabling the inference of new abilities and skills; 7 postal addresses that may be used to infer the geographical area of influence on an expert; 12 new evidences on language skills for 3 experts, which may be used by the recommender to propose experts according to the communication language defined for an educational.

Client Applications That Integrate SDE Recommendations

To date, the services offered by the SDE have been successfully integrated in two different client applications.[5] The first, Composer (Simon et al. 2013), is the application for creating and configuring learning activities that was created in the scope of iTEC Cloud. The second, AREA (Caeiro-Rodríguez et al. 2013), is an application that includes facilities to create learning plans, and it integrates the SDE's recommendations to configure the learning activities inside learning plans.

[5] Apart from an ad-hoc front-end that was developed for a pre-testing with participants (Anido Rifon et al. 2012).

Composer

As mentioned above, the iTEC Composer is the iTEC's proposal to provide support to the identification of the most suitable Tools and Resources for Learning Activities. The iTEC SDE provides additional features for the iTEC Composer. Indeed, while the iTEC Composer facilitates the production of a learning plan providing access to available Tools and Resources needed to satisfy the requirements of one or several Learning Activities, the iTEC SDE analyses the actual requirements of a Learning Activity to offer recommendations on Tools and Resources satisfying these requirements according to the specific context where activities will be developed.

The iTEC Composer is an autonomous entity that may also provide basic support to the production of learning plans independently of the recommendations provided by the SDE. The first step when generating a learning plan is to provide two key elements: (1) the Learning Activities that will be eventually included in the learning plan and (2) the Learning Context, that is, the set of parameters characterizing the context where the learning experience will eventually take place (e.g., Technical Setting, language, learning subject). Then, the teacher may use the iTEC Composer to navigate across the collection of available Tools and Resources to select the most suitable to the learning plan. Additionally, the Composer may utilize the SDE to provide personalized recommendations according to the requirements included in each Learning Activity.

AREA

iTEC initiated a collaboration line with the TELGalicia[6] research network, whose objective is to facilitate pedagogical and technological innovation in primary and secondary education in the northwest of Spain. Given the compatibility between the objectives of iTEC and TELGalicia, a collaboration with that network was initiated that had among its outcomes the adaptation of a web application named AREA in which the services offered by the SDE were integrated together with initial content available on the SDE's KB. AREA is basically a social Web 2.0 application that facilitates access to primary and secondary teachers to innovative educational proposals. AREA provides resources and tools for authoring, exploration and social curation for teachers to design their own lesson plans. Once a lesson plan has been completed in the classroom, AREA also provides structures for teachers (and also students in those cases where teachers find it convenient) to document their experiences in a similar way as it can be done with a blog, but according to the activity structure defined in the lesson plan.

One important aspect of SDE testing was that users were able to obtain recommendations on the most appropriate resources for learning stories/learning activities through. For each activity, users could consult the requirements and perform resource selection.

[6] www.redetelgalicia.com

Evaluation

At the time of writing this chapter, three testing sessions with end users have been completed. The first session with Galician primary and secondary education teachers, the second session consisted of a workshop with iTEC end users in the UK, and the third session consisted of a workshop in Oulu (Finland), also with iTEC end users.

A session was organized on 6th June 2013 in Santiago de Compostela (Spain) with 15 Galician primary and secondary education teachers. This session included the introduction of AREA and the integrated SDE recommendation features. Then, there was an open discussion about the questionnaire, that was created as part of iTEC's evaluation plan (Haldane and Lewin 2011), with a special emphasis on possible barriers and enablers, and on the suitability of the SDE for their needs. On 18th June 2013 a demonstration and testing session of the technologies developed in iTEC took place in Bolton (UK) with 25 teachers. As part of this, the SDE was presented in a workshop, and participants assessed the tool by means of a questionnaire. The SDE was evaluated in a similar way in the session in Finland.

On average, participants on the evaluations think that recommendations on non-traditional educational resources may foster innovation in the classroom. Teachers agree with the vision that new technologies may be very useful in teaching-learning environments, but one hindrance towards the realisation of that vision is the difficulty of knowing what technologies are most adequate for whom. Overall, participants think that recommendations from the SDE is one step forward towards filling the gap between existent, suitable, and useful technologies and being aware of their existence.

Conclusions and Lessons Learned

This chapter has described a recommender system for non-traditional educational resources—tools, people, events—that is based on semantic technologies and that was developed in the scope of the iTEC project, whose main findings are described in this book. As the main contributions of our research we can highlight the following ones.

We defined a semantic model that characterises the universe of discourse that the recommender uses, and that is also the basis for the definition of a common language shared between the different iTEC working packages. This semantic model was implemented as an ontology, which constitutes the core of the intelligence of the recommender. The scope of the ontology developed is very broad, as it models concepts such as learning activities, contexts, technologies, events, people, and many other elements that are specific to the educational area.

The recommender system which we have described provides recommendations for technologies, events, and people (e.g. experts). This constitutes an innovative approach, at least in the area of recommender systems applied to education. Besides, the recommendation strategy is based on the learning context, rather than on students' and teachers' preferences.

The recommender's API is publicly available, and it is ready to be consumed from client applications that want to make use of recommendations. We have described how two client applications (Composer and AREA) successfully integrate SDE's recommendations. Using AREA as a front end, we tested the SDE with final users, in three experiences with teachers in Santiago de Compostela, Bolton and Oulu, and the first results were positive.

After 4 years working in this system we can point some lessons learned. First of all, the increasing number of open resources available in the web is a huge unexplored source for resources beyond content. Many applications and resources not explicitly designed to be used for education can be actually applied to that purposed. The original objective of integrating some repositories within the SDE—i.e. the Widget Store or de People and Events Directory—was not enough to provide teachers with a sufficient number of alternatives. This issue was overcome thanks to the use of enrichment techniques allowing to easily integrate external sources.

On the other hand, traditional semantic web technologies, including the academic design of ontologies and the development of recommendations algorithms based on them, are not agile enough to adapt to the community of content and application developers. Therefore a less strict approach, based for instance, on the use of soft ontologies is required.

Finally, when resources coming from different sources are to be integrated to provide recommendations to users based on whatever criteria, an extra effort is needed to appropriately classify those resources. Again, pre-design ontologies may not work for many cases. In the light of this we suggest research into Machine Learning techniques whose application to the automatic classification of educational resources may contribute to the field of automatic metadata generation.

References

Adomavicius G, Tuzhilin A (2010) Context-aware recommender systems. In: Recommender systems handbook: a complete guide for research scientists and practitioners. http://ids.csom.umn.edu/faculty/gedas/NSFCareer/CARS-chapter-2010.pdf. Accessed 12 Mar 2015

Anido Rifon L et al (2012) iTEC—wp 10 d10.2—support for implementing iTEC engaging scenarios v2

Anido L et al (2013) iTEC—wp 10 d10.3—support for implementing iTEC engaging scenarios v3

Burke R (2002) Hybrid recommender systems: survey and experiments. User Model User-Adap Inter 12:331–370. Available via http://www.springerlink.com/index/N881136032U8K111.pdf. Accessed 12 Mar 2015

Caeiro-Rodríguez M et al (2013) AREA: a social curation platform for open educational resources and lesson plans. In: Proceedings—frontiers in education conference, FIE, pp 795–801

Connolly D (2007) Gleaning resource descriptions from dialects of languages (GRDDL). W3C Recommendation. http://www.w3.org/TR/grddl/. Accessed 12 Mar 2015

De Nicola A, Missikoff M, Navigli R (2005) A proposal for a unified process for ontology building: UPON, vol 3588, Database and expert systems applications (Lecture notes in computer science). Springer, Heidelberg, pp 655–664

Fernández-López M, Gómez-Pérez A, Juristo N (1997) Methontology: from ontological art towards ontological engineering. Assessment SS-97-06, pp 33–40. http://www.cpgei.cefetpr.br/~tacla/Onto/Artigos/MethontologyFromOntologicalArt.pdf\nhttp://oa.upm.es/5484/. Accessed 12 Mar 2015

Ferrara E, Fiumara G, Baumgartner R (2011) Web data extraction, application and techniques: a survey

Figueira J, Greco S, Ehrgott M (2005) Multiple criteria decision analysis: state of the art surveys. Springer, New York

Gago JMS (2007) Contribución a los sistemas de intermediación en el ámbito del aprendizaje electrónico utilizando tecnologías semánticas. University of Vigo

Griffiths D et al (2012) The Wookie Widget Server: a case study of piecemeal integration of tools and services. J Univ Comput Sci 18:1432–1453. Available via http://www.jucs.org/jucs_18_11/the_wookie_widget_server. Accessed 12 Mar 2015

Haldane M, Lewin C (2011) WP5: revised evaluation plan. iTEC

Herrick DR (2009) Google this! Using Google apps for collaboration and productivity. In: Proceedings of the 37th annual ACM SIGUCCS fall conference, pp 55–64

Jaro MA (1995) Probabilistic linkage of large public health data files. Stat Med 14:491–498. Available via http://www.ncbi.nlm.nih.gov/pubmed/7792443

Lakiotaki K, Tsafarakis S, Matsatsinis N (2008) UTA-Rec: a recommender system based on multiple criteria analysis. In: Proceedings of the 2008 ACM conference on recommender systems, pp 219–226

Lakiotaki K, Matsatsinis NF, Tsoukiàs A (2011) Multicriteria user modeling in recommender systems. IEEE Intell Syst 26:64–76

Liu L, Mehandjiev N, Xu DL (2011) Multi-criteria service recommendation based on user criteria preferences. In: Proceedings of the 5th ACM conference on recommender systems—RecSys'11, p 77. http://dl.acm.org/citation.cfm?doid=2043932.2043950. Accessed 12 Mar 2015

Maltz D, Ehrlich K (1995) Pointing the way: active collaborative filtering. In: Proceedings of the SIGCHI conference on human factors in computing systems, pp 202–209

Manouselis N, Matsatsinis NF (2001) Introducing a multi-agent, multi-criteria methodology for modeling electronic consumers behavior: the case of internet radio, vol 21, Lecture notes in computer science. Springer, Heidelberg, pp 190–195

Martín-Vicente MI et al (2012) Semantic inference of user's reputation and expertise to improve collaborative recommendations. Expert Syst Appl 39:8248–8258

Matsatsinis NF, Lakiotaki K, Delias P (2007) A system based on multiple criteria analysis for scientific paper recommendation. In: Proceedings of the 11th Panhellenic conference on informatics

Noy N, McGuinness D (2001) Ontology development 101: a guide to creating your first ontology. Development 32:1–25. http://www.ksl.stanford.edu/people/dlm/papers/ontology-tutorial-noy-mcguinness-abstract.html. Accessed 12 Mar 2015

Oxford English Dictionary (2014) Oxford English dictionary online. Oxford English dictionary, 2010. http://dictionary.oed.com/. Accessed 12 Mar 2015

Patterson TC (2007) Google Earth as a (not just) Geography education tool. J Geogr 106:145–152

Pazzani MJ, Billsus D (2007) Content-based recommendation systems. Adapt Web 4321:325–341. Available via http://link.springer.com/10.1007/978-3-540-72079-9. Accessed 12 Mar 2015

Pinto HS, Staab S, Tempich C (2004) DILIGENT: towards a fine-grained methodology for DIstributed, Loosely-controlled and evolvInG Engineering of oNTologies. In: 16th European conference on artificial intelligence—ECAI, pp 393–397

Plantié M, Montmain J, Dray G (2005) Movies recommenders systems: automation of the information and evaluation phases in a multi-criteria decision-making process. In: Proceedings of the 16th international conference on database and expert systems applications, pp 633–644

Prud'hommeaux E, Seaborne A (2008) SPARQL query language for RDF. W3C recommendation, 2009. W3C, pp 1–106. http://www.w3.org/TR/rdf-sparql-query/. Accessed 12 Mar 2015
Redding S (1997) Parents and learning. Educational practices series. International Academy of Education. http://www.ibe.unesco.org/publications/EducationalPracticesSeriesPdf/prac02e.pdf. Accessed 12 Mar 2015
Resnick P, Varian HR (1997) Recommender systems. Commun ACM 40:56–58
Ricci F, Rokach L, Shapira B (2011) Introduction to recommender systems handbook. http://dx.doi.org/10.1007/978-0-387-85820-3_1. Accessed 12 Mar 2015
Rodríguez AC et al (2013) Providing event recommendations in educational scenarios. In: Advances in intelligent systems and computing, pp 91–98
Roy B (1996) Multicriteria methodology for decision aiding. Nonconvex optimization and its applications. Springer, Heidelberg
Schafer J et al (2007) Collaborative filtering recommender systems, vol 4321, The adaptive web (Lecture notes in computer science). Springer, Berlin, pp 291–324. http://www.springerlink.com/content/t87386742n752843. Accessed 12 Mar 2015
Shambour Q, Lu J (2011) A hybrid multi-criteria semantic-enhanced collaborative filtering approach for personalized recommendations. In: Proceedings—2011 IEEE/WIC/ACM international conference on web intelligence, WI 2011, pp 71–78
Simon B et al (2013) Applying the widget paradigm to learning design: towards a new level of user adoption, vol 8095, Scaling up learning for sustained impact (Lecture notes in computer science). Springer, Heidelberg, pp 520–525
Uschold M, King M (1995) Towards a methodology for building ontologies. Methodology 80: 275–280
Van Assche F (2012) iTEC—wp 9 d9.2—release of the directory. iTEC, pp 3–44
Volz J et al (2009) Silk—a link discovery framework for the web of data. In: CEUR workshop proceedings
Winkler WE (1999) The state of record linkage and current research problems. Statistical Research Division US Census Bureau, pp 1–15. http://www.census.gov/srd/papers/pdf/rr99-04.pdf. Accessed 12 Mar 2015

Chapter 7
Resources Beyond Content for Open Education

Frans Van Assche, Victor Alvarez, Douglas Armendone, Joris Klerkx, and Erik Duval

Abstract While many innovations in Technology Enhanced Learning (TEL) have emerged over the last two decades, the uptake of these innovations has not always been very successful, particularly in schools. The transition from proof of concept to integration into learning activities has been recognized as a bottleneck for quite some time. This major problem, which is affecting many TEL stakeholders, is the focus of the 4-year iTEC project that is developing a comprehensive approach involving 15 ministries of education and is organizing a large scale validator with more than a thousand classrooms. This chapter reports on how the information provision on events of interest in learning as well as on persons that can contribute to learning activities, supports novel scenarios and is key for the introduction of open education in the K12 education.

Keywords Persons • Events • Repository system • Interoperability • Learning

Open Education for Schools

While Illich's (1971) vision of deschooling society did not materialize for many reasons—including the fact that taking care of youngsters is institutionalized in our western society where in many cases both parents work—many of his ideas such as the "educational webs" are more relevant than ever. Similarly, the ambient intelligent vision for education presented in Ducatel et al. (2001) was unrealistic. However, it was indicative of a shift to different forms of more learner-centred education. Nowadays ICT-facilitated approaches include personalization (García Hoz 1981),

F. Van Assche (✉) • V. Alvarez • J. Klerkx • E. Duval
Department of Computer Science, University of Leuven, Leuven, Belgium
e-mail: frans.van.assche@gmail.com; victor.alvarez@cs.kuleuven.be; joris.klerkx@cs.kuleuven.be; erik.duval@cs.kuleuven.be

D. Armendone
Swiss Agency for ICT in Education, Bern, Switzerland
e-mail: douglas.armendone@etu.unige.ch

F. Van Assche et al. (eds.), *Re-engineering the Uptake of ICT in Schools*, DOI 10.1007/978-3-319-19366-3_7

differentiation, individualization, self-regulated learning, the flipped classroom and ambient schooling (Van Assche 2004). The current focus on proactive, communicative, and participative pedagogical strategies, as well as the emphasis on social learning (Brown and Adler 2008) can be seen as a natural evolution of the learning-centric paradigm and a means to provide open access to a wealth of learning resources. Indeed, instead of one teacher for many students, the use of different kinds of resources (including human resources) is facilitated by ICT and open education in the educational process of a single student.

Open education traditionally relies heavily on the availability of open educational material such as provided in Open Educational Resource repositories (see e.g. the Learning Resource Exchange[1] and the Open Discovery Space[2] or GLOBE[3]), and more recently in Massive Open Online Courses (MOOCs). However, just providing open access materials is not sufficient within a schooling context, neither does it utilize the full potential that modern ICT offers. In a way, in today's school setting, a real learner-centred approach, including personalization, differentiation, or individualization, might turn out infeasible from a socio-economic perspective. Indeed, following Herbert Simon's (1956) *satisficing* principle, policy-makers are compelled to consider what is "good enough" education due to budgetary constraints. Hence, the challenge is to make the shift towards a more learner-centred approach within the socio-economic context of today.

Therefore, if we seek to make education for youngsters more open and more personalized, differentiated, or individualized, institutional education needs to explore *alternative interactions* that can be delivered in a cost effective manner.

Richer Interactions Through Resources Beyond Content

The rationale for looking at interactions when aiming to provide open education for youngsters is based on the observation that social presence enhances learning (Swan and Shea 2005) and that our understanding of content is socially constructed (Van Assche 1998). An informal model that illustrates the interactions in learning is given in Fig. 4.1 of Chap. 4. Typically, a learner interacts with a tutor (usually the teacher), a subject expert (usually the teacher), co-learners, education material, and the world outside the close educational environment. In a way, the learning can only be influenced through these interactions.

However, current systems are mostly focused on providing access to learning material and getting access to educational resources beyond content remains problematic. Despite social systems such as Facebook or even professional networks such as LinkedIn, or researcher networks such as ResearchGate, it is very hard to

[1] http://lreforschools.eun.org

[2] http://www.opendiscoveryspace.eu/

[3] http://globe-info.org

find a **person** willing to help with French pronunciation, a tutor for a mathematically gifted child, or co-learners in contemporary history, beyond the persons known from and immediately available in the school context. Similarly, it is not easy to find **events** happening in the world that could contribute to a valid learning experience. This vision of future education suggests increasing the current scope of openness, emphasizing the importance of providing open access to resources beyond content.

At the same time, harnessing new (forms of) interactions may have a profound impact in education and lead to increased engagement in the learning process (Beare 2013; Beldarrain 2006). Referring to the same interaction model, engagement can arise from the person, material, or environment one interacts with and/or the interaction conduit itself. From the early Web for Schools (Van Assche 1998) project up to recent TEL projects such as the Stellar project, research has pointed to this engaging potential of ICT.[4]

Therefore our project explored to what extent interactions other than those found in the traditional classroom can positively affect educational attainment and enhance engagement; specifically by making information about Persons and Events available that can enhance such interactions. By doing so, we seek to facilitate the exploration of ICT enabled *new scenarios, new roles and situations in the learning process*.

The Persons and Events Directory

The Persons and Events (P&E) Directory is part of the iTEC project. iTEC, which stands for Innovative Technologies for an Engaging Classroom, was a large-scale pilot led by European Schoolnet (EUN)[5] and involved a network of Ministries of Education, universities, leading ICT vendors, innovative SMEs, TEL researchers, teacher educators and experts in school validations and pedagogical evaluation. The aim of this collaborative project was to produce meaningful pedagogical scenarios for supporting teaching and learning in future classroom practice.

The iTEC P&E directory was designed by our research group at KU Leuven to allow registered users to find other persons, within and outside the school context, who can contribute to a learning activity and to find events that are of interest to a teacher or students in their learning activity. An illustrative user story is as follows.

Belgium has two astronauts that have visited the International Space Station (ISS). The latest, Frank De Winne, remained six months in space and was commander of ISS expedition 21. The MoE of Flanders, keen on raising interest in science, has asked him to register as an expert in the Persons and Events Directory. Mr De Winne accepted with pleasure and he agrees to be available for six chat

[4] In the Stellar 'Big Meeting' of February 2012 there was only one factor mentioned by all business stakeholders: the engagement potential of TEL.

[5] www.eun.org/

sessions with students and their teacher. The MoE sets up six chat events and registers them in the P&E directory. A few days later, Chris, a science teacher, is reading the iTEC scenario "Beam in the expert". She considers this an interesting scenario and consults the P&E directory, easily identifying experts that speak Dutch and have expertise in science. She identifies Mr De Winne and selects one of the six chat sessions that he is offering. The pupils prepare very well and during the chat session, interesting questions arise such as about the smell in the ISS if you don't have fresh air for six months...

While professional social networks such as LinkedIn were readily available, they were inadequate for our purpose; i.e. to find persons in a European multilingual network based on country, the language(s) they master, country, subject, and ways to contact them. Within the iTEC project, search options were investigated, leading to the faceted search for persons as illustrated in Fig. 7.1 (for privacy reasons the data is fictitious). Here, the search is effected using a number of filters shown on the left. The data available for the person is shown on the right. Users can indicate whether they know persons in the directory and whether they trust a person's judgement. This information is used to make recommendations to the user as elaborated in Chap. 6.

Similarly, events from across Europe can be found based on country, language, subject, event category, and event place. This is illustrated by Fig. 7.2. These events may come from different sources (see next section) and be of different types.

The interface of the P&E directory has been translated to 9 languages, and through the use of multilingual vocabularies, users can also access most of the data

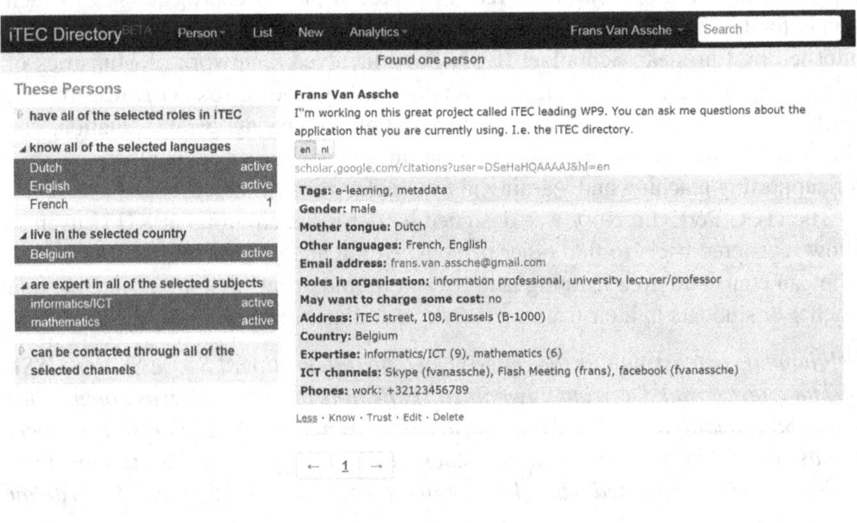

Fig. 7.1 Finding persons

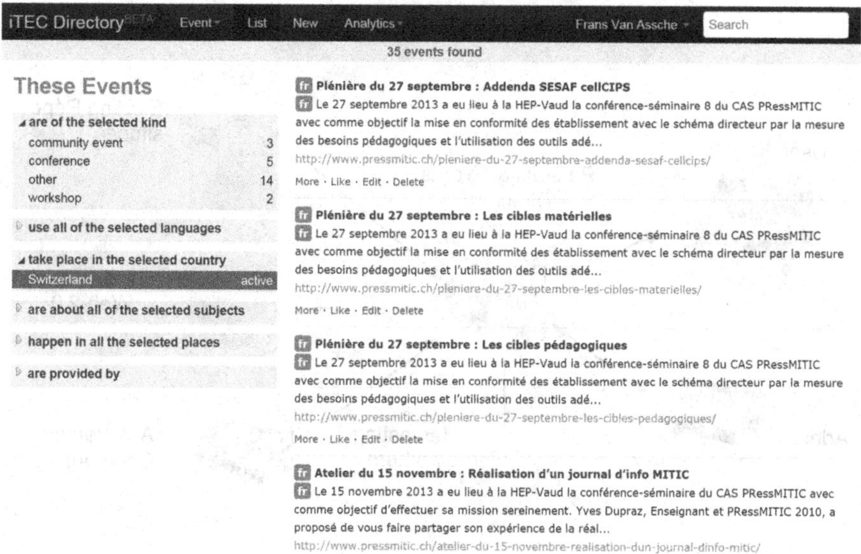

Fig. 7.2 Finding events

in their own language, while they need to be entered only once in the user's mother tongue. Also, some social data (i.e. that one likes an event) is gathered, which is then used in the aforementioned recommender system.

Technical Implementation

The implementation can be divided into three separate technical concerns: (a) how the data on Persons and Events is obtained from different sources, (b) how this data can be searched and presented, and (c) how the data can be accessed by other components.

Federated Access to Learning Resources

The Persons and Events Directory has a federated architecture. As such, the directory obtains its data from different sources depicted at the right of Fig. 7.3. The Persons and Events Directory reads RSS channels from existing educational repositories such as from Ministries of education, European portals and educational institutions. In addition, the Persons and Events Directory is harvesting from other

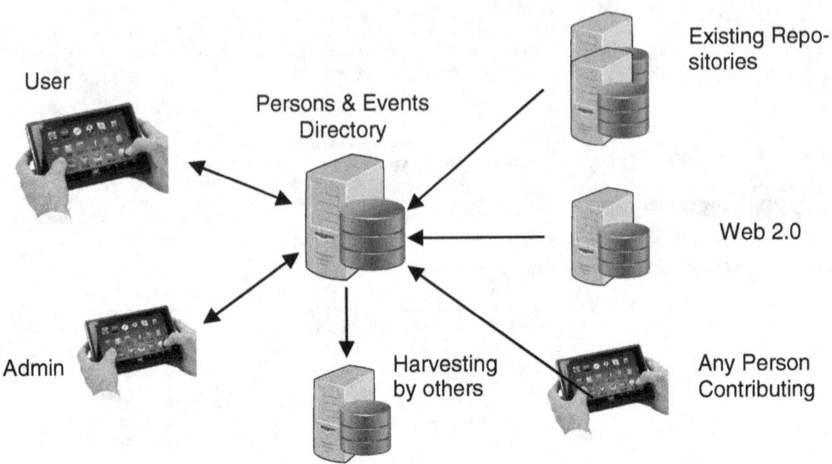

Fig. 7.3 The federated architecture of the Persons and Events directory

repositories such as the iTEC SDE repository[6] which scrapes existing web sites, transforms it into web 2.0 data structures and exposes it in either RDF triples or JSON data structures. As an example, events are scraped from CEN/ISSS, the open education portal, etc. Finally, registered users can also submit new entries to the directory.

The technical implementation involves the following components:

- A search engine for Persons and Events, implementing the combination of a full text search with a faceted search.
- An RSS harvester for the ingestion of events from external sources.
- A harvester for ingesting collections of iTEC formatted events from other iTEC components, such as the SDE repository.
- A harvesting target such that other authorized systems can harvest information from the Persons and Events Directory. This includes for example other subsystems from iTEC as well as any educational site or repository
- A vocabulary handler that ingest and handles multi-lingual vocabularies from the Vocabulary Bank for Education[7] (VBE).
- Facilities to manually submit new and enrich harvested entries about Persons and Events.

[6] http://www.itec-sde.net

[7] http://aspect.vocman.com/vbe/home

- A usage data logger implementing an application profile of the Experience API[8] (xAPI) as well as analytics tools.
- Visual analytics tools that indicate, in an objective way, the real figures for the total traffic and activity registered in the directory.

Facetted Search Engine

The search options adopted and investigated under the framework of the iTEC project has led to a faceted search for Persons and Events, which uses filters that are usually not available on other established social networks. These search filters allow persons in a European multilingual network to be found based upon a specific country, by the language(s) they master, subjects of expertise and a series of contact channels to reach them. Similarly, events from across Europe can be found using the following filters: country, language, subject, category, and place. The events may also come from different sources and be of different types.

Integration with Other iTEC Activities and Learning Tools

The Persons and Events Directory has been integrated with other iTEC tools, i.e. by harvesting other iTEC sources of information, such as the iTEC SDE repository. It also provides a RESTful API encoded as JSON strings over HTTP to access the information about Persons and Events. Consumers of the P&E API need to be able to send HTTP POST requests and be authenticated.

iTEC tools have also been classified in groups, and the P&E directory is now part of iTEC Educational Cloud (see Chap. 4) along with the Composer (see Chap. 5), the Widget Store (see Chap. 8) and the SDE (see Chap. 6). However, these various iTEC technical outputs can be further integrated for the benefit of iTEC users and the educational community. It seems, teachers and educational experts could take advantage of a more holistic and comprehensive view of the various iTEC tools, and multiple products, inside and outside iTEC. They could also benefit from the integration of the whole set of technologies available and the current information in P&E Directory.

Evaluation

The evaluation of the Persons and Events Directory addressed different dimensions: (a) the potential benefits for stakeholders, (b) the technical feasibility, (c) the usability, (d) usage and social use, and (e) other operational considerations.

[8] http://www.adlnet.gov/tla/experience-api/

Potential Benefits of the iTEC Persons and Events Directory

An initial analysis carried out with stakeholders revealed that the P&E directory could have a series of potential benefits for teachers and students attending a teacher training institution and for people in the education area in general. Although the Persons and Events Directory is already being used in real life situations with real life data, it is a proof-of-concept system and therefore the evaluation not only looks at the current system but also at the potential it has.

The potential benefits, split in three groups for better readability and comprehensibility, are enumerated as follows:

Find Resources to Improve Your Teaching Practice

1. Find support in developing advanced learning design skills, while improving the use of information and communication technologies (ICT) in the classroom.
2. Identify and make use of events during learning activities: a way to make students more interested in the topics they are studying.
3. Identify trainings and continuing professional development (CPD) opportunities in your region.

Promote Your Initiatives and Publish Your Resources

1. Gain visibility by promoting a favourite technology, service or technical tools you use in the classroom.
2. Promote self-organised events or activities taking place at your school (e.g. competitions, fairs, etc.).
3. Event organizers can promote regional and national events.
4. Post links to videos through which you share your experience and teaching practices.

Become a Member and Benefit from Networking

1. Be part of a dynamic multi-cultural community. Easily identify and contact (or be contacted by) peers and experts outside the school (locally or from other countries), willing to contribute to teaching and learning activities.
2. Persons traditionally not involved in the learning activity can more easily express their willingness to participate in the learning process.
3. Become part of a teachers' network and be contacted to take part in a wide range of training opportunities from across different European Schoolnet (EUN) projects (including workshops, courses, summer schools, and online or face-to-face events offered at the Future Classroom Lab). Teachers may also receive invitations to participate in new EUN projects.
4. Be invited to become a certified Future Classroom Ambassador in your country.

In order to evaluate the influence of these factors and enable us to better understand their potential benefits for teaching and learning, we developed new information models and designed a combined quantitative and qualitative evaluation method. The following sections deal with the evaluation of the pilot phase and elaborates on the lessons learned from the maintenance of the iTEC Persons & Events directory. This study allowed us to draw first conclusions about technical feasibility, usability and other factors that should be considered for a successful deployment of the P&E directory.

Technical Feasibility

The proof of concept development, allowed us to confirm the scalability of the system, and how it could easily be developed into a production system, due mainly to the harnessing and combination of proven scalable technologies. The concept of a *federated architecture* is today very well understood and has been in operation for some years. See for example: (Klerkx et al. 2010) and (Van Assche et al. 2009). However, in contrast to these systems, the federation presented in this chapter, uses simple RSS channels as well as simple JSON exchanges. Other technologies used are relational database systems as well as SOLR[9] for full text indexing and the faceted search. *Semantic interoperability* is facilitated by multilingual vocabularies developed in a number of European funded projects, including ETB,[10] CELEBRATE,[11] MELT,[12] and ASPECT.[13] These vocabularies are now available through the Vocabulary Bank for Education (See also section on "Technical Implementation").

Usability Evaluation

Teachers and education experts participating in the pilot study were asked to respond to surveys and provide information about their experience with the P&E Directory. This study was conducted in three workshops and during the final stage of the pilot study. The researchers carried out two different surveys, the System Usability Scale (SUS)[14] (see Table 7.1 for the questions and Fig. 7.4 for the results) and a survey specifically designed to address the assessment of the directory.

---

[9] http://wiki.apache.org/solr/Solrj

[10] http://etb.eun.org

[11] http://celebrate.eun.org

[12] http://info.melt-project.eu

[13] http://www.aspect-project.org

[14] The System Usability Scale (SUS): http://www.usability.gov/how-to-and-tools/methods/system-usability-scale.html

Table 7.1 The questions of the System Usability Scale

Q1	I think that I would like to use this system frequently
Q2	I found the system unnecessarily complex
Q3	I thought the system was easy to use
Q4	I think that I would need the support of a technical person to be able to use this system
Q5	I found the various functions in this system were well integrated
Q6	I thought there was too much inconsistency in this system
Q7	I would imagine that most people would learn to use this system very quickly
Q8	I found the system very cumbersome to use
Q9	I felt very confident using the system
Q10	I needed to learn a lot of things before I could get going with this system

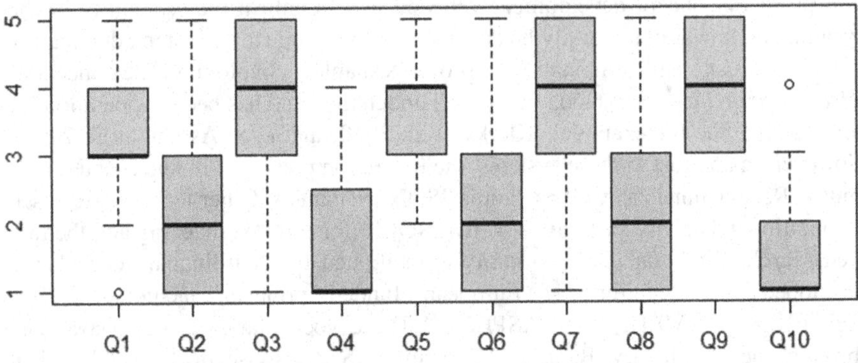

Fig. 7.4 Box plot of answers to the SUS questionnaire

Preliminary study. The usability of the P&E Directory was first evaluated using the SUS during two workshops. Together, these workshops had a mixed audience of 46 participants. The simplicity and proven effectiveness of the SUS has made it a widely used reference in usability evaluation.

By comparing the data of the two workshops, it was possible to observe how the P&E Directory scored much better with teachers than with non-teachers (i.e. authors, counsellors, experts, learners, managers and others) on the question "I think that I would like to use this system frequently". In order to validate the consistence of the answers, an intended user mismatch was introduced in the questionnaire. It is interesting to see that the answers of people that filled in the questionnaire carefully resulted in a much higher SUS score (72.13) than for people with inconsistent answers (59.47). Taking into account the number of valid answers, the usability of the P&E Directory was deemed to be "OK" to "Excellent" using an adjective rating scale.[15]

[15] Determining What Individual SUS Scores Mean: Adding an Adjective Rating Scale: http://www.upassoc.org/upa_publications/jus/2009may/bangor1.html

Similarly, it was clear that the intended audience found the P&E Directory much more usable than the non-intended audience. A closer look also revealed that teachers without previous knowledge of the iTEC project and its set of tools had more trouble to understand the purpose of the P&E Directory, which scored higher with teachers that were familiar with the iTEC approach of scenarios. In addition, the influence of other factors such as: teachers from small countries were more inclined to use resources from abroad than teachers from big countries, can make a European wide choice of resources be appreciated differently. These observations may have an influence on the mainstreaming of the P&E directory.

iTEC workshop. In a second stage of the usability study 18 experts in other areas of the iTEC project were asked to interact and perform tasks with the P&E directory. Following this, they were requested to fill out an online survey specifically designed to address the assessment of the directory as a "proof of concept", rather than a product, thus focusing on the potential benefits when developed into a full system.

In this study, the respondents highlighted the value of using the P&E directory to identify peers and experts outside the school environment who were willing to contribute to teaching and learning activities, over finding information about educational events, or promoting teaching and learning events they are involved in. This finding stressed the importance of forming a community of practice around the P&E directory. It suggests as well that a few actions are necessary to improve the way events are introduced and presented to users in the current version of the system.

In terms of perceived advantages in comparison to using other social networking sites, over 47 % of the respondents remarked the aim on pedagogical purposes and the simplicity to find very particular information about education and educational networking, while 21 % valued the structuring of data, improved search functions and filtering of information.

Final usability study. In the last stage of the pilot study, the user interface of the P&E directory included an evaluation tab with links to an online survey available in nine languages (DE, EN, ES, FL, FR, HU, IT, TR, PT). The following reproduces the final usability report developed at Manchester Metropolitan University and applies only to results obtained for the P&E directory. For a broader view on the impact of the iTEC project, please refer to Chap. 9 in this book.

The majority of the findings reported here were collected via an online survey that was delivered via SurveyMonkey and promoted via various iTEC mailing lists. The P&E survey was open between 21st May and 20th June 2014. Responses were included only if respondents had completed the survey at least as far as question 5 (the first question directly about the use of the P&E Directory).

Across all languages, a total of 132 respondents completed sufficient questions to be included in the analysis. This figure represents 48 % of the total number of registered P&E users at the time of the survey. 65 % of respondents (n = 132) were teachers; 12 % were teacher educators; and 7 % were experts. Head teachers (5 %); counsellors (5 %); managers (3 %); trainee teachers (2 %); learners (1 %) and authors (1 %) were also represented. Additional data was obtained from a small number of teacher comments relating to the P&E Directory in notes/transcripts from technology focus groups and pilot case studies.

The P&E directory and social media. Among survey respondents, Facebook was the most commonly used social media network for professional purposes (83 %; n = 132). Around half the respondents used Twitter (51 %) and a slightly smaller proportion used LinkedIn (42 %). When asked what, if any, potential advantages the People and Events Directory offered in comparison to other social networking sites (e.g. LinkedIn), by far the most frequent response was that it was focussed on education and the needs of teachers (47 responses):

"Sites as such LinkedIn are too general. This is for teachers."
"It is a more specific network it is connected to education."

Twelve respondents felt that the structure of the P&E Directory was better than existing sites:

"Easier to sort and find people."
"The people network on the P&E Directory is structured"

Other benefits mentioned were: allowing easy contact between people involved in iTEC (and other European projects) (6 respondents); the quality of information provided (e.g. currency, consistency and depth of detail) (3 respondents); the range of contact options offered (2); and the fact that people listed were likely to be willing to help if contacted (2). Nine respondents said they did not feel the P&E Directory had any advantage over existing social networking sites.

Training and support. 43 % of respondents (n = 132) had used the P&E Directory Manual to learn about the Directory. Around one-third (30 %) had received a training session from a national co-ordinator and 14 % had received one-to-one-support. However, 26 % did not indicate that they had received any training or guidance in using the Directory. 63 % agreed or strongly agreed that the information and support they had received provided all the information necessary to understand and use the People and Events Directory effectively (see Fig. 7.5).

Using the P&E Directory. Overall, respondents (n = 131) indicated that location-based searches were seen as the most useful ways of using the 'events' section of the P&E Directory (see Fig. 7.6):

- Finding information about regional or national events (59 % ranked first, second or third).
- Finding information about local events (59 % ranked first, second or third).
- Finding information about international events (58 % ranked first, second or third).

Other ways of finding events (by audience and subject) were less popular and the facility for respondents' promotion of their own events was seen as the least useful function:

- Finding information about events on particular subjects (48 % ranked first, second or third).
- Finding information about events aimed at particular audiences (44 % ranked first, second or third).
- Promoting events you are involved in (32 % ranked first, second or third).

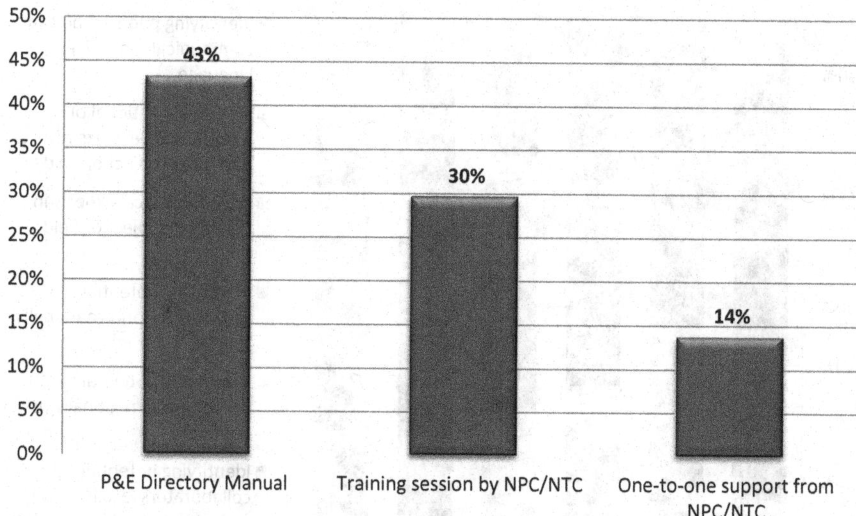

Fig. 7.5 Use of training and support materials and sessions; 132 participants responding to the question: "Which of the following have you used to learn about the People and Events directory?"

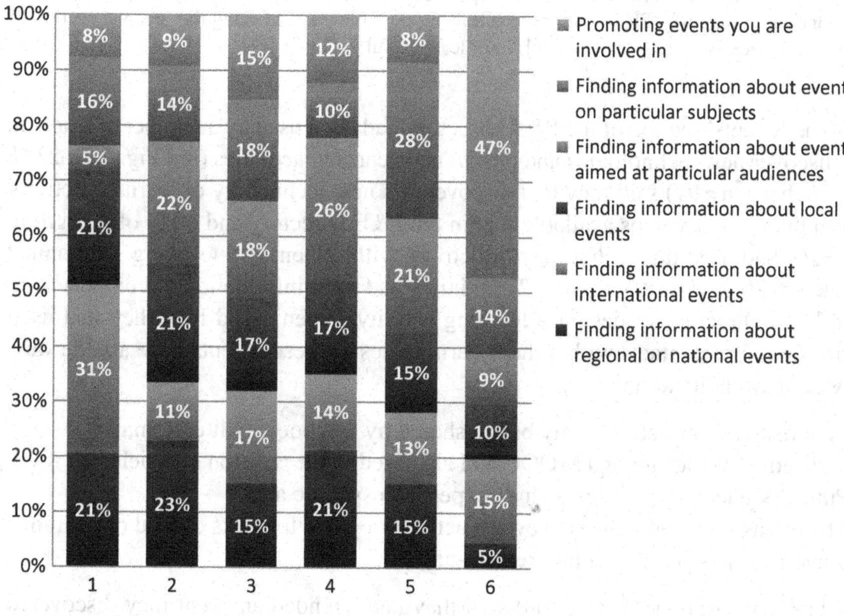

Fig. 7.6 Perceived usefulness of the events section in the P&E directory; 131 participants responding to the request: "Please order the following possible ways of using the 'events' section of the P&E directory from 1 (most useful) to 6 (least useful)"

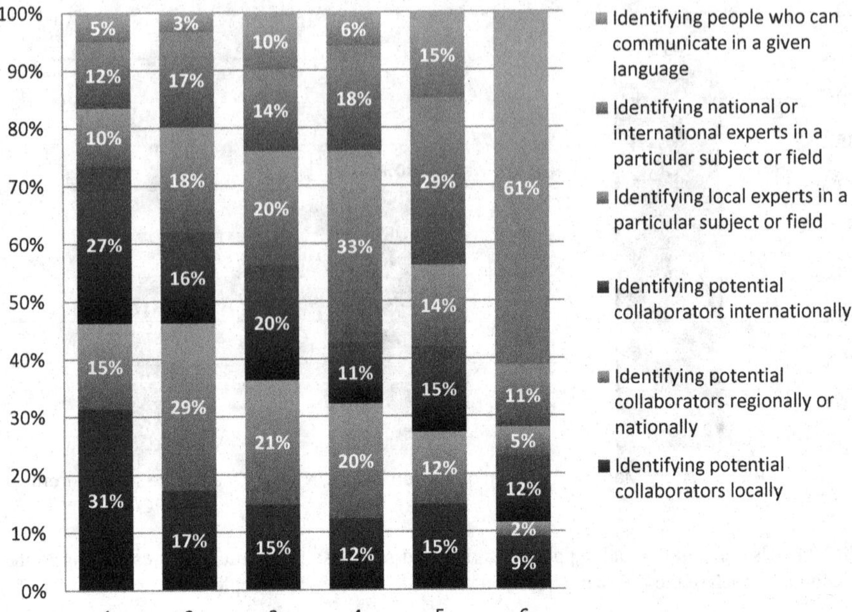

Fig. 7.7 Perceived usefulness of the people section in the P&E directory; 121 participants responding to request: "Please order the following possible ways of using the 'people' section of the P&E directory from 1 (most useful) to 6 (least useful)"

The 'events' section of the P&E Directory had been used by a number of teachers to discover new technologies and design new learning activities (see Fig. 7.7). 23 % of teachers (n=91) said they had discovered a new technology or learning activity from the teacher videos available within the P&E Directory and 60 % of this group (n=20) had used this technology or activity within their own teaching, or planned to do so. 20 % of teachers (n=92) said they had used information or contacts from the P&E Directory to design a learning activity. When asked how they had used information or contacts within their learning design, respondents gave a wide variety of answers including:

"I published information in my blogs, shared by facebook, twitter, e-mail."
"Utilised in the design of a MOOC and also used in the creation of articles on ICT."
"Put my students in contact with an expert in a specific area."
"The inclusion of references to events acted as a guide for tasks carried out within a learning activity (searching, referencing…)."

11 % of respondents (n=108) said they had attended an event they discovered through the People and Events Directory.

Turning to the 'people' section of the Directory, the facility to identify collaborators, at all levels was seen as the most useful way to use the Directory (n=121):

- Identifying potential collaborators regionally or nationally (65 % ranked first, second or third).

- Identifying potential collaborators locally (64 % ranked first, second or third).
- Identifying potential collaborators internationally (63 % ranked first, second or third).

The Directory was seen as less useful as a method of identifying experts. This may perhaps be because respondents felt less need to contact experts, or because the number of experts listed was very small. The facility to search for someone who could communicate in a given language was seen as being of limited use:

- Identifying local experts in a particular subject or field (48 % ranked first, second or third).
- Identifying national or international experts in a particular subject or field (42 % ranked first, second or third).
- Identifying people who can communicate in a given language (18 % ranked first, second or third).

Overall, the 'people' section of the Directory appeared to have been less well used than the 'events' section to date. Only 8 % of teachers (n=91) said they had contacted, or been contacted by, an expert or collaborator they identified through the P&E Directory. Just one of the other stakeholders (n=16) said they had contacted, or been contacted by, a teacher (or other collaborator) through the Directory. When asked to describe what happened and how they had worked together, two teachers mentioned email and another referred to a seminar. One other stakeholder said they were using WebEx.

Benefits of the P&E Directory. When asked to assume that the Directory had been developed into a mature product with sufficient People and Events available, at least four-fifths of respondents agreed with the following statements (see Figs. 7.8 and 7.9):

- 84 % agreed users become part of a teachers' network (n=114)
- 84 % agreed teachers and learners have access to videos of ideas, technologies and practices posted by other teachers and experts (n=113)
- 84 % agreed teachers and learners can more easily contact (or be contacted by) peers and experts outside the school willing to collaborate (n=113)
- 82 % agreed users can be part of a dynamic multi-cultural teacher community (n=114)
- 81 % agreed teachers and learners can more easily identify peers and experts outside the school willing to contribute to teaching and learning activities (n=113)
- 79 % agreed teachers can identify events to use during their lessons (n=114)
- 75 % agreed teachers and learners can promote self-organized events or activities taking place at their school (n=114).

The only statement with less than 70 % agreement was:

- 65 % agreed stakeholders traditionally not involved in the learning activities can more easily express their willingness to participate in the learning process (n=113).

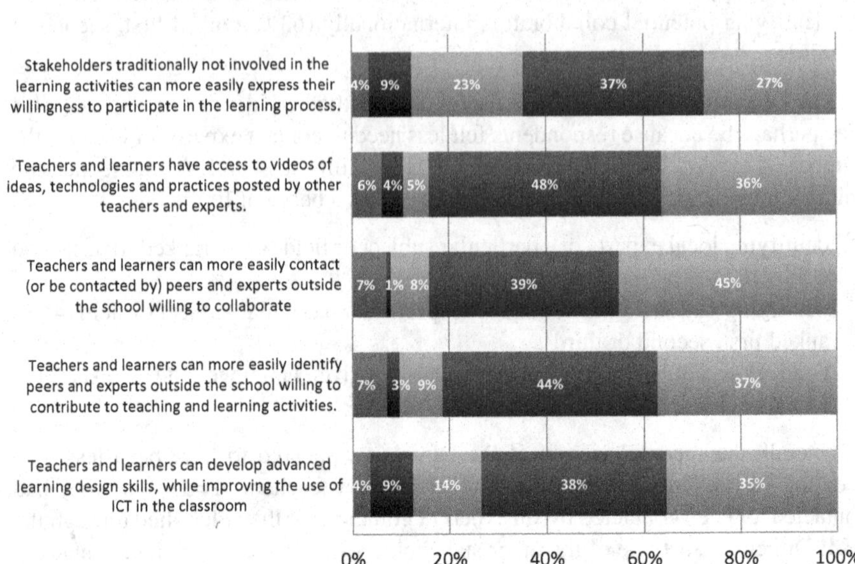

Fig. 7.8 Perceived benefits of the P&E directory (see section on "Open Education for Schools"); 114 participants responding to the request: "Assuming that the directory has been developed into a mature product with sufficient People and Events available, to what extent do you agree…"

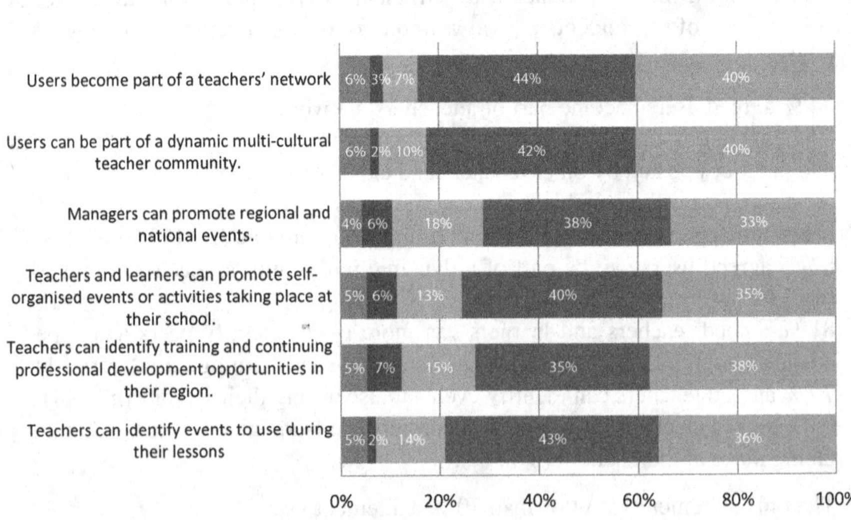

Fig. 7.9 Perceived benefits of the P&E directory (see section on "Richer Interactions Through Resources Beyond Content"); 113 participants responding to the request: "Assuming that the directory has been developed into a mature product with sufficient People and Events available, to what extent do you agree…"

When asked to describe the further potential benefits of the P&E Directory, the most common answer was improving contact with other teachers, and experts with an interest in education (17 responses):

"Creating a big community of teachers, learners and experts."
"Belonging to a large family"

Twelve referred to the capacity of the P&E Directory to act as a platform for sharing innovative ideas aimed at improving pedagogy:

"We can improve our classes by collaborating with schools around Europe."

Closely related to this, nine referred to the establishing of a European community capable of strengthening "interaction between cultures". According to six respondents, another benefit could be improvements in ICT skills as "stakeholders will improve their ICT competences".

Sustainability. 81 % of respondents (n = 106) said they would be likely to use the P&E Directory again, assuming it is developed into a mature product with sufficient people and events available. When asked for what purposes they were likely to use the P&E Directory again, respondents' answers can be categorised as: use of 'People' (either teacher or 'experts') (38 %; n = 86); use of 'Events' (21 %) and to generally improve their knowledge or teaching practice (36 %):

"I want to know more about new technology and to improve my teaching."
"To find inspiration for designing learning activities, to contact experts to invite them to participate in interactive activities with my students, to find partners for collaborative projects,..."
"I will search for events and colleagues for my projects."

When asked why there were unlikely to use the P&E Directory again, just two respondents gave reasons. One felt there was "not enough information and sharing" and the other could not see a use for it, describing it as "inapplicable".

Furthermore, 80 % of teachers (n = 89) said that they would recommend the Directory to other teachers (again on the assumption that it became a mature product). 94 % of other stakeholders also said they would be likely to recommend the Directory to their colleagues and other contacts.

Suggested improvements. Teachers (including head teachers, trainee teachers and teacher educators) were asked how the Directory could be improved to make it more valuable for teaching and learning. The most frequent response was that it needed to be more widely publicised to expand the number of entries (24 responses):

"Be promoted at a national level, better known."
"Including more people."

Seven respondents wanted to see improvements to the interface, in particular changes that would make it easier to use:

"Make it easier and quicker to register People and Events."

A further seven felt the site could be improved through more use of multimedia resources, and perhaps through links to external resources:

"Pictures, an illustration of teachers´ work."
"Examples of good/bad practice should be included."

Six respondents said they would like to see collaboration being more actively supported:

"More opportunities for collaboration."

Teachers also called for improvements to the search facility and categorisation scheme, allowing them to identify useful people and events more easily (5 responses).

"Refining the categorisation of some items in the descriptions of people and events."

Four respondents raised concerns about data security, especially if student contact details were available via the site. Three wanted to see the site translated into other languages.

There were also two people who wanted an alert service to notify them when new entries were added which matched their search criteria.

Experts and other stakeholders were also asked how the Directory could be improved to make it more valuable for people in similar roles. Although a number felt they did not have sufficient experience of using the Directory to be able to comment, six thought that the design should be improved by, for example, making it more interactive and incorporating multimedia content, or simply changing the colour scheme and layout:

"the interface design and it's too formal colour and frame designs … may cause negative bias for some users who may expect… more dynamic and interactive interface."

Three respondents said they would like to see more entries included and a further three thought the Directory could be improved by linking to other services or platforms:

"RSS feeds from other websites that promote training events or learning communities"
"An API for Integrated into other platform—e.g. other things/people you may be interested in after a search."

Other suggestions were an internal messaging or chat system (2 respondents) and more detailed information about people included in the listings (1).

Qualitative data. In addition to the P&E survey, a limited amount of qualitative feedback was received from the technology focus groups (9) and pilot case studies (8). In the teacher focus groups, teachers' use of the P&E Directory had been limited. Most had registered with the site and some had added an event.

Some teachers felt that the P&E Directory duplicates existing tools that provide information about people and events (2 focus groups). Others felt it has potential but needs to include more resources, especially at a local level (3 focus groups). Some teachers experienced technical/administrative issues such as problems logging in (2 focus groups). Suggestions to improve the Directory included a forum/chat facility; allowing RSS feeds; improved categorisation of learning stories/activities to help teachers find relevant resources; a rating system for experts and events; and training and support in the use of the Directory.

Only one teacher in the pilot case studies had made sufficient use of the P&E Directory to be able to comment on the tool, but even they admitted, "I didn't work with it enough to have a well-founded opinion". This teacher thought more content was needed and welcomed the idea of an alert service to make them aware of new people/events that might be of interest.

Usage and Social Evaluation

A visual analytics software tool developed in collaboration with the University of Oviedo was integrated in the last versions of the P&E directory with the goal of allowing obtaining and displaying usage and social information. The pilot study using data analytics was conducted from the 28th of January to the 28th of May 2014. The analytics engine enabled us to compare and contrast the qualitative evaluation by measuring the use of the P&E directory during the pilot phase. Visual analytics were very relevant because they indicate, in an objective way, the real figures for the total traffic and activity registered during the pilot phase of the project. This measure enhanced our understanding of the information and results obtained. From a user perspective, data visualisations can motivate and engage teachers and experts to use the system more effectively.

Usage dashboard. The usage dashboard (see Fig. 7.10) complemented traditional data analytics for a web site with specific usage analytics for the iTEC P&E Directory. Such an approach was meant to make visualizations easily interpretable by any user, particularly for those who were used to working with this type of analytics. The indicators were designed as simple data representations, including the following:

- Session, search and action indicators.
- Data representations for entity creation, search, action, and funnels browse—edition for people and events.

Overall, these figures confirmed previous results, such as the importance of improved search functions and filtering of information. They also highlighted the value of using the P&E directory to identify peers and experts: 4198 searches on 192 persons (ratio: 21.86) versus 2924 searches on 1659 events (ratio: 1.76).

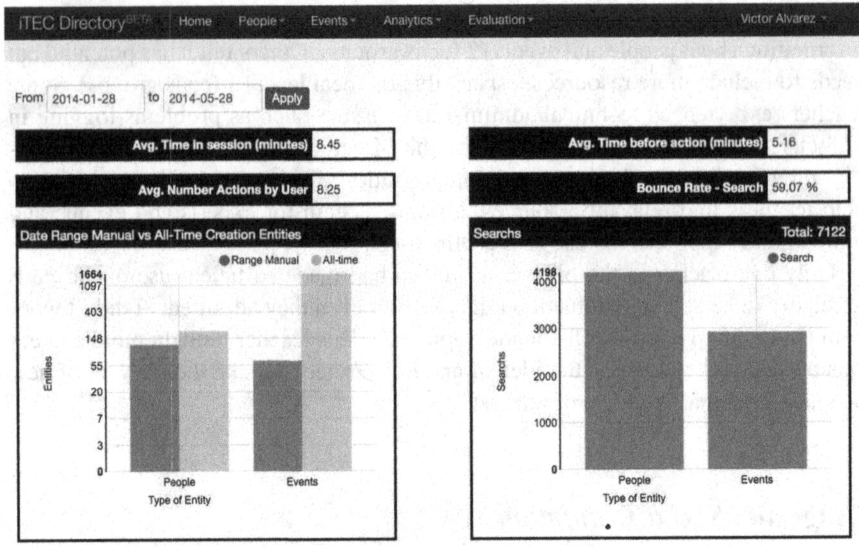

Fig. 7.10 Usage analytics of the Persons and Events directory

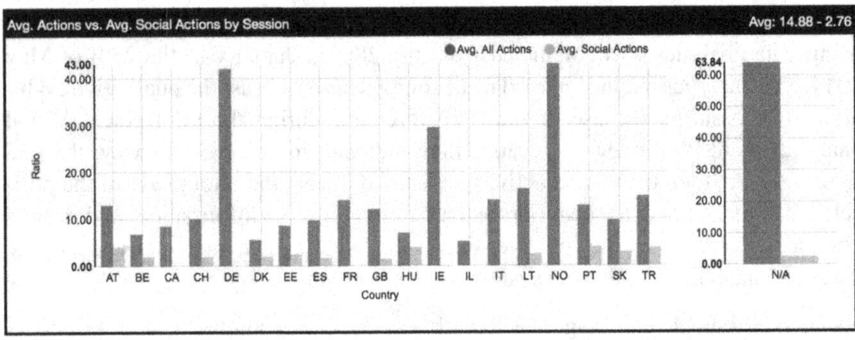

Fig. 7.11 The average number of actions compared with the average social actions

The figures allowed us to map the use of P&E features and the social connections (i.e. know and trust a person, and like an event) made by each participant country.

Social dashboard. The social data dashboard (see Fig. 7.11) aimed at drawing conclusions about how the use of the P&E directory could be related to social variables, with an analysis of country-level participation rates. The design of this dashboard included data representations for:

- "Trust" and "know" connections for people, and "like" for events.
- Entity creation and social action share per country
- Social actions rate with respect to total actions per country.

The results in this area highlighted the overall contributions of some of the partners during the study, and how the average proportion of social actions, 2.77 over 14.80 total actions (18.7 %), were disparate when analysed per country.

Google Analytics. In the final days of the pilot, the P&E Directory enhanced the usage and social analytics dashboards by adopting Google Analytics to track visitors' traffic on the website.

Other Operational Feasibility

In this part of the evaluation, we looked into factors—other than benefits, technical, and usability—that should be in place for a successful deployment of a P&E directory on a larger scale. The main factor was to find and attract good sources for persons and event descriptions. During the project, different categories were investigated and tested with teachers. The most promising event types centred around Continuous Professional Development and involved external subject experts in classroom activities. Teachers then shared their experiences. The most promising person types were those who could contribute to these events. This was investigated with a 16 item questionnaire where each question had a 5 point rating scale. Valid responses were obtained from 46 subjects.

In order to have sufficient Persons and Events available, the harvesting of events from trusted and suitable sources was essential. As such, the establishment of a network of contributing partners was key. In addition, as stated above, the semantic interoperability of harvested resources can be very much improved by an application profile for the RSS feeds as well as Atom feeds. In order to achieve such semantic interoperability it was necessary that the same network of partners would agree on the application profiles and their implementation.

Challenges and Future Developments

The P&E directory was designed to test the hypothesis that providing easy access to resources beyond content can play an important role in facilitating the uptake of ICT in schools. In this section we discuss some possible further developments and challenges related to the gathering, search, and presentation of such resources.

Web-Search of Educational Resources Beyond Content

The P&E Directory was conceived as a specialized educational networking site and some of its features are similar to those in professional networking sites that have a more general scope like LinkedIn. More specifically, it is possible to see similarities and a common trend with projects focusing on providing social networks for teachers and educational experts, such as the case of Prof-Inet in Quebec,[16] Canada. The P&E Directory was conceived to provide unique and specialized features like federated access to learning resources, and improved search functions and filtering of educational information. Conversations with users of the P&E Directory showed the importance of taking into account and investigating the main characteristics and features provided by similar tools. Users seem to expect familiar interface design principles and features already present in other social networking and educational sites.

Future implementations could make use of P&E users' search information to enrich their profile information, allow them to subscribe and get notifications about persons and events, and create recommendation systems based on pre-configured search criteria. In this way, for example, a teacher interested in Biology events in Switzerland in which French and Italian are the working languages can subscribe and receive notifications about related, relevant persons and events in multiple ways. The P&E directory would perform specific searches on behalf of the users using the database of persons and events and inform them about the results they might be interested in via the website, email or any other electronic means.

Manual gathering or editing of events data was utilized only for the pilot phase implementation of the P&E directory. It could be possible in the future, too, but not as the main method for data collection. Even with automating the ingestion of new events, there will be a role for humans to manually or semi-automatically 'tag' the items with the relevant 'subject', 'location', and possibly 'age range' and 'target audience' labels using controlled vocabularies.

Long-term sustainability of the database can only be secured if the gathering of all data is done using automated processes. Among sources to be taken into account the following have been considered:

- Event databases on MoE's national or regional web portals Visual analytics tools.
- RSS-feeds offered by various educational institutions
- Social media channels
- Websites run by relevant institutions
- Webcasts
- Blogs

Our experience with a variety of RSS sources for Events, has shown how different patterns and XML labelling schemes were used for feeds, making them very heterogeneous and, thus, difficult to harvest and match with existing vocabularies or ontology-based dictionaries. This indicated that semantic interoperability would be greatly enhanced, if an application profile could be developed for the RSS specification targeted at Events for learning.

[16] http://www.prof-inet.com/a-propos-de-nous/qui-sommes-nous/

Innovates Approaches to Data Exploration and Collaboration

The Persons & Events directory set a precedent for federated information sharing and peer networking that could be applied in a variety of educational settings, as well as in science and other fields, using a wide range innovative technologies.

An example of this is ConferExplore (Alvarez et al. 2014), a research effort from the HCI group at KU Leuven concerned with exploring the use of novel techniques in information visualisation and augmented reality to empower data exploration and collaboration in scientific events. It displays a network visualisation of persons (authors) and events (conference talks and presentations) to allow discovering of information and facilitating networking among attendees (see Fig. 7.12). This setup has two main purposes: (i) giving participants an overview of the talks and papers presented at the conference and their authors, and (ii) allowing participants to interact with visual data, discover new papers, and enable peer networking and collaboration. In spring 2014, ConferExplore became the official application of the Tenth Joint European Summer School on Technology Enhanced Learning.[17]

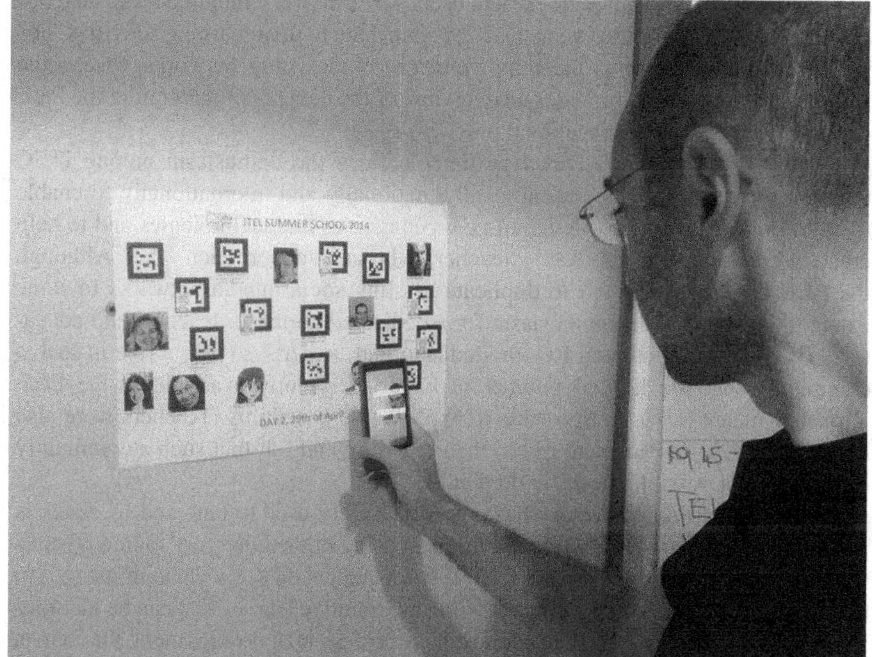

Fig. 7.12 A participant of the JTEL Summer School 2014 using ConferExplore to search scientific information and connect with their authors

[17] http://www.prolearn-academy.org/Events/summer-school-2014

Conclusions

Recent decades have brought a shift in the vision of education towards more decentralized, learner-centred and collaborative approaches. This view has found support from ICT applications, which currently facilitate proactive, communicative, and participative pedagogical strategies. Although educational technologies provide the means to go beyond the classroom settings, the main focus has been traditionally put on providing access to learning materials, while sharing educational resources beyond content remains a problem.

iTEC was a large-scale European pilot that increases the current scope of openness and emphasized the importance of providing open access to resources as a means to facilitate the uptake of ICT in education. One of the available outputs of this project is the iTEC Persons and Events (P&E) Directory, which enables the extraction of information from existing repositories and uses semantic-enhanced information to combine data from multiple heterogeneous sources and enhances search results through filtering.

The successful integration of open resources into learning activities depends largely on establishing an educational network. The P&E directory has already enabled a community of practice where users perform over a hundred daily searches to find persons and browse events that can contribute to their learning activities. The initial evaluation confirms the improvements over existing networks, asserts the interest of teachers, and provides an overview of the benefits of integrating the P&E directory into everyday educational practice.

Feedback on the P&E Directory demonstrates the enthusiasm among iTEC teachers for greater collaboration locally, nationally and internationally to enable them to improve their knowledge of new pedagogies and technologies and to help create a community of innovative teachers who can support each other. Although the P&E Directory was felt to duplicate existing social media networks to some extent, there was notable enthusiasm for a dedicated portal for teachers and educators. There may be potential for other educational 'experts' to play a role in such a community, but the limited number of experts currently available in the P&E Directory meant it was not possible to explore this possibility. Teachers were also keen to find new resources to use in their teaching and felt that such a community offered them a possible means to do that.

Although the P&E Directory has not been widely used to date and feedback is preliminary, responses suggest that interest in using of the Directory to find 'events' (in the traditional sense) is limited. However, teachers do see a value in using it to identify other teachers they can work with and to find resources that can be incorporated into their teaching and can support their professional development. Of course, this is dependent on sufficient collaborators and resources being available through the Directory.

The issues addressed during the project provide the foundation to identify areas for future work. Our experience using a variety of sources for events shows the difficulty of harvesting and matching existing information with ontology-based dictionaries, and highlights the importance of using metadata and application profiles to improve semantic interoperability. The strategy towards a further integration of the P&E directory with other educational services includes the development of "The Future Classroom Toolkit", which will integrate the key elements from across the iTEC project with other toolkits to provide a series of activities, processes, resources, tools and guidance. In parallel to the development of this toolkit, the project has developed a teacher continuing professional development programme to support the development of future classroom scenarios and learning activities.

Acknowledgements The authors are in debt to Sarah McNicol and Cathy Lewin for all their work on the evaluation of the Persons & Events Directory.

References

Alvarez V, Charleer S, De Moor T, Klerkx J, Duval E (2014) Science 2.0 and visual data exploration using augmented reality. In Proceedings of the workshop on collaboration meets interactive surfaces: walls, tables, tablets and phones, 2014

Beare H (2013) Creating the future school. Routledge, London

Beldarrain Y (2006) Distance education trends: integrating new technologies to foster student interaction and collaboration. Dist Educ 27(2):139–153

Brown JS, Adler RP (2008) Open education, the long tail, and learning 2.0. Educ Rev 43(1):16–20

Ducatel K, Bogdanowicz M, Scapolo F, Leijten J, Burgelman JC (2001) Scenarios for ambient intelligence in 2010. Office for Official Publications of the European Communities, Luxembourg, pp 3–8

García Hoz V (1981) Qué es la educación personalizada? (What is Personalized Education?), 2nd edn. Docencia, Buenos Aires

Illich I (1971) Deschooling society. Harper & Row, New York

Klerkx J, Vandeputte B, Parra G, Santos JL, Van Assche F, Duval E (2010) How to share and reuse learning resources: the ARIADNE experience, Sustaining TEL: from innovation to learning and practice. Springer, Berlin, pp 183–196

Simon HA (1956) Rational choice and the structure of the environment. Psychol Rev 63(2): 129–138

Swan K, Shea P (2005) The development of virtual learning communities. In: Hiltz SR, Goldman R (eds) Learning together online: research on asynchronous learning networks. Erlbaum, Mahwah, pp 239–260

Van Assche F (ed) (1998) Using the World Wide Web in secondary schools. ACCO, Belgium

Van Assche F (2004) Towards ambient schooling. In: Delgado Kloos C, Pardo A (eds) EduTech computer-aided design meets computer-aided learning. Kluwer Academic, New York, pp 7–18

Van Assche F, Massart D, Vuorikari R, Duval E, Vandeputte B, Zens B, Mesdom F (2009) Experiences with the learning resource exchange for schools in Europe. eLearning Papers 17

Chapter 8
The iTEC Widget Store

David Griffiths and Kris Popat

Abstract The iTEC project undertook the task of distributing resources and services for learning activities across a wide range of technological platforms in many different countries. Interoperability was achieved through the W3C widget specification and the Apache Wookie widget server. A connector framework was developed to enable widgets to be embedded in host platforms. In order to facilitate the discovery and deployment of widgets the iTEC Widget Store was developed and evaluated. This is an open source app store whose functionality is separated from the widgets which it serves. It was found that the adoption of W3C widgets beyond the project was very weak, and consequently there were few widgets available for inclusion in the Widget Store. Consequently a range of authoring functionality was made available in the Widget Store, enabling users to create their own widgets from online resources or local files. The Widget Store was also extended to enable it to handle LTI tools, including the management of authorisation keys.

Keywords Flexible services • Education • Interoperability • App store • Open source • Widget • Apache Wookie • Open social • LTI

The Role of Widgets in iTEC

The iTEC project was established to pilot innovative Technology Enhanced Learning (TEL) activities on a large scale across Europe. This presented the challenge of delivering technological support for TEL scenarios to schools using a range of different technologies in many different countries. At the proposal stage the decision was taken that in order to achieve this, the project would make use of the W3C widget specification (W3C 2011), as described in Chap. 4. A W3C based infrastructure was to be provided to enable a collection of resources and services to be collected and curated on central servers, and to deliver them to a wide range of

D. Griffiths (✉)
Institute of Educational Cybernatics, University of Bolton, Bolton, UK
e-mail: D.E.Griffiths@bolton.ac.uk

K. Popat
University of Bolton, Bolton, UK
e-mail: projects@krispopat.co.uk

F. Van Assche et al. (eds.), *Re-engineering the Uptake of ICT in Schools*,
DOI 10.1007/978-3-319-19366-3_8

platforms. It was also set out that this would be achieved using open source software and standards based systems, so that others could adopt and build on the systems developed by the project. The Wookie Widget server was identified as the technical means to achieve this functionality, so as to

> …provide a technological infrastructure which supports the mash-up and interoperation between different tools and services in order to ensure a seamless experience for teachers, learners and other stakeholders while providing the user with access to a variety of tools and services (European Commission 2010).

Wookie was originally developed by the Institute for Educational Cybernetics, located at iTEC partner Bolton. By the time iTEC commenced Wookie had been accepted into the Apache Incubator, which seeks to generate community support for software projects before they are definitively accepted by the Apache Foundation. Wookie graduated as a top level Apache project during the lifetime of iTEC. This use of an emerging open source infrastructure enabled the project to support innovative functionality by working with an evolving code base in which project staff had great expertise, while also ensuring that project outcomes were as widely available as possible. The planned work focused on the enhancement and extension of Apache Wookie, the creation of connectors which would enable Wookie widgets to be embedded in host environments, and development of tools for the authoring of widgets.

The iTEC work with widgets was therefore a means towards the projects wider research goals, rather than an end in itself. Nevertheless, although the underlying technology of W3C widgets was in place, it was not mature. Consequently there were a number of technical research questions to be addressed concerning the most effective architecture and methods to be used in managing and delivering widgets.

- What extensions are required to the Apache Wookie W3C widget API in order to support the planned iTEC functionality?
- What affordances opportunities and difficulties are raised by implementing a full separation between user interface and business logic?
- What is the appropriate outline data model for store services?
- What are the critical usability factors in designing an open online store?
- What user interface can support users in making sense of the process of managing widgets? The process of mixing functionality from a number of sources on a single Web page is conceptually complex for users who have only a vague idea of what a server is, or how a Web page is composed.

This led to the iterative design of the users' interaction with the system, not only in terms of the interface elements, but also in the underlying functionality. Indeed, as the project progressed evaluation showed that the technical solutions which were developed for delivery of tools and services worked well, but the system was not widely adopted by teachers. This led to the development team to review the assumptions which lay behind the technical plan, and to propose the development of an App Store which would make the affordances of the infrastructure clearer and more available to teachers. The architecture, features, and design of the Widget Store, as detailed below, embody our response to the research questions which we have identified. The store front of the Widget Store is shown in Fig. 8.1.

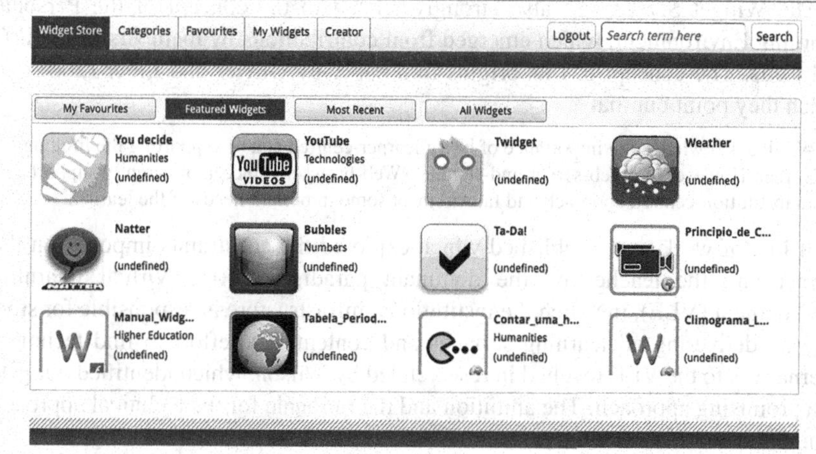

Fig. 8.1 The iTEC Widget Store

A Long-Standing Problem of Interoperability

The need for the widget infrastructure developed by the iTEC project was not only determined by the practical requirements of the project, it was also informed by an established line of work which critiqued the prevailing technical infrastructure for learning. Building on Koper's (Koper and Tattersall 2005) critique of the lack of a connection between pedagogical thinking and the structure of online applications and courses, the Learning Design movement within educational technology sought to create abstract representations of designs for learning activities which could be instantiated for particular contexts. This gave rise to the development of a wide range of tools which were intended to enable teachers to author reusable lesson plans. These include LAMS (Dalziel 2003), the Graphical Learning Modeler (Neumann and Oberhuemer 2009), the Pedagogic Planner (Laurillard et al. 2011). Within this line of work the Reload and Recourse editors (Griffiths et al. 2009) were created by a team drawn from the IEC, and the Centre for Educational Technology Interoperability and Specifications (Cetis) service run by the IEC. The Wookie Widget Server was originally designed within the TENCompetence project (TENCompetence Foundation 2010; Sharples et al. 2008) to provide flexible services for IMS Learning Design (LD) that could be selected and contextualized with the Recourse editor. These abstract descriptions of lesson plans could be provisioned, and then delivered to specific learners and teachers in particular institutions. The work reported in this chapter was in some respects an extension of this effort to provide teachers with effective tools for planning learning activities, as described in Griffiths et al. (2009).

The Widget Server was also strongly related to the concept of the Personal Learning Environment, which emerged from contributions by members of the IEC and Cetis. The concept has its origins in a paper by Olivier and Liber (2001), in which they point out that

> We all acknowledge the importance of being learner-centred and of supporting the lifelong learner. However the Web-server-and-stateless-Web-browser paradigm inherently supports an institution-centred approach and fails to meet some important needs of the learner.

A line of work was established which explored the constraints imposed on the learner and the teacher by the dominant paradigm of the Virtual Learning Environment (VLE), in which the institutional infrastructure is responsible for storing and delivering all learning services and content. The effort to find technical alternatives to the VLE resulted in research led by Wilson, which identified widgets as a promising approach. The ambition and the rationale for the technical approach behind this work was summarized in Wilson et al. (2011) as

> … an approach to challenging the dominant design through creatively subverting the VLE using highly interactive applications (widgets) that can be delivered within the VLE but also embedded by the users into other platforms, including individually-owned tools and websites. By extending the capabilities of the VLE in this manner, we can create a new conversation about the VLE that moves us away from the dominant design, but stays within the comfort zone of lecturers, managers and students who have become used to the existing model. Also, rather than attempt to 'create' a personal learning environment (PLE) that is provided to learners, we instead open up the VLE to be remixed by users to construct their own PLE using technologies of their choosing.

The relationships between these two aspects of interoperability, and the way in which they contributed to the Wookie Widget Server and the iTEC Widget Store, are described in greater detail in Griffiths et al. (2012a, b). 'The Wookie Server, a case study of piecemeal integration of tools and services'. For both aspects the central contribution of the Wookie server was to enable services and resources to be managed and delivered separately from the VLE which teachers and learners were required to use. There was a good fit between iTEC and these technologies for two reasons. Firstly, the pragmatic requirements generated by the need to deliver centrally managed services to pilots in a wide range of target platforms in different contexts were similar to those generated by the Learning Design and PLE approaches. Secondly, the focus of iTEC on innovation made it attractive to make use of a platform which enabled teachers to have access to services and resources from beyond their institutional platform, and in this it echoed the discourse around the PLE.

In practical terms, initiatives such as iTEC, which seek to develop and share innovative teaching activities and practices, are constrained by the technical affordances of existing platforms. For example, there are limitations on the use of the same tools across different learning environments, and in the integration of activities between different tools in different environments. Often the only viable approach is to leave the confines of the institutional system, and to adopt the services of a third party Web applications provider, an option which brings with it a different set of constraints relating to lack of control over functionality and data. The IMS Learning

Tools Interoperability specification (IMS Global Learning Inc. 2010–2012), which we discuss in the section on "Moving Beyond Widgets: IMS LTI Compatibility" below, has made some progress in addressing this issue, but there remains a great deal to be done. This problem is a long standing one, and essentially it remains as described by Liber and Britain in their report on Virtual Learning Environments in Universities (1999), who analyse how tools are locked-in, not only to the particular VLE platform, but also with little provision for tools to be deployed across modules or lessons in ways which would facilitate innovative pedagogical organization.

The Technical Response of the iTEC Project

The iTEC project responded to the challenges identified in the previous section by establishing a Connector Framework for use in iTEC pilots. The connector framework addresses the specific issues of interoperability between tools and platforms and the removal of technical barriers by enabling widgets to be embedded in host platforms (known as shells in iTEC). A 'connector framework' is a broad term for a set of Application Programming Interfaces (APIs) and Software Development Kits (SDKs) which allow for the instantiation of and communication between a common toolkit across a range of different platforms. Such toolkits, including Google OpenSocial Apps and 'gadgets', which were transferred to W3C in 2015, is one such toolkit (W3C 2015). The use of connector frameworks featured strongly in efforts to realize learning environments which marry centrally-provided tools with Personal Learning Environments, for example the EU-funded ROLE project (see Kroop et al. (2015)), which made use of OpenSocial. In these projects, efforts have been made to facilitate the inter-operation of widgets across the diversity of platforms where they might be used, removing barriers of authentication, data sharing and platform dependence. The connector framework in iTEC moved forward this established work by providing a service designed for managing educational tools for schools, implementing it in Apache Wookie, and piloting it on a large scale. The requirements of the connector framework for iTEC were that it should be:

- Adaptable, so that it is capable of functioning with a range of infrastructures in different schools and countries, and supporting the pedagogic adaptation of scenarios for differing school contexts.
- An enhancement of the ability of teachers and educational leaders to manage the teaching for which they are responsible.
- Capable of being centrally managed, so that the coherence of the pedagogic designs and technical offering is maintained.

As a server-side support and delivery mechanism for W3C widgets, with additional support for Open Social gadgets and widgets with specific Wookie features, the architecture of Apache Wookie was conceived within this paradigm. Wookie functions to both store and deliver W3C widgets to a range of platforms through the provision of the connector framework API. The essence of this approach to a

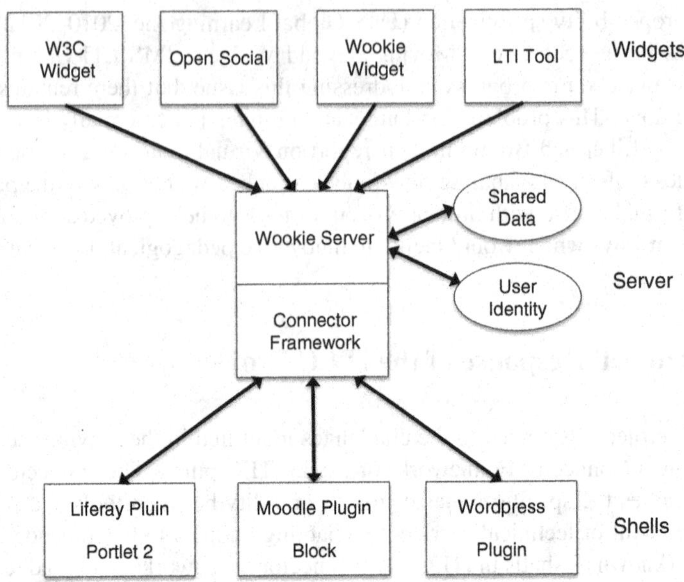

Fig. 8.2 Architecture of the Wookie Connector Framework

'connector framework' is shown in Fig. 8.2, where API calls are provided both to instantiate tools and to manage users.

The iTEC connector framework enabled developers to create plugins in new environments to allow for the linkage (including user authentication) and embedding of tools. RESTian APIs provide function calls to allow the plugin to get lists of widgets/tools, set user information, instantiate widgets or get a URL to retrieve a widget. SDKs were developed as part of this toolkit to provide easy access to these APIs in a variety of programming languages. Wookie manages the unpacking and delivery of widgets to web applications and download to devices that already support widget packages, and acts as a mechanism for managing widget users and facilitating data storage and widget interoperability. These mechanisms enable a rich set of additional tools and content (indeed anything that can be housed in a browser) to be integrated with existing shells such as virtual learning environments, social software, mobile devices and whiteboards. The technical challenge lay in taking a technology designed for delivering small, self-contained applications and allowing them to be collected, connected (mashed-up) and delivered to the specific shell requirements of iTEC.

Unlike other widget platforms (for example Google gadgets), Wookie is platform neutral, requiring for authentication purposes only a 'screen name' of a user, which is passed to it from a shell. The plugins are configured with a host URL for Wookie itself and an API key. This key is created within Wookie to identify the calling environment. It is used by Wookie for data sharing which is particularly useful for widgets that need data to be persisted and communicated between users, or for persisting data for a single user. For instance, a chat widget or a vote widget needs to send chat or vote data to the server. Using Wookie's "sharedDataForKey" function this data is accessible to other users of the same widget, given that the widget id and the API key are the same. As a result, collaborative multi-user activities can be established in Wookie with no need to create users for that particular activity. In effect, this means that the user management for a Wookie widget-based activity need only be done by the shell that instantiates the widget, thus removing one of the principle barriers to the integration of external tools.

In the standard Wookie setup there are three modes of use for a widget. These are established by a set of terms defining the role of the user. The roles, and thus modes, are: student, teacher and administrator, and in most cases teacher and administrator are the same. For some widgets this dual role allows the widget to be configured rather than used, for example, RSS feeds may need to be set up, or chat rooms to be created, etc. The way in which the roles are used is determined by the way in which a particular widget is programmed, and Wookie provides the framework for this to happen. These roles should be passed on from the host environment where possible. In the case of the Moodle plugin the roles defined in Moodle are rationalized (there are seven standard roles in Moodle hence the need for rationalization) and passed via the connector framework to Wookie which then passes them on to the widget.

Each individual plugin makes use of the Wookie connector framework, but it is a separate entity and is more akin to the environment in which it is embedded than it is to Wookie. For instance, in the case of Liferay the plugin was written in Java as a Portlet using the JSR 286 specification,[1] and it should work with any environment that supports that specification. For iTEC it was targeted and tested on Liferay.[2] Similarly a Moodle plugin was written as a Moodle block in PHP.[3] The source code for the connector framework itself is part of Apache Wookie.[4] Despite this range of technical underpinnings, the user experience in each plugin is similar for each.

The Need for a Widget Store

The connector framework was developed in the first phase of the project, together with its associated plugins for clients.[5] These provided the infrastructure that was necessary for administrators and teachers to be able to use centrally managed widgets in activities across the range of schools involved in iTEC pilots. The discovery and selection of widgets for use, however, proved problematic. The available widgets

---

[1] https://jcp.org/aboutJava/communityprocess/final/jsr286/

[2] The Liferay plugin is available at: (#http://iecbolton.jira.com/svn/ITEC/liferay_plugin/trunk/#)

[3] The Moodle plugin is available at: https://github.com/krispopat/Wookie-Moodle-Connector

[4] Apache Wookie is available here https://svn.apache.org/repos/asf/wookie/trunk

[5] The REST API for the store is documented at http://www.widget-store.org/index.html?subpage=documentation. Access to the REST API for the demonstrator version is at http://www.widget-store.org/edukapp/api/rest

were shown to users on a Web page generated by the Wookie server, and they had to scroll down to find the widget that they wanted to use. This arrangement had the virtue of simplicity, but once large numbers of widgets were made stored on Wookie it quickly became unmanageable. It was found that the connector framework software was creating its own barriers to the effective deployment in iTEC which it was seeking to promote. In seeking a way out of this impasse, the project decided to develop and deploy an app store.

Linux based operating systems have long used package managers and app stores as a means of hiding the complexity involved in finding the appropriate packages and installing software. App stores provide users with a single place to go where new functionality, tools, and activities can be added to their computers with a guarantee that they will work without further configuration. In recent years the app store approach has been adopted by mobile phone providers, but most of these app stores are currently proprietary systems tied into particular operating system architectures. With the interoperability opportunities presented by Wookie widgets, an educational app store presented itself as a way of extending the metaphor of 'apps' into the education space and providing teachers with a solution to the over-burdensome processes of discovering and installing new tools. The fact that teachers had high levels of familiarity with app stores on mobile platforms was a strong argument in favour of adopting this approach in iTEC.

While the purpose of our development work was to create an app store to meet the needs of education, the decision was taken to use industry standard technologies wherever possible, rather than to develop our own education-specific systems. By building on open specifications and open source software we were able not only to achieve more effective development, but also to make it easier to extend and adapt the functionality of the app store. The store was called the 'iTEC Widget Store' to reflect its role within the project, but it constitutes a set of open source software which can be used to build an app store for any purpose. The flexibility of the software was demonstrated by the provision of support for IMS Learning Tools Interoperability (LTI) in the final release of the iTEC Widget Store.

Building the Store

The Widget Store is built from several pre-existing software systems as well as some newly created ones. The pre-existing software systems are:

- Apache Wookie,[6] which houses, parses, manages and delivers W3C widgets.
- Solr,[7] which is used for search indexing and query language. The engine behind the discovery service.
- Shindig,[8] which is used to house, parse, and manage OpenSocial gadgets.

---

[6] http://wookie.apache.org/

[7] http://lucene.apache.org/solr/

[8] http://shindig.apache.org/

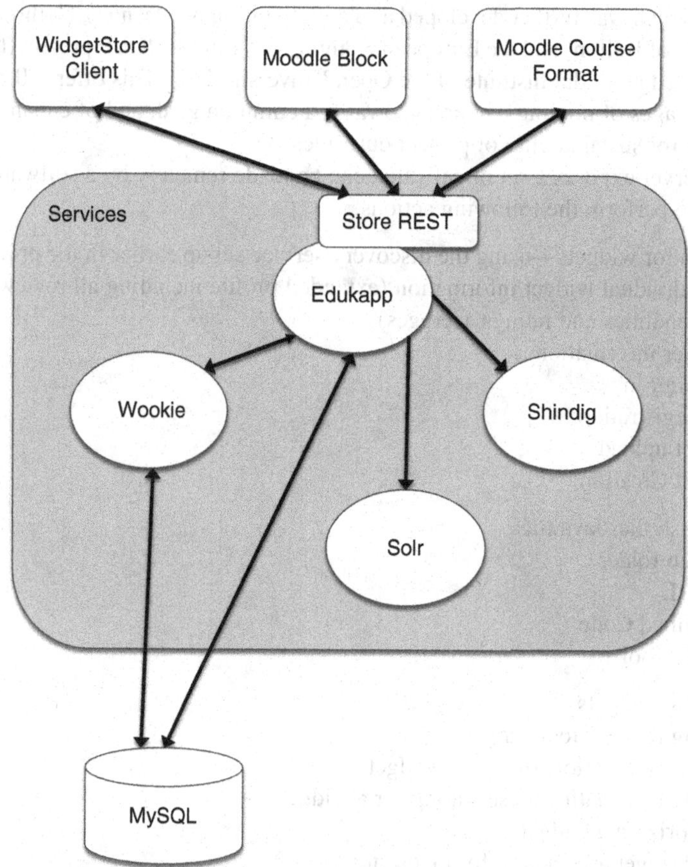

Fig. 8.3 The Widget Store architecture

The store service itself is based upon Edukapp,[9] a prototype widget app store developed with funding from both Jisc in the UK and the European Commission. This software was substantially modified and extended to include a dedicated pure REST API and also to include some model requirements particularly to describe functionalities.

A user interface for the store is implemented as a separate software package. In the case of the store implemented for iTEC, this is a pure HTML/JavaScript client, written and packaged as a W3C Widget. Figure 8.3 gives an overview of the various services that make up the store. The iTEC Widget Store as seen by the user is a client which accesses a service to manage the data for tags, functionalities, reviews and ratings. This service is based upon an open-source web application called Edukapp, initially funded by the Joint Information Systems Committee (Jisc) in the

[9] http://widgets.open.ac.uk:8080/

UK, but which was further developed as a collaboration between iTEC (through the University of Bolton) and the European Commission funded ROLE project (through the Knowledge Media Institute of the Open University UK). This offers all projects the advantages of pooling resources towards a common goal, and of enhancing the prospects for sustainability of project outcomes.

The server exposes a set of calls that can be made remotely by a software client in order to perform the following actions.

- Search for widgets—using the discovery service set up earlier in the project.
- Get individual widget information (extended profile including all reviews, tags, functionalities and ratings averages)
- Get user information
- User sign-in
- User registration
- Widget upload
- Widget Creation:
    - Flash file, Java file
    - Web folder
    - URL
    - Embed Code
    - LTI Tool
- Tagging widgets
- Adding reviews to a widget
- Assigning functionalities to a widget
- Adding or updating a user rating for a widget
- Categorizing a widget
- User/Widget association for favourites

During work on the Store the capabilities of Edukapp were greatly extended, and a number of iTEC-specific extensions were added with the aim of meeting the requirements of the project. In order for the iTEC Widget Store to be fully independent of Wookie, the Edukapp kernel was separated so that it communicated with Wookie solely through the REST API. It was also necessary to develop a means of representing and setting functionalities of widgets, as well as introducing date management capabilities. Some extensions to the data model were also required to address iTEC specific meta-data requirements, in particular the ontologies developed to describe functionalities.

The diagram shows that the Store REST API built upon Edukapp is central to communication between the store and the clients. In this case two clients are shown, One is the Widget Store Client which, as mentioned above, has been packaged as a W3C Widget. The other is a Moodle block, which allows widgets to be included in a Moodle course. The lines indicate the flow of control and information between the services. Edukapp is central to the service architecture as it makes use of the functionalities in the other services to support two different formats of widgets and searching.

The Discovery Service

In order for the Widget Store is to be usable in practice, it was essential to enable teachers to discover new tools based on search criteria. For this a 'widget discovery service' was implemented. This is a backend search engine for widgets that are stored in Wookie, and it allows widgets to be found through searches on the metadata stored in Wookie. The search engine runs as a separate service that sits alongside Wookie, and this separation allows the discovery service to be flexible and extensible. For instance, there may be a number of running instances of Wookie with interesting widgets installed in different locations. The discovery service could be configured to search all or a number of these instances.

Figure 8.4, below, shows how information flows between the discovery service interface and the Store. The user sees the search interface as a text box which is embedded in the Store. When a search term is entered the user is presented with a list of results in the store interface from which a widget could be chosen. Choosing the widget sends a request back to the store with the Widget ID. The store responds by getting an instance or creating an instance of the widget from Wookie of from its own internal data store and sends the instance information back to the plug-in or store interface so it can be displayed.

The discovery service makes use of Apache Solr/Lucene, with Lucene being a search language, while Solr is a search engine. Solr is a separate web application which, in this case, is configured to run with Wookie and the store as data sources for its indexes.. The search engine is written as a cluster of search cores, which

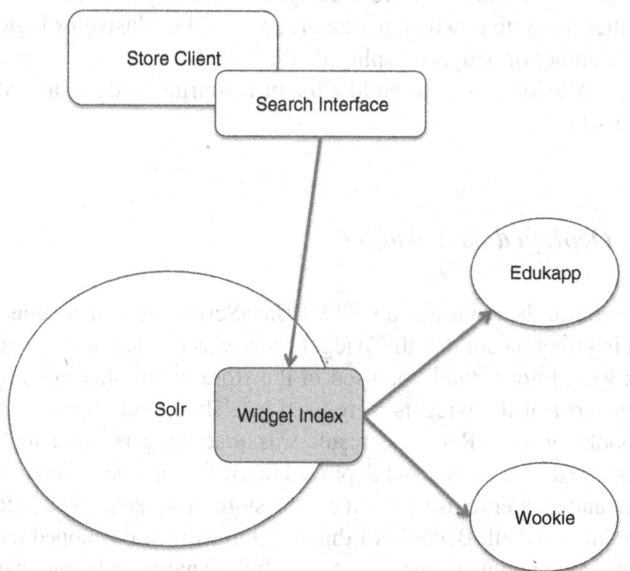

Fig. 8.4 Wookie discovery service architecture

communicate with the indexing services via REST. The list of widgets is returned in ATOM format and categories in JSON.

The discovery service sits behind the searching in indexing capabilities of the Store, and it has been extended to index data from the store as well as from Wookie. Originally the discovery service simply indexed the data contained in the config file of each widget. With the development of the store it was extended to include data from tags, categories and functionalities.

The iTEC Store extended Apache Wookie in a number of ways in order to support the functionalities required by the project. A store API was established as a separate service located along side Wookie itself. This extends Wookie's capabilities with meta-data for each widget beyond the meta-data associated directly with the widget in its config file. As a result the store is able to provide the following extensions:

- Ratings for Widgets: This enables each user to rate a widget. Each user has one rating record per widget which can be updated, and the ratings of all users can be aggregated (averaged).
- Reviews for Widgets: Reviews are composed of a block of text which is associated with a user record and a widget record. The time of creation is recorded.
- Tagging: Tags can be created by users, and those tags which have already been created can be re-used by other users.
- Functionalities: These enable users to provide a weighting value for widgets which conforms to the taxonomy for functionalities developed by iTEC (Anido et al. 2012).
- Categories: These allow widgets to be categorized according to administrator-defined words. The categories are used by the discovery service search but also a faceted filtering system, which uses a group, based exclusive-or logic to narrow down the number of widgets displayed.
- Favourites: Allowing users to build a list of favourites widgets and also to view other user's favourites.

The Store Deployed as a Widget

The first version of the store was an HTML/JavaScript site which called the REST API, which in effect meant that the Widget Store was a place on the web. However the widgets would not actually be used in the store or installed directly from the store. Rather most of the widgets were used in a shell, and within iTEC this was usually Moodle or DotLRN. The result was that widgets were to be created, reviewed and rated in one place but deployed in a different one, whereas it would be more elegant and clearer to users to access the store in the same web location as the widget container or shell. Because of this the store was re-developed the store as a W3C widget—albeit quite a large one. All the functionality and more that was in the original site was transferred to the widget. This could then be embedded in the shell in the same way as any other widget. This also had the benefit that an additional login was not required, as widgets are provided with information about the users logged into the shell. The store interface was written as html with JavaScript, and all functionality is accessed via the REST API using Ajax. Security on the REST API is handled via http authc basic. This is the recommended way of securing a REST API, as typically such interfaces do not make use of session management and the authentication is passed with each function call. This allows clients to the API to be written in any language which supports network calls, and so they are not tied to web browser technologies.

The REST API

The REST API exposes the core functionality of the store to clients and it contains a number of different modules, which supply discrete functionality. It has been designed to encapsulate the types of functionalities associated with store including reviews and ratings. Our definition of the store goes beyond this by encompassing the publishing side of the store and extended categorizations through functionalities. The modules provide these capabilities.

Creator: This handles uploading of widget packages to the store and has calls allowing widgets to be created either from Flash, Java applets, embed codes or web folder packages. Web folder packages are ZIP files with self-contained web sites in. The web site can have any kind of functionality. This zipped folder is converted to a W3C widget by the system.

Discovery: This API exposes the store's search and filtering mechanism. The calling system can also get extended profile information for particular widgets.

Tags: These functions allow widgets to be tagged and those tags to be managed. Tags can also be used to get a list of widget profiles associated with a tag.

Reviews and Ratings: These modules handle reviews and ratings for widgets, both of which are many to one. In the iTEC store each user can only have one rating per widget, and they can be changed. They are also averaged.

Functionalities: This is an iTEC specific requirement. It is a type of weighted tag associated with the widget profile that is based purely on an agreed taxonomy. In this way these functionalities are directly usable by the recommender and composer.

Users: User management is included to allow the store to be used independently of the iTEC environment. This aspect was handled by UMAC for iTEC project activities.

Statistics: Calls made to the store are recorded in the database automatically. Other calls can be made to update the statistics from external services. This is particularly useful to allow the client to track external actions outside of the REST services such as users downloading the widget, embedding it or merely viewing it. These statistics are included within the widget profile structure. The full REST API and data types are attached to the end of this document as appendices.

Widget Store Content Tools

The content available for use with the Widget Store has been constrained by changes in the wider ICT industry, and in the eLearning market. The choice of W3C widgets as an enabling technology for the project was based on the expectation that the positive trends in adoption of the specification at the time writing the proposal would be continued during the life of the project. In this we were sorely disappointed. The W3C widget specification has not achieved its goal of unifying the Web app market, and number of useful publicly available widgets is very small. Consequently the development team placed a great deal of emphasis on the provision of tools for widget creation. These were added as the project progressed, often in response to requests from users.

The first widget creation tools which were provided enabled the user to upload either a W3C Widget file or an Open-Social gadget. The user was expected to know how to create these packages already before installation. This upload feature was expanded by providing a form allowing users to create a widget using an existing Flash or Java applet. These can be uploaded and form fields ask the user for the extra metadata required for making a widget package. Sending this form triggers a widget package creation section in the store which, using templates embedded the applet in an html page, created the widget configuration file and packaged the whole thing together as a widget package, which was then posted to Wookie, indexed and made searchable. It became clear however that more was needed, and the team proposed that it would be useful to handle embed codes as a way of sharing existing widget tools, movies, content etc. Initially a special widget was developed that allowed the user to input an embed code, this then generated a widget package and installed it on the server. This functionality proved popular with users, and so it was then moved into the store itself as a widget creation mechanism. A further extension of functionality was The Web Address tool, which creates a widget from a web URL. This effectively creates a mash-up portal to another web site, and is shown in Fig. 8.5, below. Finally, the Mini Web Site creation tool was provided in response to some teachers who commented that while they taught their students to build simple web sites, it was often very difficult for them to actually publish them. The new tool enables teachers or learners to upload a zipped set of web pages, which are converted into a widget package and made available on the server.

Managing Widgets

The widget creator tools provided in the store proved effective in enabling large numbers of widgets to be created, and in the process it changed the focus of the iTEC Widget Store. The Store had originally been conceived as a means of managing resources and services provided by third parties, but its use in iTEC increasingly became as a tool which could be used by teachers and coordinators to identify and

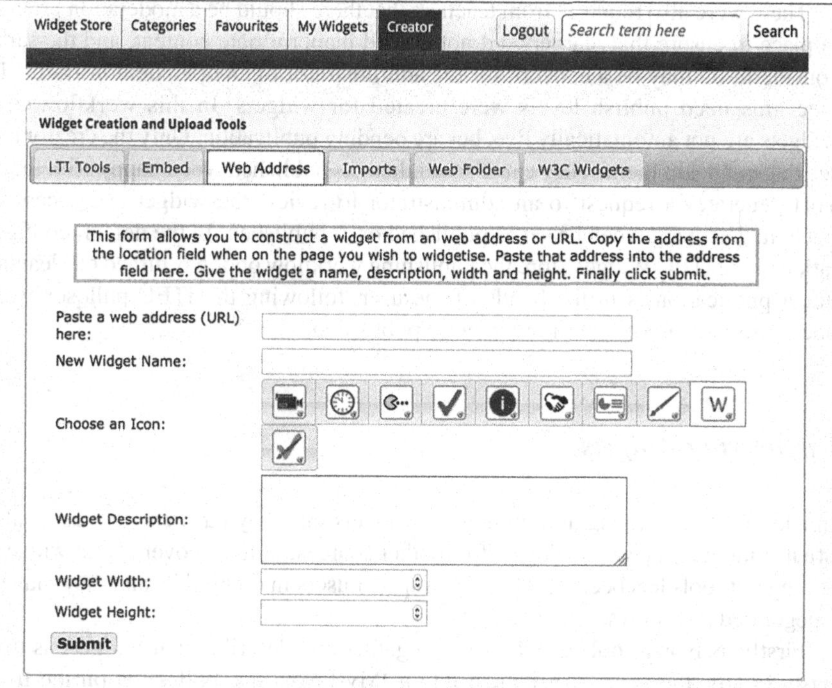

Fig. 8.5 The Web address tool

encapsulate valuable web functionality of any kind as a widget. The search and description features of the Store enabled the resulting widgets to be shared and curated.

The ease with which new widgets could be created quickly created a problem for users, who were unable to distinguish or find their new widgets among the many widgets in the store. To help users find what they needed, different types of user created widgets in the store were distinguished by a set of icons included in the widget creation tools. The icons correspond to the following categories: Collaboration Tools; Creativity Tools; Games and Fun Widgets; Research and Information Tools; Films, Videos (e.g. YouTube Embeds); Reflection and Self Organization Tools; Presentations; Quizzes and Questions; Quiz Creation Tools. Three sets of the same icons were created, with different mini icons in the corner indicating whether the widgets are flash files, web embeds or web folders. When the mouse rolls over the widget additional information is displayed, including whether the resource is an LTI tool. When uploading standard W3C widgets the creator does not get the option to add icons as they contain their own configurations and icons.

In early versions of the Store a simple list of widgets was presented to users. Selecting one of them allowed the user to delete that widget, but little more. The My Widgets area now shows the user's widgets in a table list with tools to publish, categorize, edit and delete their widgets.

There were also requests from teachers that there should be a moderation process in place to ensure that learners did not upload inappropriate content, and the same consideration may be a concern for the administrator of an open demonstrator. To meet this need publish levels were created for widgets. In this workflow new widgets are not automatically live, but are pending publication. Only the creator can see them and edit them. They can also set them as published when happy with them. That generates a request to an administrator to review the widget and accept or reject it. The widget can be set as published or unpublished. In the default configuration of the iTEC Widget Store the publishing workflow option is turned off, leaving direct publication is in the hands of the user, following the iTEC philosophy of open, crowd-sourced, community based publishing.

Discovering Widgets

In addition to managing and finding the widgets that they have created, users also often want to find known widgets from other sources, or to discover useful widgets. A range of tools has been developed to support users in doing this, and they may be categorized as follows.

Firstly, personal tools enable users to gather and describe their widgets as they wish. Firstly, they can gather them into a 'My favourites' collection on the front page of the store. This is helpful for their own reference, but it also becomes a searchable resource available under the 'Favourites' tab, enabling users to browse through the favourites collections of other users. Secondly users can add searchable tags to their widgets, making use of the tag cloud built into the Store.

Secondly, the Store defines groups of categories which can be applied by users to their widgets when they create them. Several users from different user groups had requested better searching and categories, and in response a faceted search interface for categories was designed in order to make searching simpler and more meaningful to users. Twenty-four categories in three groups were added the store, with which the creator of the widget can categorize widgets with multiple categories in their 'my widgets section'. The categories and groups can only be edited by the system administrator. Within each group of categories the discovery is accumulative, and between the groups it is subtractive. This faceted approach allows users to tailor the discovery of the widgets to best suit their needs. It acts as way of filtering down to the subjects, skills and age ranges in which you are interested.

Thirdly, the administrator can also designate certain widgets as being 'featured'. These widgets are then available to users through the 'featured widgets' in the main Widget Store tab.

Fourthly, automated discovery was supported by an API which exposed user descriptions of widgets using the iTEC taxonomies that describe the functionalities of tools. These are not specific to widgets, but rather describe the functions of tools in a general way in order to maintain maximum flexibility. This enables tools to be described in terms of 'what needs to be done' in an activity without specifically identifying individual tools. This work built on the approach adopted by the EU-funded iCAMP project (see http://www.icamp.eu) and the iCAMP tools have formed the principal inspiration behind the approach to tool description adopted in iTEC. Thus the technical description of tools (their operating environments, language, interoperability capabilities/requirements, etc.) was been separated from a description of what they do, and the iCamp approach of 'Soft Ontology' (iCamp 2006) was followed to identify the 'things to be done'. Interfaces for defining functionalities were built into the Store, with sliders with which users indicated the degree to which a widget provided a functionality. The information generated was made available as one of the services harvested by the iTEC SDE recommender service. Because the same taxonomy is used in other parts of the infrastructure, widgets could be mapped to the functional requirements of learning scenarios and learning activities. In this way the project created an over-arching architecture which related scenario description through to the instantiation of tools in technical settings. For further details of this aspect of iTEC work, see Chap. 6.

Moving Beyond Widgets: IMS LTI Compatibility

The Widget Store architecture has been designed so that the functionality offered by the store is entirely separate from the tools and resources which it makes available. This greatly increases in the range of contexts within which the Store can be usefully applied, with consequent benefits to its future viability. This flexibility was put to the test late in the project, when two separate factors indicated to the development team that it would be valuable to adapt the Widget Store so that it could work with the IMS Learning Tools Interoperability (IMS Global Learning Inc. 2010–2012). This specification shares some aspects of the widget approach, in particular a unique identifier which is passed via web type services to instantiate some web content within a frame or via browser redirect. The specification has been adopted by a number of online learning environments, such as Blackboard and Canvas, by tools producers, in particular by eBook providers. One factor which has driven this adoption is that LTI includes a secure, extensible model, which allows online objects to be sold between provider and consumer.

The first indication that the inclusion of LTI in the Widget Store would be valuable came from the inclusion of LTI services in the .LRN platform as part of iTEC pilots in Austria. This produced very promising results, and a higher level of engagement by teachers and institutions than widget-based services had been able to achieve. The second factor was that IMS Global Learning Inc. established the IMS Community App Store Architecture (CASA) initiative, which was announced at San Diego in May 2013 (IMS Global Learning n.d.). LTI has been successful as a means of enabling publishers to market their content to educational institutions while ensuring that the publishers maintain control over access to the materials.

However, the relationships involved are always between the consumer and an individual publisher; there is no marketplace where a range of possibly interesting LTI resources are made available to a teacher and presented according to the teacher's profile. This is the mission of CASA, and the LTI capabilities of the final release of the Widget Store fulfil this role. In the light of these two factors, the final release of the Store under the umbrella of iTEC added the capability to both consume and produce LTI tools.

This was not the first extension of the Store's ability to work with formats beyond its native W3C widgets and Open Social Gadgets. During the development cycles formats such as Flash, Java applets, embed scripts, ZIP folders with web sites and web addresses were added. However, these formats were invariably converted by the store into W3C widgets and stored within Wookie. LTI required a different approach as the actual content of the tool remains with the tool producer and is referenced by the host environment using a key and secret combination to secure the content. The store could already be consumed via LTI, this had been added when Edukapp was first developed and this allowed the store to be embedded in an environment that support LTI Basic or LTI version 1. Wookie could also produce LTI so any Wookie widget could be consumed via LTI. The big barrier though was that the store initially could not itself consume other LTI tools and include them in its listings, search engine or associate any of the ontological data or para-data with them.

As far as the user is concerned all tools within the store look the same. With LTI tools there are some additional complexities to accommodate when using the tools from the store, related to the additional security required to view content via LTI. These complexities arise only when installing the widgets/tools from the store into a host environment. The Store could be used by an institution in wide variety of ways. For example, it might be used as collection point for an institution to host and provide their own set of tools; it might be used by a tool producer as a catalogue of the tools they publish or it might be used by a tool reseller. There are three possible cases for the installation of the Store. Three scenarios were defined which anticipate how the store might be installed to cover this range of uses:

- Case 1: The store is installed on the same host as the shell. In this case the administrator of the store can only include LTI tools into the store using a key and secret supplied by the tools supplier. The user of the store can include and use the tools without having to worry about the key and secret.
- Case 2: The store is installed on the same host as the tool provider. In this case the administrator the store sets a special provider key and secret in the store configuration. The user of the store can only use or install a widget in their shell with a key and secret supplied by the tool (and store) provider.
- Case 3: The store is installed on a separate host to both the tool provider and shell. In this case the administrator of the store needs a key and secret from the tool producer to include the tool in the store. The user of the shell needs a key and secret from the store host (reseller key) to install the tool in their shell.

Conclusions

Like the rest of the infrastructure developed by iTEC, the Widget Store was designed to provide technical support for the pilots, which would develop an improved understanding of how to introduce information into schools in an effective way. Consequently much of the insight generated by the Widget Store may be subsumed in the results of that pilot program. We have also published elsewhere and the barriers which we encountered to adoption by teachers of the Widget Store, setting this in the context research lines which led to the Widget Store, and wider issues in the adoption of TEL. Readers who are interested in this wider discussion are directed to the papers on this topic by Johnson (2014) and Griffiths and Goddard (accepted for publication). There are, however, a number of lessons learned which are more specific to the technology, and to its affordances for education, which are worth drawing out here.

First, the technical strategy adopted by the project was justified, as the system provided all the functionality foreseen by the project plan, and indeed went substantially beyond this. The connector framework and the Widget Store not only fulfilled their functional requirements and performed well, they also led directly to major changes in Apache Wookie.

Second, the architecture, features and design of the Widget Store constitute a finding concerning the most effective architecture and methods to be used in managing and delivering widgets. This addresses the technical questions raised in the introduction to this chapter, and is based on extensive technical evaluation and pilots. This work also had practical implications for open source code projects beyond the project, in particular the deprecation of the user interface to Apache Wookie, and its replacement with an API which could be accessed by an app store, and the major restructuring of Edukapp.

Third, the choice of the W3C widget specification as the underlying interoperability specification for iTEC, as a means of gathering third party content, has not proved to be successful. The specification was chosen in the belief that it would become widely adopted on desktop and mobile platforms, providing many resources and services to consume. Indeed, when the iTEC project was planned W3C widgets were the format for Opera mobile apps and seemed well positioned to become a successful exchange format for web apps on multiple platforms. However, the business model adopted by mobile providers has given them no reason to welcome an interoperability specification, which could threaten the competitive advantage which they hope to gain from their own exclusive catalogue of apps. Consequently, the specifications for Web apps adopted by each provider vary slightly to ensure that interoperability cannot become a reality, even though at the technical level the tasks that they perform are quite similar. As a result there has not been a flow to iTEC of services and resources from the expanding mobile and tablet platforms. The shift away from the PC also had an impact on the iTEC interoperability strategy. The expansion of the use of ICT in schools was dominated for a decade by Virtual Learning Environments running on PCs, and projects which supported this platform could be confident in achieving strong penetration in the education market. In recent years, however, the technical environment of eLearning has changed, and the Virtual Learning Environment (VLE) is no longer seen as a leading context for innovative technical development or teaching practice. Indeed, in many cases the need for a VLE has been questioned. This was not unforeseen by iTEC, and the choice of W3C widgets as an interoperability specification, and the development of the Widget Store were both in part intended to unite mobile and VLE platforms. Moreover, VLEs are mostly open systems, the increasingly dominant mobile and tablet platforms are closed, due to the strategy of each provider to capture and maintain a sector of the market. The consequence for iTEC was that while VLEs can be easily adapted to work with the Widget Store and can be administrated and configured locally, or at regional level, the incorporation of the Widget Store into mobile platforms is much more problematic, as administration and configuration of the system is largely restricted to commercial providers.

Fourth, in seeking to overcome the consequences of the failure of the W3C widget specification to achieve widespread adoption, the Widget Store developed innovative functionality, which has potential value within education. The content creation tools we have developed enable the W3C widget specification to be used in a different way. As an alternative to being a means of offering interoperability between different widget publishers, the specification has been used to enable individuals to encapsulate resources and services which they find useful from anywhere on the Web, to re-publish these as widgets, and to embed them within a wide range of Web applications. Where these resources do not exist, the user is supported in publishing their own, using the 'mini web site' creation tool. This is combined with the ability of the Widget Store to describe and discover widgets in a number of ways, as described above. Evaluation carried out by iTEC showed that individual teachers were comfortable with using these tools in training sessions, and many of them could see that they could be valuable, but they did not move on to making use of them in their own practice. It seems that the functionality that was offered did not make a very convincing case to the individual teacher. Indeed, on the one hand the final round of evaluation reported that teachers who were not technologically oriented had difficulty in understanding the purpose and functionality of the technology, and/or were defeated by inadequate network connections. For example, the idea of embedding content, rather than linking to it, was new for some teachers and proved to be a challenge. On the other hand teachers who were experienced users of technology had established habits, and often preferred to stick to the tools they already knew and trusted. Thus although the Widget Store has features which could be of value to individual teachers, its use may appear to those teachers as responding more the needs of the researchers who developed it then it does to their own needs. Nor does it enable them to carry out their core tasks in ways which are difficult or impossible to achieve by other means. The iTEC National Coordinator in Italy offered a suggestion for the use of the Store which is in line with our own rationale for an alternative use of W3C widget tools, saying that "the ways in which it is used need to be expanded beyond using the widget store simply to search for useful content, for example, by focusing on the ability for teachers to share content via the widget store." However, the sharing practice is not usually a priority for individual teachers, It is, however, a major concern for pedagogic coordinators at the level of department, school or ministry. The Widget Store it possible to share and describe sets of resources which consume live services from the Web, and to embed these in training resources and in classroom practice. From this perspective it is not surprising that the most successful deployment of the Store during the iTEC pilots was achieved when its use was driven by the Ministry of Education in Portugal,[10] which provided local support and technical leadership for a community of teachers around the widget store, who created widgets from available resources and embedded them in blog posts which shared the way in which they were used. Had the pilots of the Widget Store focused on this use case more strongly at an earlier stage the Widget Store might have achieved higher levels of use. However, clarity about who benefits from a technology is often elusive, and particularly within a project with a strong focus on activity within the classroom.

References

Anido Rifon L et al (2013) D10.3 support for implementing iTEC engaging scenarios V3. ITEC Project. http://itec.eun.org/web/guest/deliverables. Accessed 2 July 2015

Dalziel J (2003) Implementing learning design: the learning activity management system (LAMS). In Crisp G, Thiele D, Scholten I, Barker S, Baron J (eds) Integrate, impact: proceedings of 20th annual conference of AscilitE, Adelaide, pp 293–296

European Commission (2010) Grant agreement for the iTEC project, Annex 1 description of work

Griffiths D, Beauvoir P, Liber O, Baxendale MB (2009) From reload to recourse: learning from IMS learning design implementations. Dist Educ 30(2):201–222

Griffiths D, Johnson MW, Popat K, Sharples P, Wilson S (2012a) The Wookie widget server: a case study of piecemeal integration of tools and services. J Univers Comput Sci 18(11):1432–1453

Griffiths D, Johnson MW, Popat K, Sharples P, Wilson S, Goddard T (2012b) The educational affordances of widgets and application stores. J Univers Comput Sci 18(16):2252–2273

Griffiths D, Goddard T (accepted for publication) Understanding teachers resistance to adopting educational technology. In Kybernetes, Special issue: Proceedings of ASC 2014, Washington, DC

iCamp (2006) Deliverable D2.2 iCamp building blocks. http://www.icamp.eu/wp-content/uploads/2007/05/d22___icamp___building-blocks.pdf. Accessed 24 Jan 2015

IMS Global Learning Inc. (2010–2012) Learning tools interoperability. http://www.imsglobal.org/toolsinteroperability2.cfm. Accessed 24 Jan 2015

[10] We would like to thank Fernando Rui Campos of the Direção de Serviços de Projetos Educativos, Direção-General da Educação, Portugal, for his sustained enthusiasm for our work, and imaginative exploration of its capabilities.

IMS Global Learning Consortium (2015) CASA Community App Sharing Architecture. http://www.imsglobal.org/casa/. Accessed 2 July 2015

Johnson M (2014) Learning design, social ontology and unintended functionalism in the ITEC project. In Design4learning conference, Open University UK. http://dailyimprovisation.blogspot.com.es/2014/09/learning-design-social-ontology-and.html. Accessed 24 Jan 2015

Koper R, Tattersall C (2005) An introduction to learning design. In: Koper R, Tattersall C (eds) Learning design: modelling and implementing network-based education & training. Springer, Berlin-Heidelberg, pp 3–20

Kroop S, Mikroyannidis A, Wolpers M (eds) (2015) Responsive open learning environments: outcomes of research from the ROLE project. Springer International Publishing, Berlin

Laurillard D, Charlton P, Craft B, Dimakopoulos D, Ljubojevic D, Magoulas G, Masterman E, Pujadas R, Whitley EA, Whittlestone K (2011) A constructionist learning environment for teachers to model learning designs. J Comput Assist Learn 29(1):15–30

Neumann S, Oberhuemer P (2009) User evaluation of a graphical modeling tool for IMS learning design. In: Spaniol M, Li Q, Klamma R, Lau RWH (eds) Advances in Web based learning—ICWL 2009, vol 5686, Lecture notes in computer science. Springer, Berlin, pp 287–296

Olivier B, Liber O (2001) Lifelong learning: the need for portable personal learning environments and supporting interoperability standards. Cetis Whitepaper. http://wiki.cetis.ac.uk/images/6/67/Olivierandliber2001.doc. Accessed 24 Jan 2015

Sharples P, Griffiths D, Wilson S (2008) Using widgets to provide portable services for IMS learning design. In Koper R, Stefanov K (eds) Proceedings of the TENCompetence international workshop on stimulating personal development and knowledge sharing. TENCompetence, pp 57–60. http://dspace.ou.nl/handle/1820/196. Accessed 24 Jan 2015

TENCompetence Foundation (2010) TENCompetence: building the technical and organisational infrastructure for life long competence development. http://hdl.handle.net/1820/2432. Accessed 28 Feb 2015

W3C (2011) Widget packaging and XML configuration, W3C recommendation 27 Sept 2011. http://www.w3.org/TR/widgets/. Accessed 24 Jan 2015

W3C (2015) OpenSocial foundation moves standards work to W3C social web activity. http://www.w3.org/blog/2014/12/opensocial-foundation-moves-standards-work-to-w3c-social-web-activity/. Accessed 28 Feb 2015

Wilson S, Sharples P, Griffiths D, Popat K (2011) Augmenting the VLE using widget technologies. Int J Technol Enhanc Learn 3(1):4–20

Chapter 9
The Impact and Potential of iTEC: Evidence from Large-Scale Validation in School Classrooms

Cathy Lewin and Sarah McNicol

Abstract This chapter presents the evaluation findings from over 2500 classroom pilots of tools and resources designed to support the development of digital pedagogy. The iTEC approach is an innovative process to support scenario-led learning design. Data collection included surveys, interviews, and classroom observations from teachers, students, policy makers and other stakeholders. This chapter focuses on the impact of iTEC on digital pedagogy; 12 key findings are presented in relation to learning and learners, teaching and teachers, and the potential for system-wide adoption of the iTEC approach. These findings suggest that through participating in classroom pilots: students developed twenty-first century `skills; students' roles changed; there was a positive impact on students' motivation; and students' attainment was positively affected. Furthermore, through participating in the project teachers enhanced their digital pedagogy; became more enthusiastic about their pedagogical practices; increased their use of technology; and collaborated more. With refinement, the scenario-led design process could support mainstreaming of innovation. The library of scenarios, Learning Stories and Learning Activities was perceived to be a valuable output. Towards the end of the project there were growing signs of awareness and uptake, particularly in countries where the approach aligned closely with current policy direction. The chapter concludes with recommendations for policy-making, the management of teaching and learning, technology provision and research.

Keywords Evaluation • Teacher • Student • Digital pedagogy • Learning design

Introduction

This chapter presents the evaluation of the large-scale piloting that took place from September 2011 to June 2014. Through iTEC, educational tools and resources were piloted with around 50,000 students in over 2500 classrooms (exceeding the

---

C. Lewin (✉) • S. McNicol
Education and Social Research Institute, Manchester Metropolitan University, Manchester, UK
e-mail: C.Lewin@mmu.ac.uk; S.McNicol@mmu.ac.uk

F. Van Assche et al. (eds.), *Re-engineering the Uptake of ICT in Schools*,
DOI 10.1007/978-3-319-19366-3_9

original target of 1000) across 20 European countries. This chapter synthesises the evidence of the impact of iTEC on learners and teachers, and the potential for system change, looking at: iTEC processes, tools and resources; classroom perspectives; and national perspectives.

European educational policy (such as Europe 2020) includes as one of its targets increasing employability and life-long learning through developing students' digital competency. There is also a need to develop students' twenty-first century skills which are increasingly important in the workplace (Dede 2010; Redecker et al. 2011). The majority of European teachers are using ICT primarily for lesson preparation; use in lessons with students is still limited despite infrastructure having improved substantially (EC 2013). There is, thus, a growing need for teachers to be supported in the development of digital pedagogy through learning design, an approach which is growing in importance but not yet widely adopted (Emin-Martínez et al. 2014). It is widely asserted that, in order to remain competitive in global markets, education and training needs to be transformed; one way to address this is to mainstream the use of technology for learning and teaching through national policies (EC 2012; Brečko et al. 2014). Given that uptake of digital pedagogy is still low, it is essential to explore mechanisms that can support system-wide change (Brečko et al. 2014). The iTEC project set out to address this through the development of processes to support such needs. The resulting iTEC approach involves the development of Future Classroom Scenarios, and the Learning Activities that are derived from them, to inspire teachers to develop digital pedagogy.

The iTEC evaluation addressed three key questions:

- How did the iTEC approach impact on learners and learning?
- How did the iTEC approach impact on teachers and teaching?
- What is the potential of the iTEC approach for system-wide adoption in schools?

The mechanisms for scaling-up pedagogical change through technology integration included: a learning design process (see Chaps. 3 and 4); professional development for teachers; and support systems such as online communities. The aim was to develop pedagogy enabled through, rather than driven by, technology innovation. This has been found to be critical to effective adoption of technology-enabled learning (Ertmer and Ottenbreit-Leftwich 2013; Kampylis et al. 2013). The iTEC approach does not focus on specific technologies, nor even digital pedagogies. It is designed to account for a constantly changing technology landscape, and enable learning design to respond the current context (at many levels in including policy, national and school).

Scenarios (see Chap. 2) were developed through bringing together a wide range of stakeholders (including teachers and students) to identify current educational trends, together with collaborative workshops tasked with developing responses to such trends. Learning Activities (see Chap. 3) were developed, in a participatory process involving teachers, by identifying design challenges, then addressing them through selecting resources and developing prototype tools. The iTEC project also developed a number of prototype technology tools to support the learning design process and classroom activities (see Chaps. 4–8).

Piloting was supported at national level by pedagogical and technological coordinators who recruited teachers, provided training and facilitated online and face-to-face communities and workshops, and undertook aspects of data collection for the evaluation. A five-day face-to-face professional development course, comprised of a suite of iTEC modules and training materials, was created. The course can be localised and adapted for use at national and regional level. These resources were also adapted for a short course and for a Massively Online Open Course (MOOC).

In the first four cycles, teachers were presented with a package of Learning Activities, exemplified through 2–3 Learning Stories (see Chap. 2). These were created centrally (involving a wide range of stakeholders) and subsequently localized by national coordinators. Localization in some cases involved a selection process at national level which meant that teachers had little, or no, choice (i.e. teachers were presented with a single Learning Story and accompanying package of Learning Activities). As iTEC technologies became available, teachers were encouraged to incorporate them into their piloting activities. Across the four cycles Learning Activities included twenty-first century skills (independent learning, critical thinking and problem solving, communication and collaboration, creativity, ICT) integrated with project-based approaches, teamwork, reflection, peer assessment, outdoor learning, involving outside experts, and students as designers and producers.

***iTEC in practice*: Implementing the Redesigning School Learning Story, cycle 3, UK**

This Learning Story required students to think about spatial design and the different motivations of people who use a particular learning space. The aim was to design a new space for future use based on identified current challenges in relation to school-based activities. Implemented in a UK secondary school as part of a Product Design course, it took 10 lessons over a period of 5 weeks. Students were divided into groups of three using TeamUp (an iTEC prototype technology). Before they started, students agreed the class ground rules and their team roles. The teacher created an Edmodo group (a social learning network designed specifically for education) to allow students to share their work, receive group messages and access resources in the 'library'. Students were presented with a design brief that the teacher had created, and were allowed to use their own mobile devices to record the issues they found around the school. They then used their own tablets to record photos, videos, make notes and record their thoughts and reflections throughout the project. Students without tablets were loaned portable video cameras. Students created a prototype and then discussed their design with future users. Based on the feedback, students then created their final design prototype, which they presented to the class. Perceived innovation included students working as producers, collaboration, easy collection of multimedia data and students developing a better understanding of the design process.

In the final cycle of the project, coordinators in each participating country facilitated the learning design process (rather than this being facilitated centrally), running workshops for scenario and Learning Activity development that involved a wide range of stakeholders including students and head teachers (in excess of 700 across both processes, the majority of whom were teachers). In this cycle, coordinators were asked to incorporate an iTEC tool for learning design (see Chap. 6) into the Learning Activity development process and to encourage teachers to use other iTEC tools (see Chaps. 5–9) either in their classroom activities or through workshops. iTEC technologies were developed to support the design process, to curate digital resources and to connect teachers.

The main outputs of the project were: a scalable scenario-led design process for developing digital pedagogy; the Future Classroom Toolkit and accompanying training provision; and an extensive library of Future Classroom Scenarios, Learning Activities and Learning Stories.

Background

Reflecting on the landscape from the conception of the iTEC project to date there have been many changes. In 2010, social media use was comparatively rare; it is now more prevalent (Aceto et al. 2014) although teachers and students still require support to use it safely in schools and to develop their skills to maximise the impact on learning (Wastiau et al. 2010). Although research evidence is limited, there are indications that social media, combined with student-centred approaches to learning, can positively impact on student achievement (Hew and Cheung 2013). There has been a huge increase in the use of tablets and smartphones since 2010, both in day-to-day life, the workplace and education (Purcell et al. 2013; EC 2013). The use of mobile devices is perceived to be important for innovation in secondary school classrooms (Aceto et al. 2014).

Game-based learning continues to be 'on the current horizon' (Groff 2013; Johnson et al. 2014); this remains unchanged. It is interesting to note that whilst its proponents remain optimistic, even evangelistic, uptake remains limited. The evidence on the relationship between games-based learning and impact on 'academic achievement' is mixed, but there is consensus that such use can impact positively on 'problem solving skills, broader knowledge acquisition, motivation and engagement' (Perrotta et al. 2013:ii). The potential of gaming and gamification warrants further research to understand why it is not being adopted by teachers. Game-making in particular has potential to support the development of computational thinking, another twenty-first century skill that advocates claim is important for life beyond education (The Royal Society 2012; Grover and Pea 2013). Game-making can lead to improved understanding of subject knowledge, creativity, increased engagement and the development of problem solving skills, critical thinking and deep learning strategy use (Vos et al. 2011; Yang and Chang 2013).

However, the typical use of technology to support teaching and learning remains rather unadventurous, confined largely to using office tools and internet searches; digital pedagogy is still undeveloped in the average European classroom despite improved provision of infrastructure and other resources (EC 2013).

Evaluation Questions and Approach

The evaluation was designed to support the development of the iTEC approach and prototype tools, as well as to assess impact on learning and teaching. Therefore, formative, rather than summative, evaluation was necessary, underpinned by qualitative data collection. Learning Activities and Learning Stories were sources of inspiration for teachers to own and adapt, rather than a fixed series of prescribed actions, resulting in wide-ranging interpretations and implementations. Given the diverse nature of the pilots, the project could not set out to provide quantitative measures of impact on student performance.

Regular surveys of teachers and learners yielded perceptions about the impact and future potential of iTEC outputs. Teachers' opinions about whether or not an idea 'works' for them are important (reflecting their experiences, understanding of the complexities of the classroom, and the particularities of their context), as are indications of intended future use (Dillenbourg and Jermann 2010; Voogt et al. 2011). Case studies, including interviews with relevant stakeholders (e.g. teachers, students, head teachers) and observations of lessons, enabled the particularity and complexity involved in the implementation of Learning Stories to be explored (Stake 1995) and provided an opportunity to triangulate teachers' claims against observed practices. In order to strengthen the evidence further, national case studies involving interviews with policy makers and key stakeholders were conducted. Assertions that are warranted by a wide range of data sources are stronger than those warranted by a single data source, irrespective of the number of 'instances' of such data (Erickson 1986). Therefore, collecting data representing a wide variety of stakeholders' perspectives about their experiences of the iTEC approach increased the robustness of the evaluation approach adopted.

Data were collected (September 2011 to June 2014) as follows:

- 68 implementation case studies (interviews: teacher, head teacher, 6–8 students, ICT coordinator; lesson observation);
- 1399 teacher survey responses (online questionnaire);
- 1488 student survey responses (online questionnaire);
- 18 teacher focus groups (with 10–12 teachers);
- 16 national case studies (online interview with two policy makers and the MoE partner lead)

National coordinators arranged for the surveys to be translated into national languages. Surveys were administered centrally using an online survey service. Data collection for classroom pilots and iTEC processes, tools and resources was undertaken by national coordinators. Co-ordinators were provided with written guidance on evaluation procedures for each cycle together with an online training session. Coordinators were also encouraged to seek advice as and when required. National case study interviews were conducted directly by members of the iTEC project team. Whilst the analyses of these interviews are presented as 'national case studies', of course they actually only reflect the view of 2–3 stakeholders, albeit directly or indirectly related to national policy making.

The evaluation has thus utilised a variety of data collection approaches and gathered the perspectives of a wide range of stakeholders including teachers, students, national coordinators, policy makers, head teachers, and school ICT coordinators. Moreover, it has taken place over the course of 3 years, embedded within a cyclical design, which enabled the iTEC approach and iTEC prototype technologies to be tested and refined.

A responsive approach to the evaluation was undertaken, refocusing in the later stages to: capture and document the innovative iTEC processes that could support mainstreaming; to shift the focus of evaluation from classroom impact to strategic impact; and to place greater emphasis on the evaluation of iTEC technologies.

How Did the iTEC Approach Impact on Learners and Learning?

The iTEC approach concerns Future Classroom Scenarios and the systematic design of engaging and effective Learning Activities involving innovative digital pedagogies. Here, we report on how iTEC impacted on the learner's classroom experience. Learners engaged in Learning Activities including group work, reflection, peer feedback, product design and producing digital (and other) artefacts, using digital tools.

Key finding 1: Teachers perceived that the iTEC approach developed students' twenty-first century skills. Their students had similar views.

Teachers and students agreed that engaging in iTEC Learning Activities developed students' skills (see Fig. 9.1). 85 % of students (n = 1488, cycle 5) agreed that they became more confident ICT users and 86 % agreed that they could now use a wider range of new technologies.

> *…the fact that classes became more appealing, and that it developed pupils' critical thinking. They began learning to listen, argue, which was something they were not used to doing; they learnt to address their own views in a relative manner and to accept the ideas of others. Then they began gathering different points of view, reflecting and making decisions. This is very innovative.* (*Portugal, teacher interview, cycle 5*)

The positive impact of the iTEC approach on the development of students' twenty-first century skills replicates findings from similar studies such as the impact of digital storytelling (Niemi et al. 2014) and one-to-one laptop provision combined with a shift to student-centred pedagogies (Lowther et al. 2012). Generic skills become increasingly important as learning becomes more student-centred, social and collaborative (Redecker et al. 2011). Assessment systems should be revised to better account for twenty-first century skills and key competences (Brečko et al. 2014). Introducing effective pedagogical approaches, together with policy reforms, will ensure that students leave education with appropriate skills for the workplace.

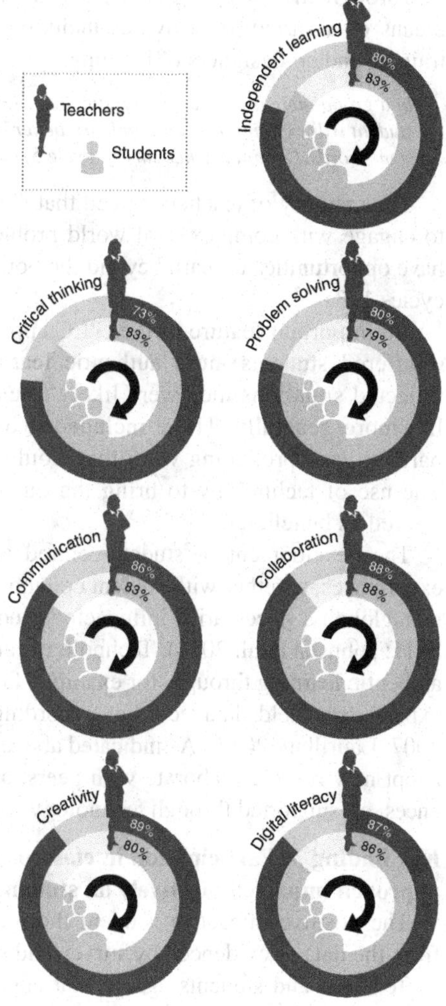

Fig. 9.1 Perceived positive impact of iTEC on students' 21st century skills. The percentage of teachers (n = 573–594) and students (n = 1444–1488) in agreement, cycles 4–5

Key finding 2: Student roles in the classroom changed.

According to the teachers surveyed, the most common way in which iTEC had made a difference to their pedagogy was that students' roles changed. More specifically, teachers referred to increased independent learning and student autonomy. This change was also noted as an important pedagogical innovation in the national case studies.

> *...you give them free rein throughout the project. People work at very different speeds and do very different things. So I have to give up some control here. I must. I have to rely on the students to actually do the job even though I can't see them all the time.* (Norway, teacher interview, cycle 4)

Through the changes in student-teacher roles, learners became 'teachers' by means of a variety of activities including as peer assessors, peer tutors, teacher trainers and co-designers of learning.

> *In a group there are always some students who do not know quite what to do and another student will explain; they seem to learn better* [*this way*] *than when I explain even with the same words*. (*Spain, teacher survey, cycle 5*)

The majority of teachers agreed that iTEC Learning Activities enabled students to engage with complex, real-world problems (76 %, n=595, cycles 2–3) and to have opportunities to learn beyond the boundaries of the classroom (86 %, n=826, cycles 1–3).

An important feature of the iTEC approach for a number of teachers was that it offered students more authentic learning experiences, which more closely reflected situations they were likely to encounter in the workplace, and in later life more generally. These included, working in teams, working with external partners, and producing work that would be seen, and used, beyond the school. The use of technology to bring the outside world into the classroom was also viewed as beneficial.

The development of student-centred and project-based, hands-on, real-world experiences, together with student collaboration, are becoming increasingly important globally, necessarily influencing student and teacher roles (Redecker et al. 2011; Johnson et al. 2014). Technology can enable teachers to more easily support authentic learning through, for example, facilitating greater access to resources and experts in the field, data recording, recording reflections and sharing ideas (Lombardi 2007; Laurillard 2012). As indicated above, the iTEC approach can help students to adopt new roles, collaborate with peers, and engage in authentic learning experiences, all supported through technology.

Key finding 3: Participation in classroom activities underpinned by the iTEC approach impacted positively on student motivation.

The positive impact on student motivation was the strongest theme emerging from the data as evidenced by survey and qualitative data.

Teachers and students agreed that engaging in iTEC Learning Activities positively impacted on students' engagement and motivation (see Fig. 9.2).

> *Overall we liked the lesson very much. The level of engagement and motivation was quite different. Peers that normally do not participate very much got involved and that was very new*. (*Austria, student interview, cycle 3*)
>
> *Pupils love activities connected with using modern tools and creating a PC game was a thing that was really motivating for them. So from my point of view, the greatest thing was the interest*. (*Czech Republic, teacher survey, cycle 4*)

This finding accords with other recent research on teacher perceptions of the impact of technology use in the classroom on student motivation and engagement (eg Pegrum et al. 2013; Perrotta 2013). Indeed, research on the impact of ICT teaching and learning frequently refers to increased motivation and engagement (Condie and Munro 2007).

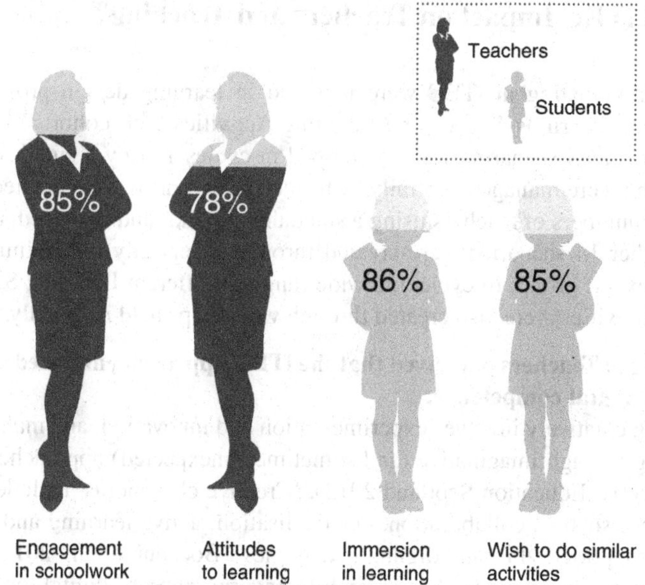

Fig. 9.2 Perceived positive impact on students' engagement and motivation. The percentage of teachers (n=826–1399) and students (n=1444) in agreement, cycles 1–5

Key finding 4: The iTEC approach improved students' levels of attainment, as perceived by both teachers and students.

67 % of teachers (n=1399, cycles 1–5) agreed that the iTEC process improved their students' attainment in subjects, as evidenced by their assessment data.

We had possibilities to improve our practical skills. We liked working together, collaborating, creating web-pages, photos, film. We have got a lot of positive assessment, high scores—it's especially inspired us. (*Lithuania, student interview, cycle 1*)

My French is not very good, I cannot read and speak it that well. But in this course it went better because I was being filmed. I wanted to do it really well. (*Belgium, student interview, cycle 3*)

iTEC has led to significant improvements [in students' learning outcomes through creating a deeper] understanding of a topic located in the curriculum and [relating it to] daily life with the use of technology. (*Turkey, teacher survey, cycle 4*)

It should be noted that the data gathered in relation to impact on student attainment focused on perceptions (although teachers were explicitly asked to respond on the basis of their assessment data) and has not taken direct account of formal assessment data.

There is compelling evidence that the use of ICT in the classroom can have a positive impact on student attainment (eg Tamim et al. 2011; Cheung and Slavin 2013) although of course many factors can influence this such as subject area, type of technology and teacher experience. In common with general evidence, although based on perceptions, both teachers and students agreed that student achievement was positively affected by technology use in iTEC.

How Did iTEC Impact on Teachers and Teaching?

Teachers participating in iTEC were involved in learning design processes and implementing Learning Stories and Learning Activities with cohorts of students. Thirty-six detailed scenarios were developed in cycles 1–4 by a small number of teachers who were managed centrally. A further 22 scenarios were created in cycle 5 by larger numbers of teachers using a standalone toolkit and managed at national level. Another 14 scenarios were created through a centrally-run training course and by an expert group. In cycle 5, a wide range of different Learning Stories and Learning Activities were also created through workshops held nationally.

Key finding 5: Teachers perceived that the iTEC approach enhanced their pedagogy and digital competence.

Teaching creatively involves experimentation and innovation, and making learning exciting through imaginative (and sometimes unexpected) approaches (Jeffrey and Craft 2004; Education Scotland 2013). 'Creative classrooms' include 'innovative practices such as collaboration, personalisation, active learning and entrepreneurship' supported through digital pedagogies (Bocconi et al. 2012:4). Thus teaching creatively demands change, and the incorporation of digital tools (requiring the development of digital competences) to support new pedagogical practices is one way of achieving this.

Facilitating iTEC Learning Activities enabled teachers to develop their pedagogy (see Fig. 9.3).

iTEC was perceived to lead to increased creative teaching.

> *Now I'm way more convinced of the need to push the school practice in this direction, because this enriches the students, offers new learning possibilities, and makes my teaching more interesting.* (*Italy, teacher interview, cycle* 2)

New forms of assessment were implemented by many teachers including peer feedback, reflection, self-assessment, online assessment and the assessment of digital artefacts. For example, reflection through blogs enabled teachers to monitor progress, developed students' metacognition and self-evaluation, and supported peer learning.

> *The significant progress was peer assessment—helped us greatly to see our work in the eyes of colleagues and examine our progress.* (*Israel, student interview, cycle* 2)

Implementing Learning Stories in the classroom encouraged teachers to innovate and experiment. Furthermore, 88 % of students (n = 1488) agreed that their teacher was using different methods to help them learn.

Teachers (cycles 4–5, n = 583) were asked to rate how different their pedagogy was when implementing the Learning Story, in comparison to what they were doing before, on a scale from 1 (not at all) to 10 (radically different). 28 % of teachers stated that their pedagogy had changed substantially (a score of 8–10). One in four teachers (25 %) perceived that their pedagogy was not markedly different to their previous teaching methods (a score of 1–4). This is unsurprising given that there

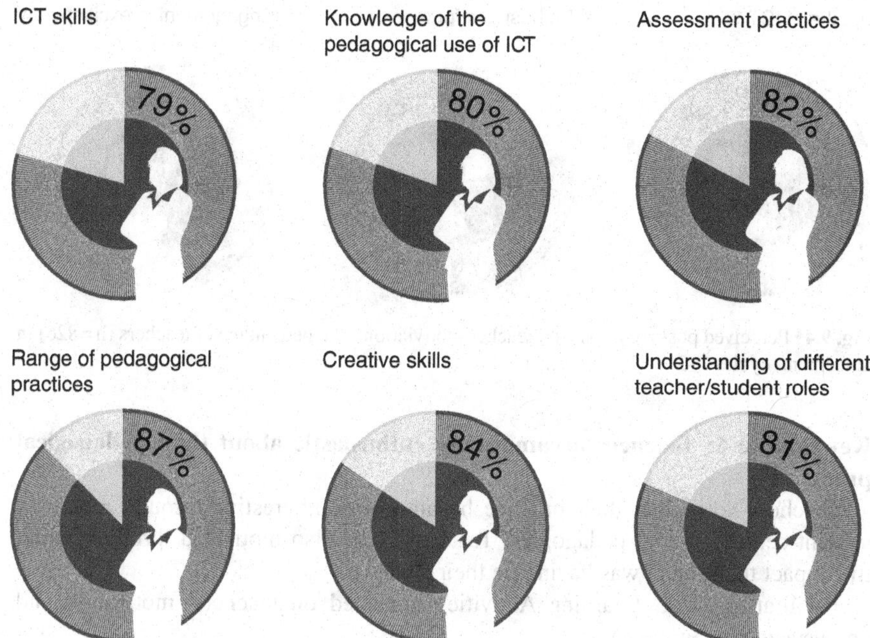

Fig. 9.3 Perceived positive impact on pedagogy. The percentage of teachers (n = 826) in agreement, cycles 1–3

was a bias towards teachers who perceived that ICT competency level was high; teachers with greater confidence are more likely to volunteer to participate in projects such as iTEC.

There was evidence of the positive impact of iTEC on teachers' digital competence throughout the project. Qualitative data echoed that of survey data in relation to the development of ICT skills, including digital pedagogy.

> *The project invites me to use more new technologies and suddenly you feel more comfortable and they can be used more easily. This is what I found.* (*France, teacher interview, cycle 4*)

Learner-centred pedagogies are essential given the growing importance of the knowledge society (Voogt et al. 2013). Current technologies readily support learner-centred activities such as collaboration and communication, and can thus easily support such pedagogical shifts (Beetham 2013). However, it should be noted that repeated attempts to change classroom pedagogy through educational reforms have not been successful (Cuban 2013). Instead, there have been what Cuban describes as 'hybrid' changes—mixes of teacher and student-centred approaches. Whilst the iTEC approach has been successful with a relatively small cohort of teachers, further work is required to understand if and how learner-centred digital pedagogies can be mainstreamed.

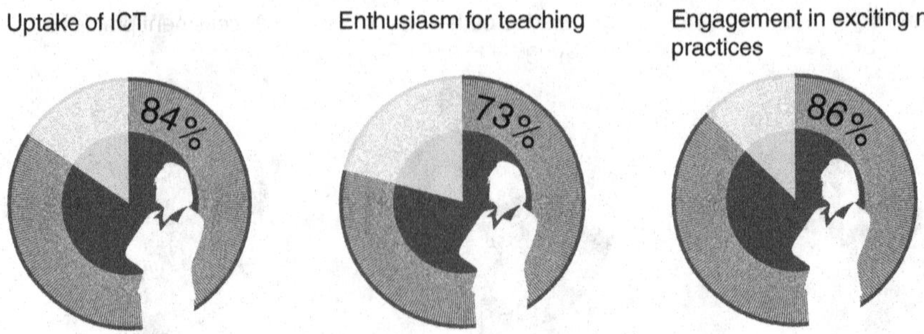

Fig. 9.4 Perceived positive impact on teacher motiviation. The percentage of teachers (n=826) in agreement, cycles 1–3

Key finding 6: Teachers became more enthusiastic about their pedagogical practices.

Teachers noted that their practice became more interesting through a shift to student-centred digital pedagogies. Teachers were also motivated through seeing the impact the project was having on their students.

Facilitating iTEC Learning Activities impacted on teachers' motivation and enthusiasm (see Fig. 9.4).

Qualitative findings echoed that of the teacher survey data with teachers reporting an increase in their own motivation.

> *The teacher feels much more motivated. His students are learning with fun and experimenting. Their eagerness gives the teacher a positive energy for his future classes and the teacher is more involved in the projects and effective teaching. (Turkey, case study report, cycle 3)*

The adoption of constructivist digital pedagogies can have a positive effect on teacher morale (Baylor and Ritchie 2002). Teachers certainly found this to be the case in iTEC; they enjoyed the opportunity to try out new ideas and increase their use of technology.

Key finding 7: Teachers stated that they used technology more frequently; it was systematically integrated throughout the learning process rather than reserved for research or presentations.

More regular, and increased, use of technology in the classroom was perceived to be new for both teachers and students. In some cases, use of technology in lessons by students per se was seen to be novel. 37 % of students (n=1293, cycle 5) said that the 'best thing about iTEC' was the increased use of technology in the classroom (the most frequent response to an open-ended question).

> *I've had this class only from the beginning of this year and the students have almost never used ICT in school so for them everything was new. (Italy, teacher survey, cycle 5)*

While the teachers involved in iTEC had used technology to support student research or presentation work in the past, they started making use of technology to interact and communicate with students; facilitate team working; support design and production tasks; assess work; and encourage students' self-reflection. This can be attributed to the learning design process, which highlights the need to include digital tools in each Learning Activity, thus ensuring that an embedded digital pedagogy is adopted.

Teachers incorporated a wider range of types of digital tools/services into teaching and learning than they had done previously (most commonly for data capture, accessing information, communication, collaboration, media sharing, media authoring and mobile learning). 60 % of teachers surveyed (cycles 1–3 and 5, n = 1048) indicated that they used digital tools/services that they had not used before. Each set of Learning Activities, presented at the start of each piloting cycle, guided teachers to try new digital tools through general recommendations for types of tools such as social networking sites, blogs and mind-mapping tools. The iTEC project also developed a number of prototype tools. These were introduced to teachers at various points in the project and incorporated into piloting activities by some of them.

Teachers (n = 583, cycle 4–5) were asked to rate how different their use of technology was when implementing the Learning Story, in comparison to what they were doing before, on a scale from 1 (not at all) to 10 (radically different). 30 % of teachers stated that their technology use had changed substantially (a score of 8–10). One in four teachers (26 %) perceived that their technology use was not markedly different to their previous teaching methods (a score of 1–4). Again, this is unsurprising given that many teachers perceived that they had a high level of ICT competence.

> *The difference between the maths lessons and the other lessons is that in these lessons we work a lot with GeoGebra, with Facebook, and with Glogster and we record things and in other lessons we don't. In the other lessons the most we can do is some work on the computer once in a while.* (*Portugal, student interview, cycle 2*)
>
> *We used technology in every step: pupils searched for all the information about the content from internet, videos, by email or from experts who visited our school. They learned to send emails to experts. They also used iPads for the first time and shot a video and edited the video by using iPads. They reflected their learning using TeamUp tool.* (*Finland, teacher survey, cycle 4*)

There are continued claims about technology's potential to enhance teaching and learning (OECD 2013). However, as already mentioned above, very few teachers in Europe use technology to support teaching and learning, other than for lesson preparation (EC 2013). Furthermore, student use is still limited, with one in five rarely using digital tools in lesson time, despite infrastructure having improved substantially (EC 2013). The adoption of the iTEC approach by teachers has led to the systematic integration of digital pedagogies in the classroom and increased use by students.

Key finding 8: Teachers collaborated more, both within and beyond their schools, a process facilitated through the online communities.

The iTEC approach led to increased collaboration between teachers. Training and support were positively received by teachers who particularly enjoyed face-to-face meetings, networking with other teachers, opportunities for hands-on experience of tools, online discussion forums, webinars and video-tutorials.

> *Working with ITEC has motivated me to engage other colleagues. It awakened a strong desire not to deal with this project on my own. The challenge is to untangle the frameworks in which we work. (Israel, teacher focus group, cycle 4)*
>
> *Another innovation is the development of a community of practice of teachers. Dissemination by teachers has taken place via a national blog and websites. There has been an increase in collaboration and interaction between teachers. (France, national case study)*

The use of national online communities was evaluated in cycle 4. Although how the online communities were used varied, they were most commonly used to share ideas and examples of good practice. They were also used to support collaborative problem solving within the online community, but this was a less frequent activity (except in communities expressly intended for this purpose).

Professional networks for teachers will become increasingly important as teachers need to continuously update their practices (Redecker et al. 2011; Johnson et al. 2014). Many teachers recognise the importance of the internet in facilitating such networks (Purcell et al. 2013). Moreover, participating in such online communities fosters a positive attitude to collaboration, sharing resources and supporting peers (Tseng and Kuo 2014). However, only one in three teachers in Europe are at schools that support collaborative approaches to learning design (EC 2013).

What Is the Potential of the iTEC Approach for System-Wide Adoption in Schools?

This section considers the evidence of the potential of the iTEC approach for system-wide adoption.

Key finding 9: The scenario-led design process can support mainstreaming of innovation, providing the process is refined.

Policy makers felt that the iTEC scenario-led design process would be an important output of the project in relation to policy-making and the potential for supporting scale-up of digital pedagogy through professional development.

> *The scenario development toolkit is seen as a real asset in Hungary…it is seen to facilitate a professional approach to developing and documenting best practice. (Hungary, national case study)*

The scenario-led design process, once finalised, also has the potential to be included in initial teacher training programmes and continuous professional development (for school leaders and teachers). For example, the scenario development process has already been integrated into a Masters level programme in Estonia and is considered to fit well with course aims; its use will continue there in future years.

Key finding 10: The library of scenarios, Learning Stories and Learning Activities was viewed by policy makers and teachers as a valuable output of iTEC to support system-wide classroom innovation.

The library of Learning Stories and Learning Activities was perceived by teachers to have the potential to lead to both pedagogical and technological innovation in the classroom (93 %, cycles 1–5, n = 1399). Policy makers noted that the library of resources provides an effective structure; the resources are sufficiently innovative without being overwhelming; and are easy for teachers to use. In addition, they suggested that Learning Activities are valuable because they provide concrete examples of novel approaches, emphasise innovation and flexibility, and encourage teachers to become learning designers. 85 % of teachers (cycles 1–4, n = 1152) said that they would use the Learning Stories they had piloted again whilst 86 % of them said that they would recommend the Learning Story to other teachers.

The iTEC scenarios and Learning Stories provide a good structure for teachers. The scenarios received a lot of attention in Estonia. (*Estonia, national case study*).

The Learning Activities are valuable because they are very practical and show teachers how a lesson can be structured. The fact that they are concrete examples, rather than general descriptions is valuable. (*Czech Republic, national case study*)

There needs to be systemic changes and/or incentives if the iTEC approach is to be widely adopted. Within school contexts, a risk-taking culture in relation to the adoption of digital pedagogy should be encouraged (Niemi et al. 2013). There is also a need to develop teacher education such that effective integration of ICT can be modelled and teachers can be encouraged to become agents of change (Twining et al. 2013; Brečko et al. 2014). In common with the literature, the evaluation has provided evidence that an incremental approach to innovation, such as that facilitated through iTEC, can be successful (OECD 2008; Kampylis et al. 2013).

Key finding 11: Awareness of the iTEC approach is growing in educational systems, and there are signs of widespread uptake.

In cycle 5, nine out of ten teachers (n = 244) said that they intended to use the iTEC approach again in the future (91 %) and would recommend it to other teachers (92 %). While 81 % of teachers (n = 244) agreed that the iTEC approach could become part of their own routine practice, only half of them (52 %) agreed that such methods could become part of the routine practice of other teachers in their school. They were particularly cautious about the potential for upscaling at national level with only 43 % agreeing that the iTEC process could become part of routine practice for the majority of teachers in their country.

Yes, it has the potential to change my future practice because now I have learnt about other ways to get my objectives, other ways to work in groups with my students, other ways to do collaborative work, and I'm going to use it in my future lessons (*Spain, teacher interview, cycle 4*)

Teachers were asked if they had shared their experience of various aspects of the iTEC approach with teachers outside the project (both within and beyond their schools). They indicated that they had shared both the Learning Story they had implemented (83 %, cycle 4, n = 331), and the iTEC approach (86 %, cycle 5, n = 244).

There is some further evidence of transfer of the iTEC approach within schools (cycles 3–5: 13 of 68 case studies), and of other teachers expressing an interest (cycles 3–5: 19 of 68 case studies; cycle 5: 54 % of teachers surveyed, n = 245). Other schools had held, or planned, training events and in many cases head teachers actively supported dissemination (an enabler of transfer). In contrast, there was some evidence of perceptions that other teachers might not be interested in the iTEC approach or would find the use of technology challenging. Similarly, teachers from cycle 5 (n=244) reported that about one third of teachers they had shared the iTEC approach with had mixed reactions and 14 % were not interested.

> *They were aware of it; K informs us regularly. She talks about it in e-mails, personal conversations and at meetings. Thus, teachers are aware of it, and are curious to know about the latest project K is involved in. This is how far we got. I think later on other colleagues may join too.* (*Hungary, head teacher, cycle 3*)
>
> *But in my school I have introduced quite a lot of ideas. A good example is mathematics, where they are making Learning Stories. There are also teachers who have started to use TeamUp.* (*Estonia, teacher interview, cycle 4*)

Transfer to teachers beyond participating schools was less commonplace, with some indications of reticence to share beyond colleagues due to lack of confidence in technical ability, the challenge of project jargon, and competition with local schools. Nevertheless, there were a small number of examples where this had happened in each cycle. For example, one teacher in cycle 4 had presented their work at a conference for mathematics teachers and in cycle 5, teachers from two countries (Estonia, Lithuania) had spoken about iTEC at national conferences. Others indicated that they believed that dissemination should take place, but this needed to be organised centrally, rather than by individual teachers:

> *More visibility on expositions and meetings for people working in education. For example at the colloquium for head teachers that is being organised annually. Every school shows what they have achieved in the past year. That is where iTEC should be made visible.* (*Belgium, teacher interview, cycle 4*)
>
> *I believe that the research and knowledge-based communities in and around city T's schools are very interested in being part of something bigger and in disseminating this to a wider audience. At the same time there are 53 primary and lower secondary schools in city T, so it's clear that sharing with other schools is a challenge.* (*Norway, head teacher interview, cycle 4*)

Key finding 12: In countries in which iTEC aligns closely with current policy direction, the iTEC approach is likely to be adopted and to influence future practices.

The national case studies were undertaken mid-way through the third year of the project, partly focusing on the impact of iTEC on ICT strategy and policy development. Although it was seen as early days, there were initial indications of potential impact in some countries. Dissemination was already taking place in many of the participating countries, with seven indicating that they had held seminars, workshops or forums, and five stating that they had held conferences.

In one country (Norway), iTEC had already been influential and had been referenced in official government consultation papers, whilst in five further countries (Austria, Belgium, Estonia, Finland, France), the iTEC project was noted to align with current policy direction, and was therefore likely to be influential in the future.

> *…this is the right time for policy recommendations to be included in the National Strategy of Education in Estonia. There is a chapter within this on 'digital culture in education'. The underlying ideas of iTEC appear to be very similar to those in the National Strategy.* (*Estonia, national case study*)

iTEC correlates quite well with other national developments, including the development of a new core curriculum, and the aim to digitalise the national matriculation exam in a few years. So, iTEC comes at a good time. (Finland, national case study)

All project partners intend to make iTEC outputs available on national portals and/or link to resources that are centrally maintained. Other future plans included: holding closing conference; producing and disseminating national publications; awareness raising events; running further training events for teachers, head teachers and/or ICT coordinators; integrating iTEC with existing online training provision; localising Future Classroom Lab modules; integration with new/ongoing projects; establishing networks of interested initial teacher training institutions (ITTs); running conferences for ITTs; co-ordinating dissemination through one or more ITTs; making initial contacts with ITTs; investigating accreditation options; and maintaining Future Classroom online communities.

Future Classroom Lab modules have already been embedded in Masters programmes and professional development courses. The University of Lisbon, a partner in the iTEC project, has been particularly proactive in bringing together representatives of ITT providers, developing a call for action document to target ITTs and policy makers. Hungary plans to localise the Future Classroom Lab modules for Hungarian teachers and has been closely involved in the preparation of the forthcoming National ICT strategy which highlights innovative learning approaches through digital pedagogies. In Italy, iTEC has become part of the Digital School strategy. Thus, an additional two countries have stated that iTEC has strongly influenced recent national ICT strategy development (Hungary, Italy).

'Bringing a technology innovation to scale in education requires a design that is flexible enough to be used in a variety of contexts and robust enough to retain effectiveness in settings that lack conditions for its success' (Clarke and Dede 2009:364). The signs of widespread uptake suggest that the iTEC approach could meet these necessary conditions of flexibility and robustness. However, few ICT innovations in the classroom survive beyond the early adopter stage (Kampylis et al. 2013). Therefore, organisational structures will need to be put in place to support the continued adoption of the iTEC approach. Policy and programme alignment is important for maximising impact (Kozma 2005); more could be done to understand the challenges and requirements in countries where this is not yet the case. Integrating the approach in teacher education will model effective use of ICT as well as the iTEC approach, and encourage teachers to become agents of change (Twining et al. 2013; Brečko et al. 2014).

Conclusions

School staff almost unanimously agree that integrating ICT into learning and teaching is necessary for ensuring students are prepared for the twenty-first century (EC 2013). However, whilst almost all teachers use technology to help them prepare, ICT has not yet become embedded in teaching and learning; use in the classroom is variable (EC 2013).

The project has created a tool kit and professional development resources to provide continued support for the approach; these resources can be (and are being) localised at national level by many of the partners who participated in the project. The main outputs of iTEC are:

- a scalable scenario-led design process for developing digital pedagogy;
- the Future Classroom Toolkit and accompanying training provision;
- an extensive library of Future Classroom Scenarios, Learning Activities and Learning Stories.

The iTEC approach, in the form of a learning design process and the library of resources created through the project, has led to the adoption of digital pedagogies and the increased use of technology in European classrooms. Most teachers were incredibly positive about their experiences of adopting the iTEC approach, plan to use the ideas in the future and have shared their experiences with colleagues. The evaluation evidence suggests that the iTEC approach can further contribute to the continued uptake of digital pedagogy, if the appropriate support systems such as professional development and online communities of practice are put in place.

Lessons Learned

Given the length of the iTEC project (4 years), it was inevitable that priorities changed, both as a result of internal and external drivers. Furthermore, the design of the project with five overlapping cycles of development, piloting and evaluation created challenges. For example, before Cycle 1 had been evaluated, Cycle 2 was at its midpoint and Cycle 3 had already begun. While formative data were shared with relevant stakeholders in iTEC, the extent to which the evaluation findings were able to input into the development of the project was more limited than might otherwise have been the case. Future large-scale pilots should take this into account and ensure that feedback can be informative and useful.

As with most evaluations, resource constraints were an issue. As the project developed, the number of themes and issues which needed to be covered in the evaluation extended, meaning additional tasks had to be added which had not been anticipated at the start of the project. Whilst adopting a responsive, flexible approach, it was not possible to evaluate all aspects of this complex project thoroughly. Whilst impossible to predict changes over time it would be helpful to prempt where possible and identify which aspects should be prioritised. Regular reviews of the aims and scope of the evaluation would be beneficial. A further tension was the need to evaluate both project processes and outcomes. Again, resource constraints meant at certain points, strategic decisions needed to be made about where resources would best be focused and this could be built into a review process from the outset.

The timing of the development of the various iTEC tools and technologies also presented evaluation challenges. The majority of the tools, and the toolkits, were only introduced in the final two cycles. This meant there was limited opportunity to gather data and it was not possible to focus on each tool in the depth which might have been possible had they been introduced into the project more gradually. Future large-scale pilots would benefit from incorporating existing technologies which require minimal refinement alongside the development of new technologies. It would also be helpful to review the management procedures for technology development so that delays can be minimised.

Naturally in a project involving such a large number of countries, language barriers presented challenges to the evaluation. This limited the amount of qualitative data which the evaluation team were able to collect directly. The approach used was to support National Pedagogical Coordinators (NPCs) in conducting qualitative evaluation activities in the national language in each country. This produced highly mixed results; while some countries supplied detailed, high quality case studies, many NPCs clearly struggled with this task, especially in earlier cycles. This situation may have been improved by including research experience as one of the selection criteria for NPCs to ensure they had the necessary skills and knowledge to collect the data required for the evaluation. An alternative approach would have been to redirect resources away from supporting NPCs in data collection and instead for the evaluation team to conduct a smaller number of case studies each cycle (with the help of translators where necessary). This would have resulted in a smaller amount of data, but of considerably higher quality (the key factor with qualitative data).

Another language barrier related to the translation of the open-ended survey responses, completed by teachers in their national language. In cycles 1–4, Google Translate was used, but this was not an adequate solution at the time as it frequently did not provide sufficiently meaningful or in-depth translations to allow the data to be coded accurately. In cycle 5, an alternative approach was adopted: responses from a limited number of countries were translated by hand, providing more accurate translations which it was possible to code with much greater granularity. The remaining data were then transcribed using Google Translate and allocated to the codes generated through analysing the data which were translated manually. This helped to act as a check that the themes emerging from a subset of countries matched those found in the wider data. Whilst focusing on data from a limited number of countries is not a perfect solution, this allowed the open-ended survey responses to be analysed in a more robust way within the resource constraints of the project.

Throughout the project, the need to report data collected from such a diverse range of countries in a meaningful way was a challenge. This was exacerbated by the differences in sample sizes between countries in each cycle. As the project progressed, we became increasingly aware of the need to stress the limits of the data and to report it in ways which were less open to challenge, even though this meant that it was not possible to provide the level of detail others wished for (for example Ministries of Education that participated in the project). Future projects of a similar scale and design would benefit from greater emphasis on qualitative data such as in-depth case studies.

Recommendations and Implications for Practice

The iTEC project has provided evidence that an incremental approach to change, at the heart of the learning design process that was developed, can be effective. The findings, and the evidence behind them gathered during the project, naturally lead to a number of consequential implications that impinge on policy making, learning management, technology provision and research. To conclude this chapter, we now present these recommendations.

Policy Making

Towards a learning culture. Mechanisms and structures should be put in place, supported through changes to formal curricular and assessment systems, to encourage the development in schools of a culture of self- and peer-reflection, continuous development, new roles, innovation and risk-taking, in order for schools to continue to be fit for purpose, to exploit new opportunities, and to meet evolving needs. Such changes should be communicated effectively to all stakeholders, including parents, in order to encourage positive attitudes. The potential of the iTEC approach and legacy resources to support this culture should be exploited in professional development, online communities, and through teacher ambassadors. This is particularly true in countries where the iTEC approach aligns closely with national policies and strategies. Opportunities to incorporate the iTEC approach in initiatives and programmes related to twenty-first century learning and change in schools should be identified.

Investigate learning outcomes. Further, larger-scale, impact studies of classroom implementations of iTEC tools, Learning Activities and Learning Stories at national level (including randomised controlled trials) could be commissioned, focusing on learning outcomes (specifically twenty-first century skills) and student attainment. The revised Future Classroom Toolkit could be validated in countries where the toolkit clearly supports current policy directions.

Build teacher capacity. Policies and support systems, including professional development, technical and pedagogical support, should be put in place to (a) develop teachers' digital competence, particularly in digital pedagogy, and (b) facilitate teachers' engagement in collaborative processes for learning design. Cost-effective online professional development, such as MOOCs and communities of practice, should be supported at national and international level, including the use of video clips and screencasts to enable teachers to share ideas and good practice. The potential for integrating iTEC assets (the Future Classroom Toolkit, Scenarios, Learning Activities and Learning Stories) created within national professional development structures and initial teacher training should be explored further. To facilitate this trainers and teacher educators would benefit from targeted development on the use of the toolkit and should be supported to use the toolkit in their own practice.

Management of Teaching and Learning

A culture of collaboration. School leaders should put in place organisational structures (e.g. embedding professional network participation in the school culture, and ensuring that teachers have sufficient time for effective networking) and incentive schemes to ensure that teachers share their experiences with other teachers, within and beyond their own school and develop positive attitudes towards teacher networking and collaboration. Teachers should establish and maintain connections with colleagues in their own school, and beyond, to share and jointly develop digital and pedagogical knowledge and skills as a community.

Twenty-first century competencies. Teachers, supported by school leaders and through professional development, should create opportunities for students to take greater responsibility for their learning, work collaboratively, engage in authentic learning experiences and develop twenty-first century skills through the adoption of digital pedagogy. This demands a shift in teacher and learner roles. It also demands a positive attitude towards change, innovation and risk-taking. As students engage in more active and student-centred learning approaches, the development of digital competence becomes increasingly important.

Technology Provision

End-user involvement. Technology providers should take account of the lessons learned through the iTEC project in relation to meeting needs, evolving pedagogical practices, motivating and engaging teachers as partners rather than end-users in product development and testing.

Product development. Of the various iTEC prototype technologies developed, the Scenario Development Environment would benefit most from further research and development with a view to its commercial development. It would be beneficial to conduct a larger scale pilot study, particularly in the countries where it was received favourably.

Research

Research topics. Research should continue to study whole school change, new ways of designing and managing learning, and pedagogies that make most effective use of new digital tools to produce desired learning outcomes. Research should build on iTEC results and investigate further how best to mainstream technical and pedagogical innovation, assessing both radical and incremental approaches in school education contexts.

National specificities. Further research should be undertaken in countries in which the iTEC approach does not align so closely with national policies and strategies to identify how the approach could be adapted to fit different needs.

Research methodology. It would be beneficial to analyse, refine and validate methodologies for large-scale evaluations of projects lasting more than 2 years, where the object of study and the technologies used themselves evolve. Developing approaches for assessing learning outcomes in such conditions would be worthwhile.

Acknowledgements We would like to acknowledge the invaluable contributions of everyone involved in the evaluation activities in the iTEC project including: Maureen Haldane who co-lead the work initially; Roger Blamire who played a major role in shaping the final evaluation report; Will Ellis for his excellent project management skills; the National Coordinators who went to great lengths (collecting data, writing case studies, translating research instruments) to support our work; all the teachers and students involved in piloting activities; and finally our colleagues from Manchester Metropolitan University—Geoff Bright, Helen Manchester, Jonathan Savage, John Schostak, Nicola Whitton, Charmian Wilby, and Adam Wood.

References

Aceto S, Borotis S, Devine J, Fischer T (2014) Mapping and analysing prospective technologies for learning: results from a consultation with European stakeholders and roadmaps for policy action. Publications Office of the European Union, Luxembourg

Baylor AL, Ritchie D (2002) What factors facilitate teacher skill, teacher morale, and perceived student learning in technology-using classrooms? Comput Educ 39:395–414

Beetham H (2013) Designing for active learning in technology-rich contexts. In: Beetham H, Sharpe R (eds) Rethinking pedagogy for a digital age. Routledge, New York, pp 31–48

Bocconi S, Kampylis PG, Punie Y (2012) Innovating learning: key elements for developing creative classrooms in Europe. Publications Office of the European Union, Luxembourg

Brečko BN, Kampylis P, Punie Y (2014) Mainstreaming ICT-enabled innovation in education and training in Europe: policy ACTIONS for sustainability, scalability and impact at system level. JRC scientific and policy reports. JRC-IPTS, Seville

Cheung ACK, Slavin RE (2013) The effectiveness of educational technology applications for enhancing mathematics achievement in K-12 classrooms: a meta-analysis. Educ Res Rev 9:88–113

Clarke J, Dede C (2009) Design for scalability: a case study of the river city curriculum. J Sci Educ Technol 18:353–365

Condie R, Munro B (2007) The impact of ICT in schools: a landscape review. Becta, Coventry. http://dera.ioe.ac.uk/1627/1/becta_2007_landscapeimpactreview_report.pdf. Accessed 25 Aug 2014

Cuban L (2013) Why so many structural changes in schools and so little reform in teaching practice? J Educ Adm 51(2):109–125

Dede C (2010) Comparing frameworks for 21st century skills. In: Bellanca J, Brandt R (eds) 21st century skills: rethinking how students learn. Solution Tree Press, Bloomington, pp 51–76

Dillenbourg P, Jermann P (2010) Technology for classroom orchestration. In: Khinel M (ed) The new science of learning: computers, cognition and collaboration in education. Springer, Berlin, pp 525–552

Education Scotland (2013) Creativity across learning 3–18. Education Scotland, Livingston

Emin-Martínez V, Hansen C, Rodríguez Triana MJ, Wasson B, Mor Y, Dascalu M, Ferguson R, Pernin J-P (2014) Towards teacher-led design inquiry of learning. eLearning Papers 36:3–14

Erickson F (1986) Qualitative methods in research on teaching. In: Wittrock MC (ed) Handbook of research on teaching, 3rd edn. MacMillan Press, New York, pp 119–161

Ertmer PA, Ottenbreit-Leftwich A (2013) Removing obstacles to the pedagogical changes required by Jonassen's vision of authentic technology-enabled learning. Comput Educ 64:175–182

European Commission (2012) Action 68: member states to mainstream eLearning in national policies. http://ec.europa.eu/digital-agenda/en/pillar-vi-enhancing-digital-literacyskills-and-inclusion/action-68-member-states-mainstream

European Commission (2013) Survey of schools: ICT in education, final study report: benchmarking access, use and attitudes to technology in Europe's schools. European Commission, Brussels. https://ec.europa.eu/digital-agenda/node/51275

Groff J (2013) Technology-rich innovative learning environments. Working paper for OECD CERI innovative learning environments project. http://www.oecd.org/edu/ceri/Technology-Rich%20Innovative%20Learning%20Environments%20by%20Jennifer%20Groff.pdf

Grover S, Pea R (2013) Computational thinking in K-12: a review of the state of the field. Educ Res 42(1):38–43

Hew KF, Cheung WS (2013) Use of Web 2.0 technologies in K-12 and higher education: the search for evidence-based practice. Educ Res Rev 9:47–64

Jeffrey B, Craft A (2004) Teaching creatively and teaching for creativity: distinctions and relationships. Educ Stud 30(1):77–87

Johnson L, Adams Becker S, Estrada V, Freeman A (2014) NMC Horizon report: 2014 K-12 edition. The New Media Consortium, Austin, Texas

Kampylis P, Law N, Punie Y, Bocconi S, Brečko B, Han S, Looi C-K, Miyake N (2013) ICT-enabled innovation for learning in Europe and Asia. Exploring conditions for sustainability, scalability and impact at system level. Publications Office of the European Union, Luxembourg

Kozma RB (2005) National policies that connect ICT-based education reform to economic and social development. Hum Technol 1(2):117–156

Laurillard D (2012) Teaching as a design science: building pedagogical patterns for learning and technology. Routledge, New York

Lombardi MM (2007) Authentic learning for the 21st century: an overview. EDUCAUSE Learning Initiative ELI Paper 1/2007. Available at: http://net.educause.edu/ir/library/pdf/ELI3009.pdf

Lowther DL, Inan FA, Ross S, Strahl JD (2012) Do one-to-one initiatives bridge the way to 21st century knowledge and skills? J Educ Comput Res 46(1):1–30

Niemi H, Kynäslahtib H, Vahtivuori-Hänninen S (2013) Towards ICT in everyday life in Finnish schools: seeking conditions for good practices. Learn Media Technol 38(1):57–71

Niemi H, Harju V, Vivitsou M, Viitanen K, Multisilta J, Kuokkanen A (2014) Digital storytelling for 21st-century skills in virtual learning environments. Creat Educ 5:657–671

OECD (2008) Innovating to learn, learning to innovate. OECD Publishing, Paris

OECD (2013) Innovative learning environments. OECD Publishing, Paris

Pegrum M, Oakley G, Faulkner R (2013) Schools going mobile: a study of the adoption of mobile handheld technologies in Western Australian independent schools. Australas J Educ Technol 29(1): 66–81. http://www.ascilite.org.au/ajet/submission/index.php/AJET/article/view/64. Accessed 25 Aug 2014

Perrotta C, Featherstone G, Aston H, Houghton E (2013) Game-based Learning: latest evidence and future directions (NFER Research Programme: Innovation in Education). NFER, Slough

Purcell K, Heaps A, Buchanan J, Friedrich L (2013) How teachers are using technology at home and in their classrooms. Pew Research Center's Internet and American Life Project, Washington, DC. http://pewinternet.org/Reports/2013/Teachers-and-technology. Accessed 28 Aug 2014

Redecker C, Leis M, Leendertse M, Punie Y, Gijsbers G, Kirschner P, Stoyanov S, Hoogveld B (2011) The future of learning: preparing for change. Publications Office of the European Union, Luxembourg

Stake RE (1995) The art of case study research. Sage, Thousand Oaks

Tamim RM, Bernard RM, Borokhovski E, Abrami PC, Schmid RF (2011) What forty years of research says about the impact of technology on learning: a second-order meta-analysis and validation study. Rev Educ Res 81:4–28

The Royal Society (2012) Shut down or restart? The way forward for computing in UK schools executive summary. The Royal Society, London

Tseng F-C, Kuo F-Y (2014) A study of social participation and knowledge sharing in the teachers' online professional community of practice. Comput Educ 72:37–47

Twining P, Raffaghelli J, Albion P, Knezek D (2013) Moving education into the digital age: the contribution of teachers' professional development. J Comput Assist Learn 29:426–437

Voogt J, Westbroek H, Handelzalts A, Walraven A, McKenney S, Pieters J, De Vries B (2011) Teacher learning in collaborative curriculum design. Teach Teach Educ 27(8):1235–1244

Voogt J, Erstad O, Dede C, Mishra P (2013) Challenges to learning and schooling in the digital networked world of the 21st century. J Comput Assist Learn 29:403–413

Vos N, van der Meijden H, Denessen E (2011) Effects of constructing versus playing an educational game on student motivation and deep learning strategy use. Comput Educ 56:127–137

Wastiau P (2010) Virtual learning platforms in Europe: what can we learn from experience in Denmark, the United Kingdom and Spain?—a comparative overview. European Schoolnet, Brussels & Caisse des Dépôts, Paris

Yang Y-TC, Chang C-H (2013) Empowering students through digital game authorship: enhancing concentration, critical thinking, and academic achievement. Comput Educ 68:334–344

Appendix
The iTEC Data Model and Vocabularies

The iTEC directory information model describes the information that was exchanged between the different components of the iTEC Educational Cloud (see Chap. 4).

Information Model Format

For each object type as well as compound data type a full specification is given. Such a specification consists of a structured set of data elements (see for example data element 10 of object type Person). Each data element has:

- A reference number. Reference numbers may be structured indicating that it is an element within a container element. For example: 'ictChannel' may consist of a tuple <name, connection>. Elements of the tuple would have a reference number 16.1 and 16.2, while the container element would have the reference number 16. Elements indicating a relationship to instances of another object type start from reference number 100.
- A name. A name which is unique within the object type or the container element. The naming convention for object types and their data elements is camel case. The object type names start with an uppercase character, the data elements start with a lowercase character.
- A description. A textual description of the data element.
- Multiplicity. Multiplicity indicates how many times a data element may occur. It can be a single integer *n*, which indicates that the data element should appear exactly n times. The most common use of *n* is 1, indicating that the data element should occur exactly once. Multiplicity may also be given as a range of two integers *n..m*, indicating that the data element should occur minimum *n* times and maximum *m* times. Finally, multiplicity can be given as *n..**, indicating that the data element should appear minimum *n* times and that the maximum is undefined. When an attribute has a maximum multiplicity greater than 1 then the values of this attribute may be ordered, which is indicated in parenthesis.
- Data type: See next section.

F. Van Assche et al. (eds.), *Re-engineering the Uptake of ICT in Schools*,
DOI 10.1007/978-3-319-19366-3

Data Types

The iTEC information model supports the following data types:

CharacterString

A string of characters in Unicode.

Number

An integer or a real. See http://www.w3.org/TR/xmlschema-2/#isoformats. An *integer* has a lexical representation consisting of a finite-length sequence of decimal digits (#x30–#x39) with an optional leading sign. If the sign is omitted, "+" is assumed. A *real* has a lexical representation consisting of a mantissa followed, optionally, by the character "E" or "e", followed by an exponent. The exponent must be an integer.

Boolean

Boolean takes the values 'true' or 'false'.

DateTime

This element is based on ISO 8601 and contains date and time information. The format follows Date and Time Formats as specified by the W3 consortium. See http://www.w3.org/TR/NOTE-datetime or http://www.w3.org/TR/xmlschema-2/#isoformats.

YYYY[-MM[-DD[Thh[:mm[:ss[.s[TZD]]]]]]] where:

YYYY = four-digit year
MM = two-digit month
DD = two-digit day of month
hh = two digits of hour (00 through 23)
mm = two digits of minute (00 through 59)
ss = two digits of second (00 through 59)
s = one or more digits representing a decimal fraction of a second
TZD = time zone designator ("Z" for UTC or +hh:mm or –hh:mm)

At least the four digit year must be present. If additional parts of the DateTime are included, the character literals "-", "T", ":", and "." are part of the character lexical representation for the DateTime. If the time portion is present, but the time zone designator is not present, the time zone is interpreted as being UTC.

Duration

This element contains information about an interval in time.

P[yY][mM][dD][T[hH][mM][s1[.s2]S]] where:

y = number of years (integer, >0)
m = number of months (integer, >0)
d = number of days (integer, >0)
h = number of hours (integer, >0)
n = number of minutes (integer, >0)
s1 = number of seconds (integer, >0; or integer >=0 if s2 > 0)
s2 = fraction of seconds (integer, >0)

See http://www.w3.org/TR/xmlschema-2/#isoformats.

The character literal designators "P", "Y", "M", "D", "T", "H", "M", "S" must appear if the corresponding nonzero value is present.

If the value of years, months, days, hours, minutes or seconds is zero, the value and corresponding designation (e.g., "M") may be omitted, but at least one designator and value must always be present. The designator "P" is always present. The designator "T" shall be omitted if all of the time (hours/min/s) are zero.

Language

In order to specify a language such as in a data element or in any language string, the following coding scheme is used. The first applicable format should be used.

1. Use a two letter code from ISO 639-1
2. Use a three letter code from ISO 639-2. See http://www.loc.gov/standards/iso639-2/normtext.html (it does not matter between bibliographic and terminology since they only differ for languages that have two-letter codes)
3. Add the ISO Country code (ISO 3166) when necessary, separated by a dash
4. Use IANA registered language tags, prefixed with i-
5. Use SIL Ethnologue 3-letter codes, prefixed with x-E-
6. Make up a name for token languages prefixed with x-t-
7. Make up a name, prefixed with 'x-' for user defined languages. A specific category of user defined languages are formal languages. They have a 'x-f-' prefix.

Examples are:

nl	Dutch
aus	Australian Languages
i-klingon	IANA registered Klingon
x-E-pcd	Picard
x-none	Not possible to identify a language
x-f-ccRDF	Creative Commons expression in RDF format

LangString

A datatype that represents one or more character strings. A LangString value may include multiple semantically equivalent character strings, such as translations or alternative descriptions. The LangString consists of a set of tuples, where each tuple consists of a language and a character string in that language.

UriId

UriId is an URI identifier pointing to an object in the iTEC back-end. It is constructed as <nameSpacePrefix>/<objectTypeName>/<integer>.

- The <nameSpacePrefix> for example for the Person and Event directory it is 'http://itec-directory.eun.org'.
- The <objectTypeName> is the object type name as given in the next section and following of this appendix.
- The <integer> is a positive integer, ending with two digits which are specific for objects generated by a given iTEC component.

  An example URI identifier is http://itec-directory.eun.org/Person/12305.

VocabularyTerm

A VocabularyTerm is a term of a specific vocabulary. In the data model it is indicated as 'Term of' followed by the name of the vocabulary or the enumeration of terms in curly brackets. An example of the latter is: 'Term of {required, recommended, nice-to-have}'. iTEC constructed a number of new multilingual vocabularies and used vocabularies from previous EU funded projects. The following vocabularies can be found in the Vocabulary Bank for Education of the European Schoolnet[1]: The example values are tokens that are used in the exchange between the different iTEC systems.

[1] http://aspect.vocman.com/vbe/

- *Age Range*. This vocabulary has values 1–24 and 25+.
- *Country*. This vocabulary is taken from ISO 3166.
- *Educational Context*. For example: {college/university, lower secondary school, post-secondary institution other than university pre-primary school, ...}
- *Event Place*. A vocabulary describing the place of an Event. For example {aquarium, art museum, garden, history museum, home, movie theatre, ...}
- *Event Type*. A vocabulary describing the type of Event. For example {conference, in service training, school event, seminar, virtual meeting, workshop, ...}
- *Gender*. Values are: {male, female}
- *General Yes-No*. Values are: {yes, no}
- *ICT Channel*. A vocabulary indicating an ICT channel through which a Person can be reached. Examples are: {facebook, jabber, linkedin, skype, twitter, ...}
- *Person Category*. A vocabulary indicating the category of a Person within the Persons and Events directory. Values are: {author, counsellor, expert, learner, manager, parent, teacher, other}.
- *Person Role In Organisation*. A vocabulary indicating which role a Person plays in an organisation. Examples are: {administration manager, advertising and public relations manager, careers adviser, comenius assistant, curriculum specialist, database architect, educational counsellor, ICT coordinator, ...}
- *Phone Type*. A vocabulary indicating an ICT channel through which a Person can be reached. The values are: {fax, home, mobile, work, other}
- *Subject Values*. A vocabulary indicating the subject of a resource or field of expertise. Examples are: {art, astronomy, biology, chemistry, citizenship, classical languages, cross curricular, design and technology, drama, economics, environmental education, ethics, european studies, foreign languages, ...}

Person

Nr	Name	Description	Multiplicity	Data type
1	givenName	Given name or first name	1	CharacterString
2	familyName	Family name or last name/surname	1	CharacterString
3	birthDate	Date of birth	0..1	DateTime
4	gender	Gender of the Person	0..1	Term from: Gender Values
5	description	Description of the Person	0..1	CharacterString
6	tags	Free tags (descriptive word or phrase) for this Person	0..*	CharacterString
7	categories	The category of a Person	0..*	Term from: Person Category Values

(continued)

(continued)

Nr	Name	Description	Multiplicity	Data type
8	roles	The primary role of a Person	0..*	Term from EUN Person Role In Organisation Values
9	img	A URL to the image of this Person	0..1	URI
10	*address*	*Postal address of the Person*	*0..1*	
10.1	streetAddress	The street address of a postal address	0..1	CharacterString
10.2	postalCode	The postal code of a postal address	0..1	CharacterString
10.3	locality	The locality of a postal address	0..1	CharacterString
10.4	country	Country of residence	1	Term from: ISO Country Code List Values
11	mbox	Email address for the account	1	CharacterString, a valid email address
12	website	Personal website	0..1	CharacterString
13	languageMotherTongue	Mother tongue	0..1	Language
14	languagesOther	Other spoken languages	0..* Ordered	Language
15	*expertise*	*Tags indicating the expertise of this Person*	*0..**	
15.1	field	Name indicating a field of expertise	1	Term from: Subject Values
15.2	level	Level of expertise	0..1	Integer: 0..10
16	*ictChannels*	*A contact channel (audio, video, chat) over the Internet*	*0..** *Ordered*	
16.1	name	The name of the channel	1	CharacterString
16.2	connection	A String by which one could connect to this Person using this channel	1	CharacterString
17	*phones*	*The phones through which a Person can be contacted*	*0..** *Ordered*	
17.1	name	The name of the channel	1	CharacterString
17.2	connection	This is the telephone number	1	CharacterString
18	*otherChannels*	*The otherchannels through which a Person can be contacted*	*0..** *Ordered*	
18.1	name	The name of the channel	1	CharacterString

(continued)

(continued)

Nr	Name	Description	Multiplicity	Data type
18.2	connection	A String by which one could connect to this Person using this channel	1	CharacterString
19	cost	Whether the Person charges for his participation or not in a Learning Activity	0..1	Term from: {yes, no, unknown}
101	knows	A relation indicating a User knows this Person	0..*	Relationship UriId
102	trust	A relation indicating a User trusts this Person	0..*	Relationship UriId
103	tool	The tools used by this Person	0..*	Relationship UriId

Event

Nr	Name	Description	Multiplicity	Data type
1	name	The name of the Event	1	LangString
2	eventStart	Starting data/time of the Event	0..1	DateTime
3	eventEnd	Ending data/time of the Event	0..1	DateTime
4	recurrence	The recurrence of this event	0..1	JSON String
5	subjects	Tags indicating the educational subject of this event	0..*	Term from Subject Values
6	description	Event description	0..1	LangString
7	tags	Free tags (descriptive word or phrase) for this Event	0..*	CharacterString
8	*intendedAudience*	*Description of the intended audience*	*0..1*	
8.1	personCategories	Category of person	0..*	Term from Person Category Values
8.2	educationLevels	Level of educational subject	0..*	Term from Educational Context Values
8.3	ageRange	Age Range is a pair of minimum and maximum values from the vocabulary	1	Term from Age Range Values
9	*location*	*Place of the Event*	*0..1*	
9.1	locationName	Name of the Place of the Event	0..1	CharacterString

(continued)

(continued)

Nr	Name	Description	Multiplicity	Data type
9.2	streetAddress	The street of a postal address	0..1	CharacterString
9.3	postalCode	The postal code of a postal address	0..1	CharacterString
9.4	locality	The locality of a postal address	0..1	CharacterString
9.5	country	Country where the event takes place	0..1	Term from ISO Country Code List Values
9.6	places	Location category of the event	0..*	Term from Event Place Values
10	types	Type of Event	0..*	Term from Event Type Values
11	conduits	Indicator whether the event is an online event or an in-person event or both	0..2	Term from Event Environment Values
12	languages	Language of the Event	0..*	Language
13	website	Website of the Event	0..1	URL
14	*organizers*		*0..**	
			Ordered	
14.1	name	Name of the organizer	0..1	CharacterString
14.2	url	URL of the organizer	0..1	CharacterString
15	cost	Whether this event is free of charge or not	0..1	Term from: {yes, no, unknown}
100	tools	Supporting tools	0..*	Relationship
				UriId

Learning Activity

Nr	Name	Description	Multiplicity	Data type
1	identifier	Learning Activity identifier	1	UriId
2	name	The name of the Learning Activity	1	LangString
3	description	A description of the Learning Activity	0..1	LangString
4	learning Outcomes	The expected learning outcome from the activity	0..*	LangString
5	ideasFor Using Technology	An explanation of why using technology makes sense	0..1	LangString
6	abstract	A summary of the main features of the Learning Activity	0..1	LangString
7	motivation	The motivation to use the Learning Activity	0..1	LangString

(continued)

(continued)

Nr	Name	Description	Multiplicity	Data type
7.1	teacher Motivation	An explanation of why a teacher should consider this activity	0..1	LangString
7.2	student Motivation	An explanation of why a student should consider this activity	0..1	LangString
8	*guidelines*		*0..1*	
8.1	gettingStarted		0..1	LangString
8.2	introduction		0..1	LangString
8.3	activity		0..1	LangString
8.4	assessment		0..1	LangString
9	creator	The creator of this Learning Activity	1	User id (UriId) LangString
10	requirements	Requirements for Learning Activity	0..*	LangString
11	*annotation*	*This category provides cataloguer's notes on the tool*	*0..1*	
11.1	rating	Free rating of the Tool as entered by the cataloguer	0..1	Number: 0..10
11.2	tags	Free tags assigned by cataloguer to the Tool	0..*	LangString
11.3	comment	Free cataloguer's notes about the Tool	0..1	LangString
12	*metaMetadata*	*This category describes the history of the tool record at the repository*	*1*	
12.1	lastUpdate	Date of last modification	1	DateTime
12.2	creationDate	Date of record creation	0..1	DateTime
12.3	deleteDate	Date of record deletion	0..1	DateTime

Tool in the Widget Store

Nr	Name	Description	Multiplicity	Data type
1	identifier	Identifier of the Tool	1	UriId
2	name	The name of the Tool	1	LangString
3	version	The version of theTool	0..1	LangString
4	abstract	A summary of the Tool	0..1	LangString
5	description	A description of the Tool	0..1	LangString
6	toolType	The type of the Tool	1	Term from: {Device, Application, Shell, Shell Component, Widget, Shell-specific Application, cloudApp}
7	widgetType	Type of widget	0..*	Term from: {Create Tool, Communication Tool, Learning Content, Simulation}

(continued)

(continued)

Nr	Name	Description	Multiplicity	Data type
8	creator	Entity who made the tool	0..*	User id (UriId)
9	*functionality*	*Utility/Functionality offered to a user*	*0..**	
9.1	functionalityID	Functionality identifier	1	Term from Functionalities
9.2	functionality-Level	Functionality level for the tool	1	Number
10	image	A URI pointing to an image file	0..1	Url
11	license	The license under which this tool works	0..1	CharacterString
12	*worksWith*	*Other tools with which this tool works (required or not required)*	*0..**	
12.1	tool	The identifier for the tool with which the tool works	1	UriId
12.2	interoperability	Description on how to let it interoperate	0..1	CharacterString
12.3	required	Indicates whether the Tool given in field 10.1 is required to run the Tool	0..1	Boolean
13	cost	Indication about Tool's usage costs	0..1	Boolean
14	accessURL	URL to obtain (or use) the tool	0..1	Url
15	language	Tool language	0..*	Term from Language list values
16	supported Formats	Supported MIMETypes	0..*	CharacterString
17	*intendedAudience*	*Description of the intended audience*	*0..1*	
17.1	ageRange	Age range of agents for whom the Tool is intended or useful	0..*	Term from General age range values
17.2	educationLevel	Education level (primary, secondary, etc.) for which the Tool is designed	0..*	Term from Educational context values
18	*annotation*	*This category provides cataloguer's notes on the tool*	*0..1*	
18.1	rating	Free rating of the Tool as entered by the cataloguer	0..1	Number: 0..10
18.2	tags	Free tags assigned by cataloguer to the Tool	0..*	LangString
18.3	comment	Free cataloguer's notes about the Tool	0..1	LangString

(continued)

(continued)

Nr	Name	Description	Multiplicity	Data type
19	*metaMetadata*	*This category describes the history of the tool record at the repository*	*1*	
19.1	lastUpdate	Date of last modification	1	DateTime
19.2	creationDate	Date of record creation	0..1	DateTime
19.3	deleteDate	Date of record deletion	0..1	DateTime

Requirement

Nr	Name	Description	Multiplicity	Data type
1	identifier	Identifier of the requirement	1	UriId
2	optionality	The optionality of the requirement	0..1	Term of {required, recommended, nice-to-have}
3	description	Description of the requirement	0..1	LangString
4.a[2]	directTool-Requirement	Identifier of a required tool	0..1	UriId
4.b	directPerson-Requirement	Identifier of a required person	0..1	UriId
4.c	directEvent-Requirement	Identifier of a required event	0..1	UriId
4.d	functionalities	Required functionalities	1..*	Term of Functionalities
4.e	*person-RequirementSpec*		*0..1*	
4.e.1	personRole		0..*	Term of Person role in Organization values
4.e.2	personCategory		0..*	Term of Person category values
4.f	*event-RequirementSpec*		*0..1*	
4.f.1	eventType		0..*	Term of Event type values
4.f.2	eventPlace		0..*	Term of Event place values

[2]The data elements 4.a to 4.f are mutually exclusive, i.e. a requirement will be about one of these elements.

Glossary of Terms Used in iTEC

Composer The Composer is a planning tool for teachers to create, adapt and share Learning Activities. It provides teachers with suggested resources, including tools and services, to use in the delivery of a selected Learning Activity, potentially exposing them to technologies they have not come across before.

Cycle The 18-month period during which scenarios, and then Learning Activities, were developed in the iTEC project; Learning Activities were pre-piloted; and Learning Activities (exemplified through Learning Stories) were validated and evaluated through large-scale pilots. Each cycle overlapped, there being five in total.

Design challenge Key issues in teaching and learning that need to be addressed in designing Learning Activities, for example barriers to engagement in learning, difficulties in understanding a concept.

Design opportunity Existing practices or circumstances that support learning and that can address design challenges (ways of overcoming identified barriers).

Future Classroom Maturity Model The Future Classroom Maturity Model is an online self-assessment and benchmarking tool. It shows a number of progressive stages of maturity in the adoption of learning technology to support advanced pedagogical practices. The tool has five levels, or stages of innovation, and five dimensions. It can be used prior to scenario creation to enable stakeholders to review current technology integration within their specific context and to inspire areas for scenarios that can be incrementally innovative. It can also be used as a means of evaluating existing scenarios.

Future Classroom Scenario A Future Classroom Scenario (FCS) is a narrative description of learning and teaching that provides a vision for innovation and advanced pedagogical practice, making effective use of ICT. A Future Classroom Scenario: takes into account issues, trends and challenges relating to the current school or educational system; provides a high level description of Learning Activities and resources; describes the roles of learners, teachers and other participants; and is not limited to the 'classroom', taking place in any context, environment or place where learning is possible.

F. Van Assche et al. (eds.), *Re-engineering the Uptake of ICT in Schools*,
DOI 10.1007/978-3-319-19366-3

Future Classroom toolkit A collection of tools and processes to support the scenario-led design process including the identification of trends, the development of Future Classroom Scenarios, and the development of Learning Activities and stories.

iTEC approach The iTEC approach is designed to bring about change in classroom practice, in order to better equip young people with the competences and attitudes to meet the opportunities and challenges of twenty-first century society and the workplace. The approach is based on Future Classroom Scenarios and the systematic design of engaging and effective Learning Activities using innovative digital pedagogies.

Learning Activities Learning Activities are concrete descriptions of discrete actions. They add practical detail and provide concrete guidance for teachers in how to deliver the approaches described in the scenarios. The Learning Activities provide details of the role of the teacher and learner, and include ideas for using ICT resources effectively. These Learning Activities are non-curriculum specific, but do provide opportunities for the development of twenty-first century skills.

Learning Story A Learning Story can be provided to describe the sequence in which the Learning Activities could be delivered, how the activities inter-relate and some example contextual information such as curriculum or subject area and learners involved. Learning Stories are useful in helping teachers think about how they could use Learning Activities in their own classrooms, but should not be considered as lesson plans for adoption, just examples for guidance and inspiration. A typical Learning Story will include 3–8 Learning Activities, which describe the resources that are needed to successfully complete each activity.

National Pedagogical Coordinator (NPC) Person in charge of coordinating the involvement of teachers in the iTEC project at national level, with a particular responsibility for pedagogical support.

National Technical Coordinator (NTC) Person in charge of coordinating the involvement of teachers in the iTEC project at national level, with a particular responsibility for technical support.

People and Events Directory The People and Events directory facilitates professional network development and collaboration for teachers. It connects teachers with similar interests, allowing them to share knowledge and experiences. It also enables them to identify people (from outside their current networks) and events that might support learning and teaching.

ReFlex ReFlex is a prototype tool that enables students to create a personal reflection space and build up a series of reflections about their learning, which are subsequently displayed on a timeline.

Scenario Development Environment (SDE) The Scenario Development Environment (SDE) is a prototype recommender system which takes into account the user's profile (for example school level and subject) and can assess the technical feasibility of a Learning Activity in a schools and provide recommendations for resources such as applications, events, widgets and lectures.

Shell A Shell is a configurable software container that (as the name suggests) acts as an empty shell allowing users to identify and add their own Resources and to integrate them in order to meet the educational objectives of a Learning Activity.

TeamUp TeamUp is a prototype tool designed to organise students into groups by interests, and also to enable the groups to record reflections on their progress.

User Management and Access Control (UMAC) UMAC is a set of components that supports user authentication and authorization throughout the iTEC Educational Cloud. It comprises three main modules: an authentication server, an authorization server and an authorization filter that controls access to the above mentioned components. Once a user is authenticated, she can use the different services dependent on her authorization.

Widget An ICT based software application or tool that provides a user with useful data or a function. Often widgets are small user interfaces that give access to information on the internet, or make use of information on the internet. The iTEC widgets can run in different shells (see above).

Widget Store The Widget Store provides a means of curating resources (widgets) and moving them easily between learning platforms, potentially offering seamless integration and facilitating interoperability. Teachers are able to create their own widgets to add to the store. Users can rate and review the widgets.

Printed in the United States
By Bookmasters

Printed in the United States
By Bookmasters